Timothy Garton Ash

IN EUROPE'S NAME

Timothy Garton Ash is a Fellow of St Anthony's College,
Oxford. After reading Modern History at Oxford, his research
into German resistance to Hitler took him to Berlin, where he
lived, in both the western and the eastern halves of the divided
city, for several years. From there, he started to travel widely
behind the iron curtain. Throughout the 1980s, he reported
and analyzed the emancipation of Central Europe from communism in contributions to the *New York Review of Books*
and other journals. In 1989 he was awarded the David Watt
Memorial Prize for his commentaries on international affairs
and named "Commentator of the Year" in the British television *What The Papers Say* awards.

He is the author of *"Und willst Du Nicht mein Bruder
sein . . ." Die DDR heute*, a book published in West Germany
about what was then still East Germany; *The Polish
Revolution: Solidarity*, which won the Somerset Maugham
Award; *The Uses of Adversity: Essays on the Fate of Central
Europe*, for which he was awarded the Prix Européen de
l'Essai; and *The Magic Lantern: The Revolution of '89
Witnessed in Warsaw, Budapest, Berlin and Prague*, which
has now appeared in fourteen languages. *In Europe's Name*
was first published in Germany, where it became a bestseller
and provoked wide debate. It has since appeared in Dutch and
Italian, and is currently being translated into French, Polish,
and Japanese.

IN EUROPE'S NAME

In Europe's Name

Germany and the Divided Continent

Timothy Garton Ash

Vintage Books

A Division of Random House, Inc.

New York

FIRST VINTAGE BOOKS EDITION, NOVEMBER 1994

Copyright © 1993 Timothy Garton Ash

The Library of Congress has cataloged the Random House edition
as follows:
Garton Ash, Timothy.
In Europe's name: Germany and the divided continent /
Timothy Garton Ash.—1st ed.
p. cm.
Includes bibliographical references and index.

ISBN 0-394-55711-5

1. Germany—History—Unification, 1990.
2. German reunification question (1949-1990)
3. Germany—Politics and government—1945-1990.
4. Germany—Relations—Europe.
5. Europe—Relations—Germany.
6. Europe—Politics and government—1989- I. Title.

DD290.25G37   1993   93-5477
943.087′9—dc20

Vintage ISBN: 0-679-75557-8

Manufactured in the United States of America
10 9 8 7 6 5 4 3 2

Contents

Author's Note

To keep the main text readable, all sources, some caveats and many interesting further details have been consigned to the notes and other appendices. To avoid littering the text with superscript numbers, each note is keyed to a few words from the passage to which it relates. The top of each page of notes tells you to which pages of text those notes refer. This sounds complicated, but in practice it is not.

Informed criticism, questions and corrections really are welcome, but would-be critics, questioners and rectifiers are asked to look in these notes and appendices as well as at the main text. I hope other readers, too, may find the notes, with their guidance to sources and further reading, and the carefully conceived maps, tables, and chronology, both useful and rewarding. However, the book can also be read without any reference to the supporting apparatus.

TGA, Oxford,
May 1993

IN EUROPE'S NAME

Prologue

European Question

Which question?

Once, Europe was cut in two. The two parts were called West and East. The division itself was often labelled 'Yalta'. It was set in concrete in the Berlin Wall.

In the early 1980s, this 'Yalta' divide became the subject of intense international debate. The legitimacy and permanence of the East-West division of Europe were questioned from the left and from the right, by the Presidents of the French Republic and of the United States, by opposition activists in Eastern Europe and peace movement activists in Western Europe, by Nato and by the Pope.

Of course the issue had never quite disappeared from the international agenda since 1945, and certainly not from the German and East European agendas. Yet the catalysts for this wider popular discussion were the declaration of a 'state of war' to crush the Solidarity movement in Poland, in December 1981, and the controversy about the deployment of new American nuclear missiles in West Germany, in the years 1980–83. The former turned attention to the external, geopolitical conditions that then precluded success for the Polish revolution, and particularly to the position of the Soviet Union in East Central Europe. The latter turned attention to the subject of European security, and particularly to the position of the United States in West Central Europe. The two debates — about freedom and about peace — then clashed and combined in convoluted ways, with many variations according to country, creed and political affiliation.

In these debates there were not a few who publicly, and even more who privately defended the 'Yalta' division, arguing that it had brought peace and stability to Europe. 'The peace of Europe,' wrote a well-known German commentator in 1983, 'depends for longer than we can foresee on the system of Yalta . . .' More diplomatic versions of this view could be heard in high places in many capitals of the West. Looking back in December 1989, the British Foreign Secretary, Douglas Hurd, said that this was a system 'under which we've lived quite happily for forty years'.

The sense that there were others who had not lived quite so happily under this system, and that their lack of happiness might materially affect our own, nonetheless clearly grew through the first half of the decade. By 1985 the goal of overcoming, or at least, reducing the division of Europe was a staple ingredient of the rhetoric of most Western governments, as well as of independent activists from Eastern and Western Europe.

Thus, for example, on the fortieth anniversary of the end of the Second World War, the leaders of the group of seven leading industrial countries (the so-called G7), together with the President of the Commission of the European Community, issued a solemn declaration in which they said: 'We deplore the division of Europe. In our commitment to the ideals of peace, freedom and democracy, we seek by peaceful means to lower the barriers that have arisen within Europe.' In the same year, the Czechoslovak civil rights movement Charter 77 issued a 'Prague Appeal' which identified the division as the root-cause of tension in Europe, and called for a gradual, peaceful transformation of the underlying 'political reality'. The concluding resolution of an international human rights conference in Kraków in 1988 all-embracingly declared that 'the goal of Europeans is to overcome the division of the continent, to unite Europe'.

In the second half of the 1980s, this debate was then transformed by the 'new thinking' on Soviet foreign policy under Mikhail Gorbachev, and by the way in which the peoples of Eastern Europe seized the opportunities that it offered. Even before he became Party leader in 1985, Gorbachev had spoken of his vision of a 'common Europe home'. Yet this image had already been used by Brezhnev on a visit to Bonn in November 1981. In the mid-1980s there was still a considerable gap between what Gorbachev seemed — at least from his public statements — to have in mind, and what either Western leaders or the European citizens advocating 'détente from below' had in mind when they spoke of 'overcoming the division of Europe'.

Here we encounter a problem that will recur throughout this book: that of distinguishing between what people said in public, what they said or merely thought in private, and, not least, what they think or say now that they thought or said then. Gorbachev made an explicit public commitment to overcoming the division in a Joint Declaration with Chancellor Helmut Kohl during the Soviet leader's visit to Bonn in June 1989. This Declaration stated that 'the Federal Republic of Germany and the Soviet Union consider the foremost task of their policy to be to draw on the historically developed European traditions and so to contribute to overcoming the partition of Europe'. Yet even here the Russian text used the more vague and general term, *razobshchennosty*, that is, 'disunity', by contrast with the specific German *Trennung*. Soviet commentators talked of overcoming the continent's economic and 'military-political' divides. One even described the Berlin Wall as a 'relic of the Cold War'. Yet at least in public they nonetheless still envisaged the co-existence of states with different 'social systems' — to use the misleading Soviet term.

Gorbachev himself put this quite starkly in his speech to the Council of Europe at Strasbourg in July 1989, just three weeks after his visit to Bonn:

> I know that many in the West see the presence of two social systems as the major difficulty. But the difficulty actually lies elsewhere — in the widespread conviction (sometimes even a policy objective) according to which overcoming the split (*raskol*) in Europe means 'overcoming socialism'. But this is a policy of confrontation, if not worse. No European unity will result from such approaches.

The reference to two social systems is significant. Gorbachev did not say that there were many social systems in Europe: the Swedish social system, for example, as opposed to the Swiss social system, the Danish and the Polish, the Hungarian and the Dutch. He said that there were just two, East and West, 'socialist' and not. By implication, the common European home should be built in spite of, and around, this central difference.

President Bush, by contrast, had declared in a speech at Mainz in West Germany, in May 1989: 'Let Europe be whole and free.' This, he averred, was 'the new mission of Nato'. 'In the East,' he said, 'brave men and women are showing us the way. Look at Poland, where Solidarity — Solidarność — and the Catholic Church have won legal status. The forces of freedom are putting the Soviet status quo on the defensive.' And the first of his four proposals 'to heal Europe's tragic division' was to 'strengthen and broaden the Helsinki process to promote free elections and political pluralism in Eastern Europe'. He went on to underline this message by demonstrative visits to Poland and Hungary, the two East European countries furthest down that path.

Thus, while the gap between the Soviet leader's proclaimed vision of a 'common European home' and the American leader's proclaimed vision of 'overcoming the division' was much narrower in summer 1989 than it had been in 1985, let alone in 1981, it was still perceptible and important. What changed this decisively in the second half of 1989 was not further movement from above on either side, but movement from below, in the centre. In events which, taken together, may be called a revolution, the countries of Eastern Europe took matters into their own hands. They did this in different ways, with varying degrees of élite and popular participation, and diverse outcomes — but all rejected the previous system, which had described itself as socialism.

While these changes certainly went faster and farther than Gorbachev and his closest associates had hoped or expected, they accepted them with quite extraordinary grace. Above all, they steadfastly refused all siren calls to preserve the 'Yalta' order by means of the instrument with the help of which it had been imposed in the first place, and then restored in 1953, 1956, 1968, and even, indirectly, in 1981: the Red Army. This renunciation of what had been known as the Brezhnev Doctrine had emerged slowly and painfully in the evolution of the 'new thinking'. The new doctrine of free choice and renunciation of force had been expressed in general terms in Gorbachev's speech to the United Nations in December 1988. Still, at the beginning of 1989 no one could be quite sure that when put to the hard test it would actually be applied to Eastern Europe. In October 1989, on American television, the Soviet Foreign Ministry spokesman Gennady Gerasimov then gave a colourful name to the successor to the Brezhnev Doctrine: 'We now have the Frank Sinatra Doctrine. He had a song, "I had it my way" (sic). So every country decides, on its own, which way to take.'

In January 1945, anticipating a preliminary Anglo-American summit meeting on Malta, to precede the Yalta conference in February of that year, Churchill jovially telegraphed to Franklin Roosevelt: 'No more let us falter! From Malta to Yalta! Let nobody alter!' In one of history's nicer coincidences, it was again on Malta, in December 1989, that there took place the Soviet-American informal summit which was an important milestone on Europe's road from Yalta. 'The post-war split of the continent,' said Gorbachev in his 1990 New Year's address, 'is receding into the past.' The Soviet Union's acceptance of the end of communism in Eastern Europe, the demise of the Warsaw Pact and the unification of Germany then marked the decisive breakthrough. By the beginning of 1991, it was no longer appropriate to talk of the 'Yalta' division of Europe. Many lines of division in Europe remained, and new ones would emerge, but this single, central divide was finished. The 'iron curtain' was no more. The Berlin Wall would soon be rubble and rusty wire.

If one argued in the 1980s that the question 'how, by peaceful means, might the "Yalta" division of Europe be overcome?' was the European question, this was considered by many to be a rhetorical exaggeration. Some said that the European question was that of how the relative economic decline of (Western) Europe, 'Eurosclerosis', might be halted or reversed. Others said that the European question was that of the development and further integration of the (West) European Community — sometimes called the 'construction of Europe'. Others again said that the European question concerned the future relationship of this community with the United States of America, especially in defence arrangements: in other words, that hardiest perennial, 'whither Nato?'

So it would perhaps be more modest and precise to talk of the Central European question. Yet throughout modern European history, the Central

European question has had a habit of becoming, sooner or later, the central European question; and this is what happened again in the 1980s.

Yalta

Two key terms emerged, or rather re-emerged, in these debates: 'Central Europe' and 'Yalta'. The matter of Central Europe is present throughout this book. A word should be said about Yalta. That Yalta became the prevailing shorthand for the division of Europe there can be no doubt. When President Mitterrand wished to express indignation at the imposition of martial law in Poland he said 'anything that helps us to get out of Yalta (*sortir de Yalta*) is good', although he warily concluded 'so long as we never confuse our desires with today's reality.' When Zbigniew Brzezinski wrote about the United States and the European question, his chosen title was 'The Future of Yalta'. The notion of 'Yalta' was equally prominent in East European opposition thinking, usually in the forms 'post-Yalta' or 'anti-Yalta'.

One might ask why Yalta, rather than Potsdam, or Tehran, or, for that matter, 'Hitler' or 'Stalin', became the all-European symbol of partition. It is also important to ask what relation Yalta — the Crimean conference of 4–11 February 1945 — bears to 'Yalta'. Almost certainly, earlier political-military decisions in the Second World War, including those at the Tehran summit conference of 1943, were more fateful even for Poland than the confused and ambiguous conclusions of the Crimean conference. In fact, 'Yalta' is drastic and misleading shorthand for the results of a long historical process, whose beginnings have to be traced back at least to August 1914, and which was not finally completed until August 1961, when the partition was set in the concrete of the Berlin Wall. The history of the Cold War is an essential part of this story, but so is that of the 'Thirty Years' War' of 1914 to 1945 — of what the historian Hajo Holborn called 'the political collapse of Europe'.

This history was retold as myth in the debates of the 1980s. Assertions about the solely negative impact of the Cold War underpinned West European social democrats' arguments for détente. Assertions about Western failures over Yalta figured largely in American neo-conservatives' criticism of détente. Some of the professional historiography, too, had a sharp political edge, which usually consisted in the explicit or implicit posing of 'if' questions ('what would have happened if . . .?'), or the canvassing of alleged 'missed opportunities'.

One of the most characteristic fallacies of this politicised if-historiography was the silent projection of certain conditions of the present into the past. A good example was furnished by the German historian Rolf Steininger. In the conclusion to his influential and well-documented book about Stalin's March 1952 offer of German reunification in return for

German neutrality, Steininger quoted a 1984 West German poll according to which fifty-three per cent of those asked were in favour of reunification in a 'bloc-free' Germany: 'a Germany,' Steininger wrote, 'such as Stalin offered in 1952'. As if the West Germany to which Stalin made his offer was the West Germany of 1984 — prosperous, stable, experienced in democracy, embedded in countless non-military structures of Western association and co-operation. Here the historian's task is to point out how different things then were.

Yet as one explores the putative alternatives of the 1940s and 1950s one sometimes feels that there is nothing new under the sun. It is remarkable how few arguments of the 1980s were not anticipated in some form — and often more eloquently and concisely — in the arguments of those earlier years. Writing in 1981, John Lewis Gaddis observed that, due to Washington's institutional amnesia, 'debates over the future of containment tend to be little more than reruns of those between George Kennan and Paul Nitze three decades ago.' *Mutatis mutandis*, much the same might be said of European debates about disengagement.

When a Christian Democrat member of the Bundestag, Bernhard Friedmann, emerged in 1987 with a proposal to put the German question on the superpowers' disarmament agenda, one of West Germany's most experienced retired ambassadors, Wilhelm Grewe, exploded in a letter to the *Frankfurter Allgemeine Zeitung*:

> How can one explain that an active politician . . . should put on paper reflections, questions and proposals without noticing that everything, but *everything* that he says, has already been said, written, proclaimed, doubted, answered countless times in the course of the last forty years — and then put aside for the time being as unreal, utopian and impractical?'

Of course we cannot here begin to explore all those historical 'ifs'. Yet it is essential to bear in mind the questions that the Yalta shorthand begs. Even if the conclusion of such an exploration were to be that, indeed, there were no real 'missed opportunities', that already in 1945 the division of Europe was as near inevitable as anything ever is in human history, it would still clearly be true that the way in which the division was completed, sealed and acknowledged, between 1945 and 1961, must have shaped the nature of the division and the way in which the division was subsequently regarded.

A unique divide

'The United States and its allies have always insisted,' the US Secretary of State, George Shultz, said before an East European tour in 1985, 'that the division of Europe is artificial, unnatural and illegitimate.' As an historical statement this is seriously open to question. There had been times since 1945 when the United States' 'insistence' on this point was less than audible, and it was more as a critic than as an ally of the United States that Charles de Gaulle insisted on Europe 'from the Atlantic to the Urals'. But if 'always' is taken to mean 'for a few years' — a fairly usual meaning of 'always' in politics — then the assertion was true. As we have already observed, by 1985 some version of this formula had become a staple ingredient of Western rhetoric. But what on earth did it mean?

If the division of Europe was 'unnatural' then what was Europe's natural state? Unity? If yes, in what form? Or was it rather — and more plausibly — that this particular division was unnatural as compared with other past or putative forms of division: for example, the 'Westphalia' division, the 'Vienna' division, the 'Versailles' division, the division into multi-national empires or the division into sovereign nation-states, each enjoying government of the people by the people for the people? Even if the last is what was meant, one is bound to say that Europe has never been natural yet.

The objection is not a frivolous one. While a Pole, a Hungarian, a Czech, a German and an American might all have heartily assented to the proposition that the division of Europe was 'unnatural', each would have meant something different by it. An older German, for example, might have taken this to mean that the division of the German nation into more than one state was unnatural. A younger West German might have regarded as the most unnatural thing the presence of American nuclear missiles on German soil.

And what would a Pole, Hungarian or Czech have meant by this proposition? Probably, some variant or combination of the following: what was 'unnatural' was that he as an individual, his society and/or his nation were denied certain rights, freedoms, opportunities and/or powers that individuals, societies and nations enjoyed elsewhere (chiefly, in 'the West', meaning essentially Western Europe and North America) and/or that his compatriots, his society and his nation had enjoyed — or were fondly believed to have enjoyed — in the past. There were thus two fundamental reference points: the real or imagined present-day West, on the one hand, the real or imagined past on the other. Different people would stress different aspects and use different vocabularies. One Polish acquaintance would use the traditional imagery of romantic nationalism, another, concepts from Hegel. One Hungarian would stress the violation of individual human and civil rights as defined in Anglo-American political thought, and find his model for a natural and truly European order in the (West) European Community. Another would consider that Europe fell from its natural state with the Treaty of Trianon.

Plainly, this division of Europe was not easy to define. And plainly it changed over time. Relations between the governments and peoples of, say,

Hungary and Austria, were not the same in 1988 as they were in 1968. Nonetheless, a rudimentary working definition — a rough sketch map — is important for our purpose.

Many attempts have been made to correlate this division with earlier and, it has sometimes been said, deeper or underlying divisions of Europe, starting with the *limes* of the Roman empire. The boundaries of the original European Community (or strictly, European Communities) of six member-states can be shown to correspond quite closely to those of Charlemagne's empire in the year 814. Several economic historians have argued that the lands to the east of the River Elbe took a different, and tendentially more 'backward' course of economic development from the sixteenth century onward. The cautious empiricist will note signal exceptions on both sides of such boldly drawn lines: with, for example, developed Silesia and Bohemia to the east, and less developed Spain and Portugal to the west. Moreover, one can point to what are arguably even deeper lines of division — such as that between Western and Eastern Christianity — running far to the east of the Yalta line.

Whatever the validity of these deeper correlations, this division of Europe was distinguished from — and at least arguably more 'artificial' and 'illegitimate' than — earlier divisions of Europe, by virtue of its historical arbitrariness, its absoluteness, the asymmetrical roles of partly extra-European, nuclear-armed superpowers, and the congruence of military, political and economic differences.

Many border lines in European history have been drawn arbitrarily, but few more so than those of which the last details were finally agreed by the Soviet representatives in the so-called European Advisory Commission on 13 August 1945, and which became the Berlin Wall on 13 August 1961. Frontiers have always divided peoples, but no frontier in modern European history has divided peoples as completely as did those between Eastern and Western Europe at their most impenetrable. The cliché once expressed a truth: these frontiers were like an 'iron curtain'. While the movement of people between Eastern and Western Europe did increase as the iron curtain grew more permeable, this was as nothing compared with the increased movement of people within each part of Europe.

Both West and East European states depended, in ways they had not before 1945, on partly extra-European, nuclear-armed superpowers. But the westward and eastward dependencies were far from symmetrical. East European states depended on their immediate continental neighbour; West European states depended on a power removed from them by several thousand miles of ocean. France and Britain had their own nuclear weapons; no East European state did. Nato defended West European states against a real or imagined Soviet threat; the Warsaw Pact defended East European states against a real or imagined Western threat, but above all against their own peoples.

West European states had a larger combined population than the United States; East European states, taken all together, had less than half the population of the Soviet Union. According to Western specialists, what the Soviet Union took out of the East European economies in the first decade after 1945 was roughly equivalent to what the United States put in to West European economies through Marshall Aid. Comecon and the European Community were no less asymmetrical. The former included the super-power, the latter did not. The EC was increasingly a genuine common market; Comecon never was.

Most East European states had been poorer than most West European states before the war. Most East European states were poorer than most West European states at the beginning of the 1980s. Despite the indubit-able fact of industrial development in Eastern Europe since the war, most of these countries' relative economic position vis-à-vis Western Europe had not significantly improved. In some cases — notably that of East Germany — it had actually worsened, and in all cases it threatened to worsen still further. Although the statistics in this field were even more treacherous than usual, the economic gap between East and West in Europe, as experienced in everyday life, was plainly visible in the figures for the provision of telephones or car-ownership.

In the internal orders of the European states there had also been asymmetrical developments. At Stalin's death, East European states were clearly more like each other, more closely integrated (at least formally) both with each other and with the 'protecting' superpower, than were those of Western Europe. Since that time, however, East European states had tended to diverge whereas West European states tended to converge. By the beginning of the 1980s, virtually all the states of Western Europe were combined in or closely associated with an historically unprecedented form of European Community, to which they had voluntarily sacrificed part of their sovereignty. Whereas for much of the post-war period several of them had been dictatorships (Spain, Portugal) all of them were now liberal (or 'bourgeois' or 'capitalist') democracies. In their internal polit-ical, economic and legal orders they were at once increasingly alike and increasingly interdependent. If they were economically and politically more dependent on each other they were also less dependent on the United States. The one — signal — exception to this rule was defence.

East European states, by contrast, had diverged not only from the Soviet model but also from each other. Although on paper their political systems might still look very similar, in practice their real internal political and economic structures had become increasingly diverse, complex and diffi-cult to categorise. No single term — 'totalitarianism', 'authoritarianism', 'state capitalism', 'really existing socialism', 'dictatorship over needs' — was adequate to embracing this diversity and complexity. With apologies to William Empson, one might describe the East European states in the

1980s as six types of ambiguity. If West European states had voluntarily surrendered part of their sovereignty to the European Community, East European states had generally attempted to claw back some of the sovereignty which they involuntarily surrendered in the 1940s and 1950s. While these states were to a significant degree economically dependent on each other, they had not made any major virtue out of this necessity. By contrast with Western Europe, their own bi- and multilateral associations in the region had not made them, individually or collectively, economically or politically, less dependent on their superpower 'protector'.

Things were even less clear at the level of society and culture. Was there ever such a thing as an 'East European society'? Did East German society have more in common with Polish society than with West German society? Or Hungarian with Romanian rather than Austrian? Was there any meaningful sense in which one could talk of an individual man or woman as 'an East European' as opposed to 'a West European'? When Czech, Hungarian and Polish intellectuals initiated a cultural-historical revival of the idea of 'Central Europe' in the early 1980s, they aimed to challenge precisely these simplistic dichotomies.

Nonetheless, for all this complexity and diversity, and for all the relative softening over time, there was still, even in the 1980s, one great divide. Every ordinary first-time visitor in either direction could tell you that. There was a reality of 'Eastern Europe', a reality of 'Western Europe', and you knew when you had crossed the line. You knew it at the line. Even if you did not actually see the 'iron curtain' with barbed wire and guard dogs, there were — coming from the West — the stricter border controls, the politically determined import restrictions, the compulsory exchange of hard currency. Beyond the line, there were a hundred aspects of everyday life, large and small — the cheap paper forms in quadruplicate, the queues, the newspapers, the smell of the air — in which, for all the differences, Budapest was still more like Warsaw or even Bucharest than it was like Vienna. And that was even more true as you penetrated into the individual's experience, not only in politics and direct relations with the state, but at the workplace, in hospital, at school or university.

In historical perspective, what was most remarkable about this divide was the congruence of military, political, economic, ideological, cultural and social differences. To be sure, after the Peace of Augsburg the rule in Central Europe was *cuius regio, eius religio*. But under 'Yalta' it was much more than just *religio*. Never before had so much flowed from so little. If you happened to live at the bottom end of the Friedrichstrasse in central Berlin, you got liberal democracy, the Americans, the European Community, the Costa del Sol, the Volkswagen and McDonald's. Your brother, who lived three blocks up the street, got communism, the Russians, Comecon, the Black Sea, the Trabant and *soljanka*.

One final remark is necessary to complete this rudimentary sketch map.

The description of Europe as being cut in half by one great divide should not obscure an important eastern sub-divide. Without venturing into the inspissated jungle of cultural-historical argument about the eastern frontiers of Europe, whether Russia is part of Europe, or where historic Central Europe begins and ends, let it simply be stated that there were major parts of the Soviet Union — for example, the Baltic republics — which were historically and culturally European. Those parts of Europe, or elements of 'Europeanness', inside the Soviet Union were, however, in a different political position from, say, Hungary or Czechoslovakia. Although their fundamental aspirations might be the same, their possibilities for realising them were not.

For the period covered in the main part of this book — until 1989–90 — it is meaningful to talk of 'the Soviet Union' as one thing, and of 'Eastern Europe' as another. This political 'Eastern Europe' may briefly be defined as those parts of historic Central, East Central and South Eastern Europe which in the 1940s and 1950s were organised into party-states on the Soviet model, with limited sovereignty, closely tied to the Soviet Union by public and secret arrangements, and incorporated into Comecon and the Warsaw Pact.

Here then is what we mean by the 'Yalta' division of Europe: distinguished from previous divisions of Europe by its historical arbitrariness, its absoluteness, the asymmetrical roles of partly extra-European, nuclear-armed superpowers, and the congruence of military, political and economic differences.

Healing?

What would it mean to 'overcome' this division? What, to use more emotive words, was to be understood by the 'restoration', 'reunification' or 'healing' of Europe? It will already be apparent that very different answers could be — and were — offered to these questions. American policymakers suggested that the healing of Europe meant ending communism in Eastern Europe while preserving Nato in Western Europe. Soviet policymakers suggested ending Nato while preserving communism.

Clearly, overcoming the division had an external and an internal aspect. The external aspect, concerning relations between Western and Eastern Europe, had two main dimensions. First, there was the relationship between Western and Eastern states, and perhaps between Western and Eastern groupings of states such as the OECD, the European Community and Comecon. Secondly, there was the relationship between peoples and between individual people: possibilities of travel, emigration, family reunification, cultural, academic, commercial or technological exchanges, and so forth. The internal aspect concerned relations inside the two parts, and this might also be said to have two dimensions. Firstly, there were the relationships of states with their nuclear-armed superpower and with other states in their own part. Secondly, there were the relationships of states to their own societies and to their own citizens.

Even if the basic terms of this crude outline were accepted by most West and East European participants in the debates of the 1980s, very different emphases were placed, and radically divergent accounts were given of the connections between different points on the agenda. Thus it was, for example, a matter of the hottest dispute, how much and what change was needed in Western Europe as against how much and what change in Eastern Europe, and what the causal relationship might be between the one and the other. With a few exceptions, even those who saw a deep symmetry between the situation of Western and Eastern Europe within their respective 'blocs' would have agreed that, however imperfect the relations between state and society might be in Western Europe, these relations were worse in Eastern Europe (some would have said 'in degree', most 'in kind'), and that in this regard there was, to put it mildly, more need for change in Eastern than in Western Europe.

Many politicians and commentators in Western Europe did, however, maintain that the position of West European states vis-à-vis the United States was in important respects comparable to the position of East European states vis-à-vis the Soviet Union; that the more independent West European states became from the United States, the more independent East European states might become from the Soviet Union; and that these states, being more independent, would then better be able to satisfy the aspirations of their societies for more freedom, respect for human rights, contacts with Western Europe and so forth, thus 'restoring Europe' internally as well as externally.

Of course this argument came in many variants, from the exaggerated and crudely deterministic version offered by parts of the peace movement and the Greens in the early 1980s to the cautious and statesmanlike German Gaullism of ex-Chancellor Helmut Schmidt. Yet even Schmidt went so far as to say (in 1986) that 'in the second half of the 1980s the extent of Western Europe's standing up for itself is, for West Europeans *and for East Europeans* the measure of Europe's standing up for itself overall' [author's italics].

Independent intellectuals and opposition activists in Eastern Europe, by contrast, tended to argue the case from the other end. East European states, they said, could only be more self-reliant and peaceful partners for Western Europe when they could rely on the support of their own societies. The less these states could depend on their own populations, the more they would have to depend on the Soviet Union. And they could only rely on the support of their own societies when they showed more respect for human rights and popular aspirations.

Since this debate was initially couched in terms of peace rather than European unification, these East Europeans said: Europe has not been at peace since 1945, it has only been in a state of 'non-war', because the countries of Eastern Europe have not enjoyed that 'internal peace' which the countries of Western Europe have, by and large, enjoyed. 'Without internal peace,' wrote Václav Havel in 1985, 'that is, peace among citizens and between citizens and the state, there can be no guarantee of external peace.' And, echoing the reflections of Immanuel Kant nearly two centuries earlier, he went on: 'a state that ignores the will and the rights of its citizens can offer no guarantee that it will respect the will and the rights of other peoples, nations and states'. If West European peace activists said that peace — meaning, in the first place, nuclear disarmament in Western Europe — would bring more respect for human rights in Eastern Europe, East European oppositionists replied that only respect for human rights in Eastern Europe would bring that real condition of European peace in which it would be safe for Western Europe to disarm.

Here too we have simplified a complex argument. The contrasting positions reflected different interests as well as different analyses. Yet this controversy well illustrates the lack of neutral or common definitions. Even with an agreed diagnosis, doctors may propose widely different cures. Here they started with neither a common diagnosis of the sickness nor even a common definition of health.

I

German Answers

The divided centre

Germany was central to this European question in two senses. First, it was central because it was in the centre. There is a long line of German historians who have argued that the most distinctive features of German history, and particularly of German foreign policy, are primarily a consequence of Germany's geographical position without well-defined natural frontiers in the middle of Europe: the famous *Mittellage*. Germany, they say, is only to be understood as a 'land of the centre'. Yet Polish historians have observed that Poland is also a land without well-defined natural frontiers in the middle of Europe; and rather different consequences have flowed for the two countries from this similar, indeed shared, geographical position. Meanwhile Prague has vied with Warsaw and Berlin for the title of 'the heart of Europe'.

Nonetheless, Germany's geopolitical situation in 'Yalta' Europe was unique. No other country had the line between East and West running through its middle. Germany was the divided centre of a divided Europe. Berlin, Germany's once and future capital, was the divided centre of the divided centre.

The second sense in which Germany was central is closely related to this unique geopolitical dilemma, but far from merely determined by it. This is the centrality of Ostpolitik. It is no accident that Ostpolitik is one of relatively few German words to be used in the English language, alongside Weltanschauung, Angst and Schadenfreude. For if one examines the policies of the major Western powers towards Eastern Europe over the twenty years from 1969 to 1989, one soon finds that the policy of the Federal Republic was the most consistent, the most extensive and the most intensive. In relations with the Soviet Union, the United States self-evidently remained in a class of its own, at least until Gorbachev's visit to Bonn in June 1989. But in terms of direct action in Eastern Europe, the Federal Republic was already second to none in the 1980s.

In 1985-86, the then Charter 77 spokesman Jiří Dienstbier wrote a manuscript entitled 'Dreaming of Europe'. He wrote it in his spare time while working as a stoker, for, like many intellectuals who had resisted Gustáv Husák's so-called 'normalisation', he was prevented by the party-state authorities from obtaining any but menial employment. In the Preface to the 1991 German edition of this book, Dienstbier, now, incredibly, Czechoslovakia's Foreign Minister, recalled that as he looked around from his boiler-room in the mid-1980s to see how the dream goal of overcoming the Yalta division might be achieved, he 'found in the West only the positions of individuals and a single larger conception, Brandt's Ostpolitik, which reckoned with a Europe other than the one to which we had all accustomed ourselves during the Cold War'. We shall try to explore, in this book, how accurate that judgement was, in relation both to Brandt's Ostpolitik and to the concepts and policies of other states, governments, movements and individuals, in West and East. But that it looked this way to the intellectual stoker in Prague is itself revealing.

Before turning specifically to Ostpolitik, however, we must look briefly at the general terms and context of German answers to the European question. For no one offered more (or longer) diagnoses of the Yalta sickness than the Germans, and no one was more fertile in proposing cures.

Let us start with the end. What would be the healing or peaceful restoration of Europe? In the 1980s, one mainstream German answer was: the 'normalisation' of relations between Western and Eastern Europe. A notable early use of the term 'normalisation' in this context was in the Soviet Union's diplomatic note of 7 June 1955, proposing the opening of diplomatic relations with the Federal Republic. On his visit to Moscow in September 1955, Adenauer took up the word, at the same time firmly insisting that the division of Germany was 'abnormal'. An important Bundestag resolution of June 1961, based on a report by the Sudeten German Social Democrat, Wenzel Jaksch, called on the federal government 'to seize every available opportunity . . . to achieve a normalisation of relations between the Federal Republic and the East European states'.

Normalisation then became a central term of the social-liberal Ostpolitik of the early 1970s, which the Free Democrat Foreign Minister Walter Scheel described as 'nothing but the attempt at a political normalisation on the basis of the realities that we find here and now.' The term was then used in the Federal Republic's actual treaties with the Soviet Union, Poland and East Germany, the three most important of the so-called 'Eastern treaties'.

This story will be told in more detail below. The point here is simply that by the 1980s the word 'normalisation' had become a regular and central component of German responses to the European question. In a tirelessly repeated formula, West German politicians of all parties said that they wanted to change not the frontiers in Europe but the quality of frontiers in Europe. They wanted to rid the frontiers of their divisive character, to make them ever more permeable. The iron curtain should be turned into one of velvet, or even of lace. The crossing between East and West Germany should be as normal as that between West Germany and Holland. Relations between the Federal Republic and Poland should be as normal as relations between the Federal Republic and France.

This answer was, to use an old schoolteacher's phrase, good as far as it went. But it did not go very far. We may leave aside for the moment the fact that the very term 'normalisation' had a sinister ring for most people in East Central Europe, where it was used in this same period to describe the attempt to return a European society, by force, to Soviet norms: as in Czechoslovakia after 1968. This coincidence — and the relationship between the two kinds of 'normalisation' — is far from irrelevant to some problems in the Federal Republic's relations with those countries, but its significance can only be understood in context.

Immediately relevant, however, is the fact that, by the standard of relations between European states in the past, or by the standard of relations between most states in the world, the relations between the Federal Republic and the French Republic or the Kingdom of the Netherlands were, by the 1980s, very far from normal. They were quite abnormally good. The frontiers were abnormally open and the relations between peoples as well as governments were abnormally close. And the essential precondition for this was not merely the elementary will to reconciliation and co-operation on the part of governments and peoples, but also the basic compatibility of political, economic and social systems.

On reflection, therefore, this was to set a quite exceptionally high standard, since to achieve such an abnormal 'normality' would self-evidently require fundamental political change inside Eastern Europe. Yet at other times the achievement of 'normality' was measured, in German usage, against the exceptionally low standard of freedom of movement between the two German states. By this standard, relations between Austria and Hungary were already almost perfect in the mid-1980s, although at that time Hungary still had a fundamentally different political and economic system. The erratic standard of 'normality' is well illustrated by a passage in Helmut Schmidt's 1978 state of the nation address in which he suggested that the goal for the relationship between the two German states should be that 'gradually a situation of matter-of-course normality should be achieved, such as has so far been achieved for example in our relationship with the Polish People's Republic'. Normality?

European peace order

These ambiguities are still more apparent when one looks at the concept of a 'European peace order' (*Europäische Friedensordnung*). By the end of the 1960s, this phrase had been adopted by politicians of all the major parties as a common formula for the long-term goal of Ostpolitik. It seems to have appeared for the first time in the July 1957 Berlin Declaration of the Federal Republic and its Western allies, the United States, France and Britain. It was used fitfully, but with growing frequency, through the early 1960s, before being accorded prominence in the first government declaration of the 'Grand Coalition' of Christian and Social Democrats, in December 1966. It was then used repeatedly by both the Christian Democrat Chancellor, Kiesinger, and the Social Democrat Foreign Minister, Brandt. It was also taken up in Nato's December 1967 Harmel report, a text which German policymakers would cite religiously for more than two decades thereafter. Helmut Schmidt expresses a sentiment which many, if not all, leading West German policymakers would have endorsed, when he writes in his memoirs that this European peace order 'has seemed to me down all the years to be the most important thing'.

But what did it mean? Here again, there were many versions of the vision, most of them remaining at a high level of conceptual imprecision. Nonetheless, one may tentatively discern two different sorts of public definition, which relate to the broader debate about the healing of Europe. The first was indicated by Walter Scheel in a Bundestag debate in 1970. The objective of the new Ostpolitik, said Scheel, was to bring about a European order 'in which countries of different political orders and social systems are equally members'. The object was not a 'compromise' between liberal and communist orders, but co-operation between countries, organisations or communities with different social and political orders. 'Only thus can there be a European peace order which embraces all of Europe, and not, as some imagine, through "pulling over" one or other side into the political system of the one or the other.'

Seventeen years later, Scheel's successor as Foreign Minister and leader of the Free Democrats, Hans-Dietrich Genscher, declared in a reflective exposition of his foreign policy credo: 'The development is inexorably towards a European peace order, in which peoples, even in different social and state orders, can advance in peaceful competition and without fear of each other.' Writing in early 1988 about this process of knitting together Eastern and Western Europe, the grand old lady of West German liberal journalism, Marion Gräfin Dönhoff, added the following observation: 'last week influential politicians of various affiliations in Vienna assured me that their relations with Budapest are now better than in Austria-Hungary under the Monarchy. So the difference between the social systems need be no obstacle.'

The clearest, though also the most extreme statement of this version of the goal came from the Social Democrat Egon Bahr, one of the most fertile and influential practitioners, strategists and ideologists of Ostpolitik from the early 1960s to the late 1980s. In a little book entitled *Towards European*

Peace. A Response to Gorbachev, published in 1988, Bahr wrote that a
system of collective security was the 'necessary structure of international
law' for a European peace order. Such a system of collective security,
which he suggested could be achieved by the end of the century, 'would
be equivalent to European peace.' Although at one point he observed in
passing that in this European peace 'the western principles of the Helsinki
Final Act . . . would become binding in international law', its achievement
was clearly envisaged prior to, and irrespective of, a change of the political
system in Eastern Europe.

In this peace, Bahr wrote, the contradictions between East and West
would remain 'to be historically resolved'. What the Soviet system might
develop in conditions of guaranteed peace 'could be very exciting'. There
would be a 'guaranteed peaceful political competition of systems and
economic co-operation' for which a proper 'culture of dispute' should be
developed. And, in perhaps the clearest statement, he wrote of 'growing
co-operation in unchanged political structures. Abnormal normality.'

Now one cannot, of course, simply assume that such public statements
reflect the sum total of the private hopes or intentions of the speaker or
writer. That states and statesmen should disguise their real goals is hardly
a novelty, and in most Western countries there is a continual debate about
how loudly and explicitly governments should embrace the goal of political
change inside other countries. In an interview in 1973, Egon Bahr quoted
von Moltke to the effect that 'everything that one says must be true, but
one must not say everything that is true'. 'That,' commented Bahr, 'also
applies to politics.' How these public statements related to private intentions is therefore a question that we shall have to consider in more detail
below. The point here is simply to sketch the publicly articulated vision.

The vision of a 'European peace order' publicly articulated by leading
Christian Democrats in the 1980s made a sharp contrast. From the
moment they came to power in 1982, Chancellor Kohl and his closest
associates roundly asserted the centrality of the issue of freedom, not
merely to the German question, on which they were vocal, but also to the
European question, as I have defined it here. The Social Democrats in
government had firmly and consistently maintained that the Federal
Republic's Western ties in the European Community and Nato were the
sine qua non of their Ostpolitik. But the Christian Democrats, returning to
government, brought a strong public re-emphasis of shared Western values
as well.

Indeed, these re-emphasised Western values took centre stage in the
rhetoric of their Ostpolitik. People in Central and Eastern Europe,
Chancellor Kohl declared simply in his 1984 state of the nation address,
wanted to be free, as people in the Federal Republic were free: 'And
therein lies the real problem of the German and European division, in the
denial of freedom and self-determination for the people in Central and

Eastern Europe.' The European peace order, he said in his 1987 address, would be one in which 'the basic freedoms are realised, undivided and unlimited, for all the peoples of Europe . . .'

'The clear articulation of our own goals and values,' said a key figure in the Kohl Chancellery, Wolfgang Schäuble, 'also serves the predictability of relations [with communist states]. Concealment would more likely be understood as an attempt to deceive, and arouse mistrust.' In the same speech, in 1986, he made a distinction which could have come straight from the writings of independent intellectuals and opposition activists in Poland, Hungary, Czechoslovakia and, not least, the GDR. Talking of the ruling Socialist Unity Party in the GDR he said: 'To be sure, it verbally subordinates its policies to the priority of securing peace. But by "peace" it understands rather the absence of war than the free development of the citizen in a state which is also inwardly at peace.' And Chancellor Kohl might have been quoting the Polish Pope when he declared that 'Peace begins with respect for the absolute and unconditional dignity of every individual human being in all departments of their life.'

So these leading Christian Democrats' public vision of the 'European peace order' explicitly linked the issue of peace between East and West to the question of freedom inside Eastern Europe, marking the symbiotic relationship between external and internal peace, and thus at least implicitly accepting that reducing or overcoming the division of Europe was as much a matter of changing internal relations between state and society inside Eastern Europe as it was of changing external relations between East and West. Freedom is the precondition of unity, they tirelessly repeated, for Germany, but also for Europe. How far their practice reflected this theory is another question, which will also be addressed below.

Two questions or one?

The governments of centre-left and centre-right were at one, however, in proclaiming deep harmony, if not complete identity, between German and European interests. Chancellor Kohl echoed Chancellor Schmidt in observing that 'the division of Germany is simultaneously the division of Europe'. Foreign Minister Genscher said simply: 'the division of Germany is the division of our European continent'. To work by peaceful means for European unity is 'above all a matter for the Germans', said President von Weizsäcker. 'To overcome the division of Germany is simultaneously to overcome the division of Europe', wrote Chancellery Minister Wolfgang Schäuble, 'it is as important for Europe as it is for us Germans.' 'German foreign policy' was always and simultaneously 'European peace policy'. There was no contradiction at all between West European integration and Ostpolitik: each served the other. Ostpolitik, as Walter Scheel most plainly put it, was 'an expression of the identity of our interests with the interests of Europe'.

That the German and European questions were very closely related is obvious. That there was such a sublime harmony of interests is not. There are good reasons for subjecting these claims to a little closer examination. For a start, it is characteristic of most European nation-states in modern history that their representatives assert or assume a harmony, or even identity, between what they see as national interests and what they claim to be European interests. One could cite countless examples from France, Poland, Italy, Russia or Hungary over the last two centuries. It was Bismarck who observed that 'I have always found the word "Europe" in the mouths of those politicians who wanted from other powers something they did not dare to demand in their own name ...' The all-European phenomenon acquires, however, a particular edge in the case of Germany.

To mention Hitler in this context may seem perverse. Yet it is remarkable to look again into Max Domarus's collection of Hitler's speeches and to find just how often and how eloquently Hitler spoke of Europe: of Europe at peace, of respect and equal rights for European neighbours, of 'European co-operation' and Franco-German reconciliation, and then again of peace and friendship. 'No man ever spoke with greater feeling of the horror and stupidity of war than Adolf Hitler,' wrote his biographer Alan Bullock. One might add: no one spoke more movingly of Europe. All of which is to say only this: that 'Europe' is one of those large words — like 'peace' — which have been so terribly abused in the twentieth century, that it should be a basic intellectual and moral requirement to use them not loosely, vaguely, or instrumentally, but sharply, precisely, and for themselves. Apart from that, any comparison with Hitler is not relevant.

A more relevant comparison is with Gustav Stresemann. Willy Brandt, Helmut Kohl and Hans-Dietrich Genscher themselves all either made or accepted the comparison of their policies with those of the foreign minister of the 1920s. Yet even in the case of Stresemann there was a strong element of using 'Europe' — both semantically and diplomatically — as a means to the achievement of national ends.

So also with Konrad Adenauer. Germany in 1945 was not only physically and morally degraded, it was also totally deprived of sovereignty. Adenauer's first task, the first task of anyone who aspired to the title of German statesman, was therefore, beside the physical and moral restoration, the recovery of sovereignty. The struggle to achieve, first the bare minimum of local self-government, then statehood in part of the nation, then sovereignty for that state (with important powers and prerogatives reserved to France, Britain and the United States), then a growing 'room for manoeuvre' for that sovereign state: this is a leitmotif of the history of the Federal Republic. It runs through all Chancellorships over four decades.

Now the first ladder out of the morass was marked 'Europe'. The conservative historian Michael Stürmer has put it thus: 'The only opportunity left to Germany [after 1945] was to play the Western game, to be the most European nation among the Europeans, and to translate Germany's geostrategic position into political negotiating power.' The Cold War turned Germany's position as the divided centre of the continent from a further liability into a partial asset — although only for the Germans in the Western zones of occupation.

For Adenauer, the enterprise of building Europe clearly had two sides. On the one hand, the Germans, whose capacity to steer their own course he sometimes doubted, were to be bound in to a larger European community, to which they might yield some of the traditional authority and powers of a nation-state. On the other hand, participation in a (West) European community was a way for (part of) Germany to recover such authority and powers. In many respects, West Germany immediately took the West European path. The 1948 Hague Congress on Europe was the first major international meeting where German representatives again took their seats as free and equal partners, democrats among democrats, Europeans among Europeans. The Council of Europe, which grew out of that meeting, was the first body in which the West German state became a full and equal member. The founding of the European Coal and Steel Community in 1951 proved, in the event, to be the first step towards building a political European Community through the pursuit of common commercial and economic policies. In 1952, the treaty which Adenauer hoped would mark the decisive breakthrough to sovereignty was umbilically linked to a treaty forming a European Defence Community. But although Franco-German reconciliation would later became a cornerstone of German policy, in 1954 the plan for a European Defence Community was defeated — in the French National Assembly.

The second ladder out of the morass was therefore marked 'Nato'. Although German membership of Nato was linked to membership of a so-called Western European Union, and with a special, unique commitment of British troops to serve in Germany, the essence of Nato was clearly the alliance with the United States. While Adenauer kept an open mind for all possible tactical and strategic variations, in the German interest, he nonetheless repeatedly insisted on West Germany's need of the United States to counterbalance the Soviet Union in the centre of Europe. For the very survival of the Federal Republic, he argued, the ties with the United States were more important even than those with France. While the renegotiated treaties of the autumn of 1954 were known as the Paris treaties, they linked the recovery of sovereignty and the commitment to a military alliance with the United States.

These Western treaties of the early 1950s were the first great leap on the (West) German path back to independence. The second great leap came twenty years later with the Eastern treaties of the early 1970s. The former enabled the Federal Republic to operate as an independent state in the West; the latter enabled it to operate as an independent state in the East.

One could write the history of Central Europe over the forty years from 1949 to 1989 as the story of attempts by European peoples to become once again the subjects rather than the objects of history. For Poles, Hungarians and Czechs this meant primarily the attempt to regain control over their own internal affairs, for to regain control over their external affairs was hardly to be dreamed of. It meant endeavouring to restore, by reform or revolution, what might be called 'internal sovereignty', with citizens becoming willing, participant and enfranchised subjects rather than un-willing, non-participant and disenfranchised objects of state policy. The key concept which Pope John Paul II used when discussing civic aspira-tions was that of '*podmiotowość*', inadequately translated as 'subjectness' or 'subjectivity', and meaning precisely the condition of being fully a subject rather than an object of history.

The majority of Germans were early given full control over their internal affairs, full 'internal sovereignty'. Like all citizens of liberal democracies, they had to work — sometimes even to struggle — to preserve and enhance this control. But the striving to become subject rather than object found its clearest expression in foreign policy: both in the struggle for external 'freedom of action' as a sovereign state and in deciding how to use that freedom. This is one of many ways in which the recent history of the Germans is at once very similar to and quite different from the recent history of other Central European peoples. The Pope said Solidarity was an expression of the Poles' 'subjectivity'. One might say that Ostpolitik was an expression of the Germans' 'subjectivity'.

This consistent and patient struggle for what Willy Brandt in his seminal government declaration of October 1969 called 'a more self-reliant German policy' required the support of allies and neighbours to an unusual degree. All major Western countries were increasingly interde-pendent in foreign policy (especially in foreign economic policy), and all major West European countries were specifically dependent on the United States for their defence. But West Germany had more ties than any. It had the residual dependencies resulting from defeat and occupation, and the new dependencies of the Cold War, including a direct dependence on the Western allies for the security of West Berlin, and, as a non-nuclear power on the front line of the Cold War, a special dependence on the nuclear-armed superpower to the West to counterbalance the nuclear-armed superpower to the East. At the same time it had the multifarious, voluntary ties and dependencies resulting from its attempt to rehabilitate itself in a larger West European, Atlantic and world community. Europe was the first ladder out of the morass, but the ladder also became a fence — as French politicians always intended that it should.

One of the oft-repeated formulae of West German politics was that German unity could only be achieved with the 'understanding', 'agreement' or 'support' of Germany's neighbours. Like several other commandments of Ostpolitik, this combined a political with a moral message. The implicit moral message was that it would be wrong for Germany to push through reunification against the will of her neighbours. The political message was that she hadn't a chance of doing so anyway. The moral and the political messages were not, however, precisely congruent. For example, in a somewhat unusual formulation, Chancellor Schmidt declared in his 1979 state of the nation address that German unity was not to be had 'without the assent of the East European peoples'. Yet if Moscow, Washington, Paris and London agreed to German reunification, could even a unanimous chorus of Poles, Hungarians, Czechs, Slovaks, Romanians, Bulgarians, Albanians, Slovenes, Serbs and Croats do anything at all to prevent it?

Now clearly no other Western state was as directly interested as the Federal Republic was in reducing or overcoming the division of Europe. What is more, those West European countries that did express some serious interest in reducing the division of Europe were not equally interested in reducing the division of Germany. Helmut Schmidt writes in his memoirs that when he became Chancellor in 1974 ' . . . there was hardly a government in Europe which genuinely regretted the partition of Germany. That was more the case in Washington or distant Peking.' In sum: 'The world thus seemed to be quite content with the division of Germany; illogically it was much less content with the division of Europe.'

To rebuke the world for being illogical was marvellously characteristic of Helmut Schmidt. It was also not entirely logical. In other contexts, Schmidt himself, like Brandt before him, spoke with perfect understanding of the fears that European neighbours might have of an united Germany of more than seventy-five million people in the heart of Europe. 'We love Germany so much that we are glad there are two of them,' as François Mauriac had famously remarked. The attitude of Germany's European neighbours, moreover, was shaped not merely by fears of Germany but also by ties of tradition and affection with other countries. Was there anything really illogical in Austrians caring more about the lot of Hungarians, or Frenchmen caring more about the lot of Poles than either might about the lot of Germans?

To say that you could not overcome the division of Europe without overcoming the division of Germany was, at first glance, iron logic. It was like saying: the division of an apple is the division of the core. You cannot have a united apple with a divided core. But Europe is not an apple. In fact, logically or illogically, both possible variants of a German-European disjuncture — a united Germany in a divided Europe, and even a divided Germany in a united Europe — had at different times been envisaged, not merely in theory, but in the practice of major Western partners of the Federal Republic. There was a time in the 1950s when policymakers in Washington seriously discussed the 'policy of strength' somehow pulling the rest of Germany fully into the West: thus creating, at least temporarily, the variant of 'united Germany in divided Europe'. (The phrase was used in American State Department discussions.) The Gaullist vision of Europe from the Atlantic to the Urals, by contrast, came close to being one of a united Europe around a divided Germany. In general, France, although sporadically interested in overcoming the division of Europe, was also the Western power least interested in overcoming the division of Germany.

The relationship between the German and the European questions was thus extremely complex. They were two questions, but so long as the Federal Republic considered itself to have a basic national interest in overcoming the division of Germany, it had overwhelming national reasons for desiring that the two questions should be taken as one. The Federal Republic therefore wanted its Western neighbours and allies to be as concerned as possible about the European question, while at the same time building the German question into the centre of the European one. In notes for a conversation with de Gaulle in December 1966, Willy Brandt put it simply and eloquently: 'The trench that divides my country also divides Europe. Anyone who fills in that trench also helps my country. We have no other prospect than to overcome the division of Europe.' And twenty years later, Chancellery Minister Wolfgang Schäuble explained: 'Our chance lies in the fact that the division of Germany is simultaneously the division of Europe.'

The rhetorical assertion of sublime harmony between German and European interests was but the most obvious symptom of this national interest, and the simplest means to securing it. This involved at least one major ambiguity in the use of the word 'Europe'. For the phrase 'unifying Europe' was applied both to the process of integration inside the (West) European Community and to the larger enterprise of overcoming the division of Europe. It then became not merely obvious but tautologous to observe that European unification served the cause of European unification. Yet, in practice, the tension between further West European integration and the search for closer ties with Eastern Europe and the Soviet Union was a recurrent theme of German foreign policy debates. The Social Democrats under Kurt Schumacher attacked Adenauer's policy of Western integration for closing the door to the East, and specifically to national reunification. Franz Josef Strauss and others attacked Brandt and Scheel for neglecting the cause of West European integration in pursuit of what Strauss then described as the chimera of a greater Europe (*Grossraum Europa*). When in government, however, each party proclaimed the harmony of interests.

Yet, plainly, rhetoric alone would not suffice. 'The unity of the Germans,' said Willy Brandt in his January 1970 state of the nation address, 'depends . . . not in the first place or solely on the wording of treaties, but rather on how far we can win other states as friends, not so much on Potsdam 1945 but much more on overcoming the division of Europe in the 1970s, the 1980s and, if it must be, in the 1990s, Ladies and Gentlemen.' And other states are not won as 'friends' by sweet words alone. In its own interest, the Federal Republic had not only to say but to do things that at least some other states or peoples felt to be in their interest too. But what things, and for which states or peoples?

Of course it would be ungenerous, and against the evidence of deeds as well as words, to imply that German policy-makers or opinion-formers did not have a large measure of disinterested, idealistic, historically informed and morally sensitive concern about the lot of those other Europeans who suffered most from the 'Yalta' division. Most certainly they did. The one by no means precludes the other. But on the evidence of their own authoritative statements, we are certainly obliged to ask how far what happened in the 1970s and 1980s was — to use a formula from the late 1960s — the Europeanisation of the German question, and how far the Germanisation of the European question.

Was Ostpolitik a European answer to the European question, a German answer to the European question, a European answer to the German question, or simply a German answer to the German question? And if, as the architects of Ostpolitik would immediately object, it was all of the above, then in what proportions?

The European interest

Not everything that is called European is, in fact, European, and not everything that is European is so called. The Europeanness of Ostpolitik may be asserted. It has yet to be proved. But how can it be proved or disproved? What are the criteria, and who the judges of Europeanness? One criterion has already been suggested: that of motives. A policy is European because those who practise or support it genuinely believe that they are acting for Europe. But this is a very weak and slippery criterion. For do we really understand even our own motives? And what if others think otherwise? 'Do not do unto others as you would they should do unto you,' said George Bernard Shaw. 'Their tastes may not be the same.'

A second approach would be to try and advance a clear definition of what is European, or in the European interest, and then measure various policies and approaches against this. Thus one could say, for example, that it is European to respect certain, explicitly specified, human and civil rights, protected by due process of law, while it is not European to repress or murder people because of their race, colour or creed. Plainly, such a definition is prescriptive rather than descriptive.

This procedure has the merit of taking the discussion into the sphere of rational argument. The meaning and implications of competing interpretations of Europeanness or the European interest can usefully be explored, and compared with other vital and closely related concepts such as the West, peace, or Thomas Mann's *Humanität*. But logic provides no tools for making a final decision between these rival claims. Assertions about what is European are not falsifiable. There is no philosophical essence of Europeanness. A Christian will mean one thing, an atheist another. There will be a Polish interpretation of the European interest, a French interpretation, and a German interpretation — indeed there will be several Polish, French and German interpretations.

Who decides? After the experience of European barbarism in this century, most inhabitants of Europe could probably now agree on a basic, minimum list of what is not European. But beyond this basic code of irreducible human rights, itself still breached in several European countries, there is a vast area of profound disagreement between people who consider themselves Europeans. How, if at all, are these differences to be resolved or reconciled?

The best answer we can come up with is: liberal democracy as an epistemological principle. Like individual men and women, so also individual states and nations differ. Their interests, perceptions, tastes and aspirations conflict. These differences and conflicts cannot be resolved — although they may be illuminated — by scientific enquiry. Nor can they ever be wholly reconciled. But in deciding between rival claims in any pluralistic community or society, the freely expressed wishes of the majority are a primary criterion of rightness. We do not say 'the majority is always right'. There are certain rights that every minority must always have. But the larger the majority, and the more clearly expressed its wishes, the greater is the burden on the minority to, at the very least, consider its position.

To apply this rough-and-ready criterion to the internal affairs of a state is already difficult. To apply it to international relations is even more so. For here there are at least three sorts of putative majority involved. There is the putative majority of states, where the relevant set of states may range in size from two to nearly two hundred, and the definition of the relevant set will itself be disputed (especially where the boundaries of states and nations do not coincide). There is the will of the majority in the state conducting the policy at issue. Last, but by no means least, there is the will of the majority in the state(s) directly affected by that policy.

Even in democratic Western Europe it was a real question how far the will of the majority was really translated into domestic, let alone into foreign policy. But what about Eastern Europe, where — until 1989 — neither the ballot box nor even the opinion survey came to our aid? There was real meaning in the statement 'Mrs Thatcher speaks for Britain', 'President Mitterrand speaks for France', and even 'Chancellor Kohl speaks for Germany' — much as many Britons, French and Germans would have disputed it. But who spoke for Czechoslovakia in the 1980s? Gustáv Husák or Václav Havel? And who for Poland? Wojciech Jaruzelski? Lech Wałęsa? The Pope?

Yet the fact that a criterion is difficult to apply does not make it less important. To adapt Churchill's famous remark about democracy: this is the worst possible criterion we have, apart from all the other criteria that have been tried from time to time. Thus, to apply it to our theme, if a head of government, a politician or a writer declares 'what we are doing, or propose to do, is in the European interest', but the majority of their European neighbours reply 'no, my friend, that is not in the European interest', then it is not in the European interest. The head of government, politician or writer may passionately believe that it is. He may have powerful arguments to support this belief. He may, he should, attempt to convince his neighbours by the force of these arguments. But if they remain unconvinced, then he must yield — or abandon the claim to be working for Europe. This is the stern criterion that we shall apply to German Ostpolitik.

II

Ostpolitik

Was there one?

Was there one German Ostpolitik? To judge by party-political debates in the Bundestag or the West German media, you might doubt it. Throughout the history of the Federal Republic, from the 1950s to the 1980s, critics inside successive governing coalitions as well as in opposition loudly maintained that the government had no Ostpolitik worthy of the name, that if it existed, it was not consistent, or that, even if it existed and was consistent, it was not in the German interest. This sound and fury demonstrated nothing more nor less than the centrality of Ostpolitik to West German politics. In no other major Western state was policy towards the Soviet Union, let alone that towards Eastern Europe, the subject of such constant attention. The general conduct of East-West relations might be a major issue in an American or French Presidential election, but nothing that any American or French politician said about this issue would be a statement about the future existence of the United States or the French Republic.

German arguments about Ostpolitik have been arguments about the future of Germany. Social Democrats in opposition to Adenauer's Ostpolitik (or lack of one) in the 1950s certainly believed this to be the case. So did Christian Democrats in opposition to the Eastern treaties in the early 1970s. And some Social Democrats and Greens in opposition claimed to believe it still, or again, in the 1980s.

One reason for the persistence of these party-political differences about Ostpolitik was simple. In the 1970s, the Federal Republic had, if one counted the Christian Social Union as a separate party, four political parties that won more than five per cent of the popular vote in federal elections and were therefore represented in the Bundestag. With the arrival of the Greens, who first entered the Bundestag in 1983, this rose to five. At any given moment, two or three of these parties would form a coalition government, and two or three would be in opposition. Each party therefore had to define itself, when in power, against its coalition partners as well as against the opposition and, when out of power, against its opposition rivals as well as against the government. Since there were several state elections every year, as well as the federal election every four years, these differences had constantly to be thrust before the noses of the electors.

If I was a Free Democrat, I had to keep distinguishing myself both from the Social Democrats in opposition and from my Christian Democrat partners in government. If I was a Social Democrat, I had to keep distinguishing myself from both the Free Democrats in government and the Greens in opposition. And so on. Hence one of the most characteristic terms of West German politics '*sich profilieren*', meaning roughly 'to establish your profile', and its derivatives, such as *Profilierungsbedarf* (the need to profile yourself) and *Profilneurose* (profile neurosis). Moreover, each of these parties contained any number of individual rival politicians, many of whom felt themselves particularly qualified to speak out on this or that: either because they were designated national party spokespersons, or in their capacity as heads or members of a state (*Land*) government (some of which came close to conducting their own miniature foreign policies), or simply as backbenchers. Ostpolitik, increasingly popular with the voters, was an attractive subject on which to make your mark. It is always easier to solve the problems of the world than to solve those of your own household.

In the history of Ostpolitik, personal, party-political and electoral motives are therefore constantly intertwined with national and international ones. This was true of Willy Brandt, especially while he was the Social Democrats' candidate for Chancellor in the 1960s. It was eminently true of Hans-Dietrich Genscher, whose statements and moves as Foreign Minister cannot possibly be interpreted without bearing in mind that he was also the leader of a small party which had constantly to struggle to enhance its 'profile' and hence its ability to surmount the five per cent hurdle in successive state and federal elections. It was true of Chancellor Kohl, who, to take an especially piquant example, reportedly had an aide lean on the East German authorities to delay the opening of the Brandenburg Gate at the end of 1989, so that he, rather than Hans-Dietrich Genscher, could get the main television footage and kudos — tele-kudos? — at the opening. Examples could be multiplied.

The major parties had, moreover, to reckon with particular constituencies which directly impinged on their conduct of Ostpolitik. The most important of these constituencies was undoubtedly the millions of Germans who fled or were expelled after the Second World War from their homes east of the Oder and Neisse rivers and south-east of the Erz mountains. In the early years of the Federal Republic, these refugees and expellees made up nearly one fifth of the new state's population. They were a formidable constraint on Konrad Adenauer's freedom of action in relations with the East. At the beginning of the 1960s, the umbrella organisation of the different regional groups of refugees and expellees, the Federation of Expellees, claimed three million members. Thirty years later it would still claim some two million members (although some of these were in fact the children of refugees and expellees, who, in an extraordinary provision, formally inherited 'expellee' status).

Even if the representativeness of some highly active leaders of the Federation of Expellees might seriously be questioned, they remained, even in the 1980s, a significant influence upon the policy of the Christian Democrats. They were a force inside the Christian Democratic Union itself. They were even more of a force inside the Christian Social Union, where Franz Josef Strauss liked to describe the Sudeten Germans as Bavaria's 'fourth tribe'. And they were a force because they could, explicitly or implicitly, threaten to divert their votes to a right-wing party such as the *Republikaner*, or simply to abstain from voting. Even with Germany's system of proportional representation, this two or three per cent of the vote could make a great difference. As we shall see, Chancellor Kohl's public prevarication on full recognition of the Oder-Neisse line is explicable only in relation to this constituency.

The Social Democrats, too, had to pay close attention to the expellees in the 1960s and 1970s. At least one expellee Social Democrat, the Sudeten German Wenzel Jaksch, actually played a notably constructive part in the early years of Ostpolitik. The defection to the Christian Democrats of a leading Social Democrat expellee member of the Bundestag, Herbert Hupka, over the Eastern treaties, helped to undermine the Brandt government's already small parliamentary majority in 1972. But altogether this constituency was not as important to the Social Democrats, and its importance to them diminished further over the 1970s.

The Social Democrats did, however, have to reckon very seriously in the 1980s with another constituency: that of the peace and ecological movements. If expellees could threaten, explicitly or implicitly, to abstain or to vote for the *Republikaner*, those active in the peace and ecological movements could threaten, explicitly or implicitly, to abstain or to vote for the Greens.

There was, in short, a whole domestic politics of Ostpolitik. Yet in the 1980s one increasingly had the impression of rather artificial attempts to suck the politician's nectar of controversy out of what was, in fact, the flower of consensus. This was particularly true of policy towards East Germany. An opposition's business is to oppose. But it is quite difficult to oppose a government for doing almost exactly what you yourself did while in office, and with more immediately visible success. The consensus on policy towards East Germany was in fact reflected in a February 1984 joint resolution of all the main parties in the Bundestag, with only the Greens voting against. The consensus was obviously less complete on other East-West issues, and particularly on defence and disarmament. Yet even here one often had the sense of distinctions without differences and mountains made out of molehills.

We need a 'security partnership' with the East, said the Social Democrats in the 1980s. Impossible, cried Eberhard Diepgen, then Christian Democrat governing mayor of Berlin; but what we could have is a 'security *Teilhaberschaft*'. 'Not to obscure the difference between *Teilhaberschaft* and partnership,' Diepgen solemnly declared in 1987, 'is a matter of openness, which we need between East and West, but also inside the West.' Clearly this is a vital difference. Impatiently we turn to our German-English dictionary and read: '*Teilhaberschaft*: . . . partnership.'

Not all the distinctions are as meretricious as this. Indeed, the precise terms in which German politicians and intellectuals described the Federal Republic's relationship with the East as opposed or compared to its relationship with the West mattered in and for themselves. It makes some difference whether I call a woman my wife, my girl-friend or my mistress. What makes more difference, however, is whether we are married (and to whom). But what matters far more than either of these considerations, the semantic or the legal, is how we actually behave to each other, and to others.

Now in terms of actual behaviour there can be no doubt about the continuity of West German government policy towards East Germany, Eastern Europe and the Soviet Union through the two decades from 1969 to 1989. A crucial test of this continuity was the transition from a social-liberal to a conservative-liberal coalition government in 1982–83. A measure of continuity was guaranteed by the fact that the Free Democrats not merely remained in power, but continued to hold the Foreign Ministry. The phrase 'hold the Foreign Ministry' is chosen advisedly, for Hans-Dietrich Genscher, having been Foreign Minister for eight years already, from 1974 to 1982, and remaining Foreign Minister for a further ten years, until 1992, had an extraordinary influence on the personnel and practices of the West German foreign service. And that was, of course, a very significant part of what people in Eastern Europe saw as Ostpolitik in practice, whatever Chancellors in Bonn might say in theory.

Yet the continuity of Ostpolitik across the change of government was more than just the continuity of Genscherism. As important was the extraordinary degree to which the Christian Democrats took over almost wholesale the policies and approaches that many (though not all) of them had attacked with notable acerbity in the early 1970s. Franz Josef Strauss furnished an example at once extreme and classical. No one had been more eloquent in denouncing the Eastern treaties. No one was now more eager to pick up the threads of friendly intercourse with the communist regimes in East Berlin and Moscow. Within less than a year of returning to power, he could boast of having personally orchestrated a government-guaranteed one billion DM loan to the GDR, on very favourable terms. In 1984, he helped arrange another credit of comparable size. As soon as Mikhail Gorbachev would invite him, he flew himself to Moscow, and few Western visitors were more fulsome in praise of their Soviet host.

We have observed already that the Western treaties of the early 1950s and the Eastern treaties of the early 1970s were two major steps in the external emancipation of the Federal Republic. (A third major step was thus, as it were, chronologically due in the early 1990s.) Each step was fiercely contested at the time, but then accepted by the major party which had opposed it. The Social Democrats' theoretical acceptance of Adenauer's western integration was spelled out by Herbert Wehner in June 1960, in a remarkable speech to the Bundestag which concluded with the words: 'Divided Germany . . . cannot abide an incurable enmity of Christian and Social Democrats . . .' Practical acceptance was then demonstrated by the Social Democrats in government after 1966.

The Christian Democrats' acceptance of Brandt's Ostpolitik is less easy to date precisely. It was a long, complex, not to say confused process. One might argue that theoretical acceptance was expressed already in the May 1972 'Joint Resolution' of all parties in the Bundestag in connection with the ratification of the Moscow and Warsaw treaties. This reaffirmed both the formal legal positions of the Federal Republic on the German question and the basic priorities of the Adenauerian integration of the Federal Republic into the West. Alternatively, one might argue that theoretical acceptance was only finally expressed in an encyclopaedic resolution of the Christian Democrats' June 1988 Wiesbaden party conference, snappily entitled 'Christian Democratic Perspectives on Germany-, Foreign-, Se- curity-, Europe- and Development-policy.'

In between there were many smaller steps. Christian Democrats cont- inued to criticise what they had seen as excessive haste and unnecessary concessions in the negotiation of the Eastern treaties. In 1975, they were the only major parliamentary party in Western Europe to vote against the Helsinki Final Act — something that they would live to regret. By the end of the 1970s, leading Christian Democrats would nonetheless advocate a policy of 'realistic' and 'illusion-free' détente, based on both the letter and, increasingly, the spirit of the Eastern treaties negotiated under Brandt and Scheel. '*Pacta sunt servanda*', Franz Josef Strauss had declared immedi- ately after the ratification of the treaties, and the parties' interpretations of what it meant to keep those treaties gradually converged in the decade between 1972 and 1982.

There was, to be sure, still a significant change of rhetoric at the transition from social-liberal to conservative-liberal government. The new Chancellor brought a blunt neo-Adenauerian reaffirmation of the absolute priority of Western integration, on the one hand, and of the long-term commitment to reunification on the other. An insistence on the restatement of formal, legal positions on the German question was accompanied, as we have already observed, by a public reassertion of Western values, including individual liberty and national self-determination, as the basis of a lasting 'European peace order'. Yet if one looks at what the government actually did in its relations with East Germany, Eastern Europe and the Soviet Union, the continuity was overwhelming.

When Chancellor Kohl paid a long-delayed visit to Moscow in October 1988, one of the country's leading left-liberal commentators, Theo Sommer, was moved to write: 'And there is no break in the continuity of Bonn's Ostpolitik. As Brandt laid it down, and Schmidt played it in, so it is advanced by Kohl.' Earlier in the same year, Chancellor Kohl himself had declared: 'Despite all the party-political disputes of the last decades, we may speak in this connection, with pride, of "our policy".' In a review of the first volume of Helmut Schmidt's memoirs, Franz Josef Strauss observed that 'on the main lines [of West German foreign policy] there are no more differences between him and me.' In a speech to celebrate Willy Brandt's seventy-fifth birthday, President von Weizsäcker said that next to the 'reconciliation with the West, which Konrad Adenauer brought about', Brandt had placed the 'understanding with the East'. The latter did not supersede the former, however. 'Both parts have come together in an integrated whole, which since then has not seriously been put in question — a treasured common good.'

As the Federal Republic celebrated its fortieth birthday in May 1989 it was thus possible to state with confidence: there was *one* Ostpolitik of the Federal Republic of Germany. All the major parties represented in the West German parliament agreed on the main lines of this policy, although the Social Democrats wanted to build on the common foundations in a direction that was not at all agreed. Bonn governments had pursued this policy for two decades with a consistency rare among Western states. This alone seemed sufficient reason for most of Germany's neighbours, in East and West, to describe it as *German* Ostpolitik, much though the other German state might object to such a usage. Leading Bonn politicians themselves spoke of their foreign policy simply as 'German foreign policy', with no qualifying 'West' or 'Federal'. They often referred to their Ostpolitik as 'the German Ostpolitik' — a usage sanctified by *Duden*.

A further good reason for adopting this usage lay in the notion of national interest which informed the basic political consensus about Ostpolitik in Bonn. The concept of 'national interest' is complex even in relatively straightforward cases. It involves objective factors such as natural resources and frontiers, but is never wholly susceptible to objective definition. In Europe in the 1970s and 1980s, the concept was perhaps most simply and clearly applied in France, for here the interests of nation and state might be considered as virtually conterminous. But in Poland, for example, most people would certainly not have considered the interests of the Polish nation to be conterminous with those of the Polish People's Republic.

No case was more complex than that of Germany. What did a West German politician, diplomat or intellectual mean when he talked and thought — or talked without thinking, or thought without talking — about the national interest? Clearly a large part of this meaning had to be: the interests of this state, the Federal Republic. With many politicians an additional, far from trivial, sense was: the interests of his or her state, meaning Bavaria, Baden-Württemberg, Schleswig-Holstein or the Saarland. Yet politicians in divided Germany could not think simply in terms of the interests of the state, traditionally called *Staatsräson*, the German version of *raison d'état*. Virtually all had some larger sense of national interest (Josef Joffe called it *raison de nation*) which included, at a minimum, the interests of the more than sixteen million Germans living inside the frontiers of the German Democratic Republic. This sense was, however, often further extended to include the interests of those several million inhabitants of Eastern Europe and the Soviet Union, from the Banat to the Volga, who were Germans according to the somewhat curious definition in West Germany's Basic Law (see below, p. 234f). But then again, on an extraordinary range of issues this large concept of national interest came down in practice to the interests of one half of one city: West Berlin.

The concept was thus as many-layered as the language used to convey it. Citizens of the United Kingdom might talk of the nation and mean either the state — Britain — or one of four peoples — the English, the Scots, the Welsh or the Irish. On most issues of foreign policy, however, if a Scotsman or a Welshman talked of the 'national interest' he probably meant the interests of the one state — Britain. Germans had to distinguish between *Nation*, *Volk* and two states, between *Staatsnation* and *Kulturnation*, between interests of the nation, the state (Federal Republic), the states (Bavaria, Saarland etc) and the half-city-state (West Berlin). In practice, of course, no one could ever distinguish between all these senses and interests, so they came tangled together in various combinations and usages. That some larger notion of 'German interest' informed all mainstream West German approaches to Ostpolitik cannot, however, seriously be doubted.

In a word

Thus far we have discussed the modifiers — 'one', 'German' — but not the noun. What was Ostpolitik? 'A designation for the policy of the Federal Republic of Germany towards the states of the Warsaw Pact,' said *Meyers Grosses Universal Lexikon* in 1984. *Duden* (1980) had 'the (especially Federal

Republic of Germany): policy towards the socialist states of East Europe and Asia; the German Ostpolitik.' *Brockhaus-Wahrig* (1982) was more precise:

1. ⟨general⟩ policy towards Eastern countries
2.1. ⟨in broader sense⟩ the foreign policy of Western countries towards the East-block states
2.2. ⟨in narrower sense⟩ the policy of the Federal Republic of Germany towards the Soviet Union and its allied states in East and East Central Europe; the Bonn Ostpolitik.

These definitions rightly recognise the transferred usage of the term. For, as mentioned earlier, Ostpolitik has become an English word. *Langenscheidt*'s concise German-English dictionary says simply: '*Ostpolitik* ostpolitik'! *Chambers English Dictionary* (1988) defines this English word as 'the West German policy of establishing normal trade and diplomatic relations with the East European communist countries; any similar policy.' The Second Edition of the *Oxford English Dictionary* (1989) has (somewhat inaccurately): 'German policy towards Eastern Europe, associated mainly with the Federal Republic of Germany's cultivation of good relations with the Communist block during the 1960s, but applied also, by extension, to the policies of other Western countries regarding the East as a whole.'

The OED's first quotation comes from Terence Prittie's *Germany Divided* (1961). Prittie writes that the Russians 'will scarcely overlook Hitler's statement . . . "The goal of Ostpolitik is to open up an area of settlement for one hundred million Germans".' This somewhat disconcerting comment reminds us of earlier, less cosmopolitan usages of the term. Thus in Henry Picker's record of Hitler's *Table Talk* we read, for 31 March 1942: 'Today's German Ostpolitik — the boss remarked at supper, stimulated by a remark of Bormann's about Heinrich I — is without historical parallel.' Indeed.

In his 1971 Nobel Peace Prize address, Willy Brandt said he did not actually like the term 'Ostpolitik' as a label for his own policy, partly because it was poisoned by this earlier German usage. Yet it is striking that, as the dictionary definitions indicate, in German as in international usage, the term 'Ostpolitik', unlike, say, *Lebensraum*, or even *Mitteleuropa*, has been almost entirely disassociated from pre-1945 usage. In West Germany, 1945 was often referred to as the *Stunde Null* ('hour zero') and this it proves to be for the word Ostpolitik. But what, then, to use another favoured West German phrase, was the *Erste Stunde* ('hour one') of the new German Ostpolitik?

'Twenty-five years ago yesterday, on 9 September 1955, the German Ostpolitik began . . .' declared, on 10 September 1980, the outstanding Christian Democrat expert on foreign policy, Alois Mertes. He referred to

Konrad Adenauer's first trip to Moscow, and the opening of diplomatic relations with the Soviet Union. This was, of course, also a party-political statement. For Mertes thus insisted that the Ostpolitik was not, as Social Democrats and Free Democrats generally implied, their patent discovery and, so to speak, intellectual property. Other analysts have placed the milestone at the 13 August 1961, with the shock of the building of the Berlin Wall; others again, in December 1966, with the formation of the Grand Coalition of Christian and Social Democrats in Bonn, including Willy Brandt as Foreign Minister. The historical justification of these claims will be considered more closely below.

Yet whatever the historical reality, for most Germans, and certainly for most of Germany's neighbours, the term 'Ostpolitik' is inextricably associated with the man who said he did not like it. It was, as Jiří Dienstbier wrote from his Prague boiler-room, 'Brandt's Ostpolitik'. There was certainly *an* Ostpolitik of the Federal Republic before 1969. But *the* Ostpolitik means, in the first place, Chancellor Brandt and the social-liberal coalition from 1969. It means the negotiation of the whole complex of the Eastern treaties, and the titanic struggle to win their acceptance in the Bundestag and in the country at large. It means the election of November 1972, which became almost a plebiscite on Brandt's Ostpolitik. It means the hope-filled crowds at Erfurt shouting 'Willy! Willy!', on Brandt's first official visit to East Germany in March 1970. It means Willy Brandt falling to his knees in Warsaw before the monument to the heroes of the ghetto uprising: one of the great symbolic moments of post-war European history. It means the policies of 'normalisation' and the pursuit of a 'European peace order' based on the full diplomatic recognition of the sovereignty and existing frontiers of East European states, and the virtually full recognition of East Germany as an independent state.

In the second half of the 1960s the policy initiated by the Grand Coalition was called the 'new' Ostpolitik, but by the 1980s the adjective 'new' had been silently absorbed into the noun. No serious analyst would deny that major elements of the thinking behind Brandt's 'new' Ostpolitik were present already in the early to mid-1960s, and even in the late 1950s. What Bonn governments did after 1969 cannot be understood without knowing what they tried to do before 1969. Yet for all that, the simple statement can be made: the child German Ostpolitik came into the world in the years 1969–72. The success had many fathers, but the midwives were definitely called Willy Brandt and Walter Scheel.

Ostpolitik was born as the German version of détente. Ostpolitik may therefore also be described as détente policy: *Entspannungspolitik*. Indeed so closely associated is the term Ostpolitik with the years 1969 to 1972, and so important is the notion of *Entspannung* (literally 'relaxation') to an understanding of German policy, that one is almost tempted to use the term *Entspannungspolitik* rather than Ostpolitik to describe our theme. But unlike the word Ostpolitik, the hectasyllabic *Entspannungspolitik* has not made a great international career.

Moreover, just because it is so central, the notion of *Entspannung* is also imprecise and controversial. The word *Entspannung* was used already by Konrad Adenauer in the early 1950s, before de Gaulle had popularised its precise dictionary equivalent *détente*, and well before Americans had turned the French word into an English one. In the 1960s, and in subsequent German usage, it had to serve both as a description of other states' policies of détente, and as a prescription for diverse German versions of détente, which, however, were themselves heavily influenced by the French and American versions that the term was also used to describe. In the early 1970s, it seemed to acquire a clear meaning: *Entspannungspolitik* = (new) Ostpolitik. But already in 1975 the newly arrived Foreign Minister, Hans-Dietrich Genscher, felt it necessary to qualify the noun-prescriptive *Entspannungspolitik* with the adjective 'realistic'.

In West Germany, as in much of the West, the Soviet invasion of Afghanistan, the Polish crisis, and the so-called 'second cold war' between the Reagan administration and the Brezhnev-Andropov-Chernenko leaderships, were said to have spelt an 'end to détente' and even 'the failure of *Entspannungspolitik*'. In a Joint Declaration at the end of Brezhnev's visit to Bonn in 1978, the word *Entspannung* appeared seven times in two pages. In the Kohl-Genscher government's May 1983 'Programme of Renewal', the word *Entspannung* did not appear once. But by the late 1980s it was back again. In an official government documentation of 'The Ostpolitik of the Federal Government', published in 1986, this Ostpolitik was described as a 'realistic and illusion-free *Entspannungspolitik*'.

In sticking to the simpler, internationally recognised term 'Ostpolitik', one should nonetheless keep in mind those intimate and formative ties with the notion of détente in general, and the social-liberal version of détente in particular.

One further caveat is due. In official Bonn usage, a distinction was made between Ostpolitik and Deutschlandpolitik. Ostpolitik was held to denote policy towards Eastern Europe (*Osteuropapolitik*) and the Soviet Union (formerly *Russlandpolitik*) whereas Deutschlandpolitik meant policy towards East Germany (occasionally described simply as *DDR-Politik*) and Berlin, although it also included the Federal Republic's political-theological approach to the whole German question, the unresolved legal-symbolic-political issues arising out of the post-war settlement, the lack of a peace treaty with Germany, and so forth.

The division between Ostpolitik and Deutschlandpolitik was, however, very far from clear. It was unclear because a quarter of what was once Germany was now Poland, or, in the case of the area around Kaliningrad (formerly Königsberg), the Soviet Union. Such crucial issues of *Osteuropapolitik* as the recognition of the Oder-Neisse line, or the status of the remaining German minorities, were thus always and simultaneously issues of Deutschlandpolitik. Secondly, the distinction was unclear because, as we shall see, the concerns of Deutschlandpolitik in the narrower sense remained absolutely central to the whole Ostpolitik. You could not begin to understand the latter without looking at the former. Indeed, one of the salient features of Ostpolitik was precisely that it attempted to integrate into one seamless whole the three areas, Deutschlandpolitik, *Osteuropapolitik* and *Russlandpolitik*.

The term 'Ostpolitik' is therefore used here — as in fact it was often used even in Bonn — to denote all three areas of policy, and the attempt to combine them in one integrated strategy. At the same time, one cannot entirely overlook the distinction, however imprecise. Whereas Soviet and East European policy were clearly regarded as foreign policy, Deutschlandpolitik was treated in Bonn as half-domestic policy. West German leaders repeatedly emphasised that for them East Germany 'could not be a foreign country'.

The distinction was also enshrined in the policymaking process. In the 1950s and 1960s, Deutschlandpolitik, as well as being a central concern of the Chancellery, was the business of a separate ministry, the Ministry for All-German Questions. With the recognition of the GDR in the early 1970s, operative policy towards the GDR came under the direct control of the Chancellery, although there was still significant input from what was now (in 1969) curiously re-named the Ministry for Intra-German Relations and from the Foreign Ministry, as well as from other Ministries on specific subjects. The Federal Republic's 'Permanent Representative' in East Berlin reported directly to the Chancellery, but had to operate within this complex political-bureaucratic geometry. A crucial part was, however, played by informal East German emissaries, direct correspondence and telephone conversations between Erich Honecker and successive Chancellors, as well as similar contacts with other key West German figures such as the Social Democrats' 'Uncle' Herbert Wehner, and the Bavarian premier Franz Josef Strauss.

Soviet and East European policy was, as you would expect, the direct responsibility of the Foreign Ministry. Yet because of the Chancellor's overall responsibility for the main lines of foreign policy — the *Richtlinienkompetenz* laid down in theory by Article 65 of the Basic Law, and in practice by Konrad Adenauer — and because of the crucial permissive function of Soviet and East European policy for the pursuit of Deutschlandpolitik, the Federal Chancellery played a very important part here too. In the record of bilateral relations with the Soviet Union and East European states, the role of the Chancellor and his advisers continued to be crucial. Chancellors from Adenauer to Kohl also used their own unofficial intermediaries and 'back channels' to cultivate direct relations with Soviet and East European leaders.

As the Foreign Ministry had a department for matters concerning Berlin and Germany as a whole, jealously watching the development of Deutschlandpolitik, and not accidentally a school for diplomatic high fliers, so the Federal Chancellery had its own department for foreign affairs, closely observing the conduct of the Foreign Ministry. Naturally enough, the relationship could often be tense. When Egon Bahr moved from the Foreign Ministry to the Chancellery in 1969, the State Secretary of the Foreign Ministry, Ferdinand Duckwitz jokingly observed: 'so now we are setting you down behind enemy lines, in the Chancellery.'

Such rivalries are, of course, nothing peculiar to Germany. One thinks of the tension between National Security Adviser and Secretary of State in the United States, between President and Prime Minister in France, or even between No. 10 Downing Street and the Foreign Office in Britain. What was peculiar to West Germany, however, was the coincidence of the bureaucratic division with a party-political one. In the Grand Coalition, the Christian Democrat Chancellor Kiesinger lived in uneasy *cohabitation* with the Social Democrat Foreign Minister Brandt. After 1969, a Free Democrat held the Foreign Ministry, with a Social or Christian Democrat as Chancellor. As a result, many of the much-publicised differences between Chancellor and Foreign Minister were those of politicians competing to 'win profile', or trimming to their own particular constituencies, rather than differing on issues of substance. By comparison with most other Western states, the West German political process nonetheless secured a high degree of consistency and continuity in Ostpolitik, not least because the same people dealt with the same issues over very long periods, both in the ministries and in the political parties. There was an important contrast here with France, and even more with the United States.

The task of describing this single, consistent, increasingly consensual German Ostpolitik is, however, complicated by another, more general problem. For towards the end of the twentieth century, foreign policy is not what it was. It is no longer the exclusive domain of nation-states. For most European states, and for the Federal Republic more than any, foreign policy was increasingly a matter of working through multilateral institutions. It was a jungle of acronyms: Nato and WEU for security policy; EC, G7, GATT, CoCom, IMF and World Bank for financial and economic policy; the CSCE ('Helsinki process') for almost everything else. In addition, there was the multilateral co-ordination of national foreign policies, in Nato and through the mechanism of European Political Co-operation between the member states of the European Community. All this greatly complicates the life of the diplomat — and of the analyst.

For if we wish to compare the Soviet and East European policy of the Federal Republic with, say, those of France, Britain, or the United States, we have to consider at least four distinct although intersecting planes. First, there is the area in which these states pursue common goals or interests through common instruments (Nato, EC, CoCom etc). Secondly, there are areas in which these states pursue common goals or interests through separate instruments: for example, through their own bilateral relations with this or that East European country. Thirdly, there are areas in which these states pursue different goals or interests through common instruments: or more precisely, through attempting to direct the common instruments in their own direction. Finally, there are the areas in which these states pursue different goals or interests through separate instruments.

The last-mentioned are the most obvious and easily identified differences. But in the 1970s and 1980s, with the progressive 'multilateralisation' of Western foreign policy, the third area became ever more important. Increasingly, differences between the major West European powers were articulated in a complex, political-bureaucratic negotiation of a supposedly common policy, rather than by direct disagreement or simply by going separate ways. The most obvious example in the 1980s was arms control, where specific German interests played a crucial role in the formation of Western positions. One might talk, in this context, of indirect Ostpolitik. This particular kind of difference is, however, especially difficult for the analyst to identify precisely — let alone to trace through the day-to-day rounds of multilateral *engrenage*.

The difficulty is increased by what Hans-Peter Schwarz has described as a hallmark of West German foreign policy: 'an insatiable striving after international harmony on all sides'. This 'harmonisation need' (*Harmonisierungsbedürfnis*), as Schwarz neatly labels it, may to some extent be characteristic of all modern, liberal industrial states, and particularly of those 'trading states' — such as Germany and Japan — whose prosperity depends to an unusual degree on keeping good relations with a wide range of trading partners. But beyond this, certain specific German reasons may be suggested.

One might, for example, regard this as a particular emanation of that general yearning for synthesis which Ralf Dahrendorf and others have argued is characteristic of German political thought as a whole. Schwarz himself stresses a more recent cause. Having by 1945 become enemies of almost everybody, he says, the Germans after 1945 felt an overwhelming need to try to be friends with almost everybody. This psychological explanation can also be expressed in terms of political thought. If the Germany that reached for world power in the first half of the twentieth century was acting (or justifying its acts) on a Social Darwinian understanding of international society, then West Germany in the second half of the twentieth century seemed at times to have gone to another extreme, with an almost utopian vision of international society. In the early twentieth century, the German left used to sing 'You must rule and win,/ Or serve and lose,/ Suffer or triumph,/ Be the anvil or the hammer.' (The words are Goethe's). In the late twentieth century, the (West) German left seemed at times to be reaching for an understanding of politics in which there were simply no hammers at all.

The vision of eternal peace, friendship and harmony, itself most powerfully articulated by German philosophers, was rejected by the historian Heinrich von Treitschke in the 1870s as an 'unmanly dream'. Seeing where manly dreams had led, many Germans in the 1970s re-embraced the older dream of eternal harmony. Here was, so to speak, the negation of Treitschke's negation.

It has also been suggested that this yearning for synthesis may partly result from Germany's position as a 'land of the centre', between East and West. This position, it is suggested, led Germans into the temptation of believing that they could interpret East to West, and West to East, while themselves combining in synthesis the best of both worlds. What is clearly true is that Germany's position as the divided centre of a divided continent after 1945 produced an acute objective need to try and harmonise ties with Eastern and Western partners, as well as a further temptation to see Germany's role, as the Christian Democrat Jakob Kaiser put it in 1947, not in the politics of 'either/or' but in those of *sowohl-als-auch* (roughly: as-well-as-and).

Whatever the precise combination of ingredients, this 'harmonisation need' was a hallmark of German foreign policy in this period. It resulted, as we have seen already, in a constant conflation of German and European or German and Western interests. Thus, for example, West German policymakers never tired of citing Nato's 1967 Harmel report as the bible of East-West relations. Here, they said, was a common definition of common goals to be realised through common instruments. But at least one reason why German policymakers so often cited the Harmel report is that it was a document which placed the division of Germany at the centre of Western concerns. Moreover, coherent as the Harmel concept of a 'double-track' of defence and détente might be, both defence and détente could be variously defined.

In the public presentation of West German foreign policy, it was further suggested that the harmony could extend not only to the interests of other Western states, but to those of the Soviet Union and East European states as well. In the rhetoric of Ostpolitik it was almost implied that the great work of reconciliation, détente and co-operation, the seamless web of ever-closer ties, cultural, economic, human and political, would bring benefits equally to all. There would be, so to speak, all winners and no losers. In more realistic discourse there was talk of an *Interessenausgleich* between West and East in Europe: a reconciliation or balancing of interests. This at least had the merit of recognising that, in international relations as in all human affairs, interests conflict. Part of our task is therefore to peer through the harmonising rhetoric, and through the tangle of acronymic multilateralism, to determine: who gains? Which usually also means: who loses?

Causes and sources

In this attempt we shall have to consider three main kinds of party. First, there is the Federal Republic, and the broader national goals that it defined as 'German interests'. Secondly, there are its Western neighbours and partners, above all the United States, France and Britain. Thirdly, there are East Germany, the Soviet Union and the other East European states. In considering this third category, however, we have to make a further vital distinction between the interests of the (undemocratic) states and those of their societies. This last distinction is all the more vital because West German policymakers themselves sometimes failed to make it very clearly.

Yet one of the most distinctive features of East-West relations in Europe in the 1970s and 1980s was that they increasingly consisted of attempts to influence domestic social and political developments on the other side of the 'Yalta' division. In the early 1970s, Pierre Hassner observed that a sort of 'hot peace' was increasingly replacing the Cold War. 'The main characteristic of the "hot peace",' Hassner wrote, 'is neither force nor co-operation, but the constant reciprocal influence of societies within the framework of a competition whose goals are less and less tangible, whose means are less and less direct, whose consequences are less and less calculable . . .'

Of course these influences, of states on societies, societies on societies, societies on states, worked in both directions. The Soviet Union had certain hopes of the peace movement in West Germany, the United States had certain hopes of Solidarity in Poland. Neither superpower produced, far less controlled, either social movement, but both could hope to influence both. The debate about Western policy towards Eastern Europe at the end of the 1980s was largely a debate about influencing domestic social, economic and political change in those countries. In the event, the whole 'Helsinki process' turned out to be as much about societies as about states. Television, radio and travel were as important as any meetings between statesmen. Yet such influences are extraordinarily difficult to pin down. What was the political effect of cultural exchanges? How did Western economic policies affect Eastern political economies? How does one distinguish between the effect West Germany had on East Germany by virtue of its mere existence, prosperity, democracy etc, and the influence it had by reason of conscious policy?

All assertions about the connections between Western policies and Eastern politics are therefore highly speculative. It was increasingly difficult to disentangle the specific contribution of German policy in the whole multi-dimensional web of East-West relations in Europe. The attempt will nonetheless be made. There was one German Ostpolitik. It was pursued with remarkable consistency for two decades. What did it achieve for Germany, and what for Europe? Having peered at just a few of the fearsome complexities of defining the 'German interest', let alone the 'European interest', the reader will observe that these questions are more easily asked than answered.

Answers may be offered most firmly in the area of West-East German relations. Although the overall East-West context — what Erich Honecker liked to call the *Grosswetterlage* — always remained crucial to German-German relations, the picture is not confused by the substantial impact of a different Western policy directed specifically at the GDR. This is less true of, say, Poland and Hungary, where distinctive American, French, British, Italian or Austrian approaches made a significant impact. It is even less true in the case of the Soviet Union, for which US policy was of the first importance. Reasonably well-founded statements can nonetheless be ventured about the development of bilateral relations between the Federal Republic and the states (and societies) of Eastern Europe and the Soviet Union.

Much more difficult are the areas of multilateral action, whether of Western co-ordination in Nato, European Political Co-operation and the Group of Seven, or of East-West co-operation or negotiation, in Helsinki review conferences, arms control talks and the like. On these there is at once too much and too little information, and the identification of a particular 'German line' is a delicate and questionable operation.

In offering answers so soon after the event, there is also the problem of historical perspective, and the closely related problem of sources. As Reinhart Koselleck has pointed out, from the time of Thucydides until the eighteenth century the fact of having been a witness to events was considered to be an advantage for the historian of those events. In an age when so much of history is made in personal encounters at summit meetings, on the telephone or on television, this may again be considered to be the case. Unlike in the nineteenth century, much of what is most important may actually never be written down. So there is nothing to compare with being there.

The main disadvantage of the witness is that he does not know the long-term consequences of the events he witnesses, and therefore cannot see them in historical perspective. Of course the perspectives do not cease to change with the march of time. 1989 affects our view of 1789. Yet certainly our perspectives on the distant past change more slowly than those on the more recent past. In the case of Ostpolitik, however, the revolution of 1989 and the German unification of 1990 do furnish a perspective unusually well-defined for such recent events. This story has a beginning, a middle and an end. While the Federal Republic of Germany may in future once again have *an* Ostpolitik, *the* Ostpolitik analysed here came to an end in 1989–90, albeit, arguably, with an important epilogue stretching to the final withdrawal of Soviet/Russian troops from German soil.

Yet the very sharpness of this historical break also brings peculiar difficulties of its own. For the historian, there is the danger of what Bergson called 'the illusions of retrospective determinism'. The story of Ostpolitik can so easily be written — or rather, re-written — teleologically, as if it led smoothly, inexorably and majestically to the dual crescendo of revolution and unification. *Post hoc, ergo propter hoc.* For the politicians, such re-writing of history is a matter of self-justification, of winning 'profile' and therefore votes. But one finds that even participants and witnesses no longer active in political life tend, almost without exception, to adjust their memories of their own words and deeds so they fit better into the direction that history has actually taken.

How can one guard against retrospective determinism and the tricks of memory? In the first place, of course, by taking the public record of what people actually said and did at the time. In the case of the Federal Republic's relations with the Soviet Union, Eastern Europe and, above all, East Germany, this public record is very extensive indeed. Between official publications, journals of record, memoirs and the press, German Ostpolitik is exhaustively — not to say, exhaustingly — documented. Yet if one does not find in these acres of paper the views that participants now claim to have held, they have an obvious retort: '*of course* we couldn't say that publicly! It would have alerted the other side to our true intentions. A bridge player does not show all his cards!' This difficulty, which we have touched on already in looking at public definitions of the 'European peace order', is a substantial one. For such tactical caution was a marked characteristic of Ostpolitik in general, and social-liberal Ostpolitik in particular.

In order to establish how much truth there is in retrospective claims of foresight and concealed strategy one would clearly need to examine all the relevant internal government papers, and above all the most secret ones. These papers are, however, mostly closed for thirty years, if not for longer. Even when they are all opened, the participants could still say — from the grave, or the pages of their memoirs — 'yes, to be sure, these thoughts were so secret that we did not even confide them to the most secret of secret papers!' But the credibility of such claims would be, at least, significantly qualified. Unless we want to wait until all the secret records are available, however, we cannot hope to have even this degree of historical certainty.

Public words and deeds have a weight and importance of their own, irrespective of private motives or unspoken calculations. In any case, an open society, participants, witnesses and the media expose between them a good deal of the private and unspoken. After the canonical thirty years, the revelations are generally less revelatory than one might expect. In this case, moreover, we are able to qualify the general disadvantage of the unavailability of official papers by virtue of several circumstances.

Firstly, the two most important addressee states of Ostpolitik, the Soviet Union and the GDR, have ceased to exist. According to legal provisions made by the now all-German Bundestag, the records of East Germany's ruling Communist Party, of its other parties and mass organisations, and of its State Security Service, are supposed to be made available to scholars with no application of the thirty-year rule, although with some important restrictions. (Regrettably, and illogically, such an enlightened provision is apparently not to be applied to the papers of the former East German Foreign Ministry.) For this book, extensive use has been made of such documents from the communist party and State Security Service ('Stasi') archives as were available to the author in this very early stage of the opening of the archives. Yet these already provide fascinating insights into the 'Eastern' side of the story of Ostpolitik. Clearly there is a great deal more to come, and as the documents are worked through so we may hope that the tentative analysis made here of policy towards the GDR will be put on a broader and firmer footing. At the time of writing, both the legal and the practical position with the Soviet and East European archives was less clear.

The demise of these states has meanwhile opened up another, more immediate source. For their former senior functionaries are ready to talk as they would never have done before. Of course their testimony is also full of retrospective self-justification. But fortunately their retrospective self-justification tends to pull in an opposite direction from that of West German politicians and officials. Where, for example, a West German politician may be tempted to play down, with hindsight, the degree of his or her understanding or intimacy with East German leaders, the former East German leader will be inclined to play it up. There is thus a nice compensatory symmetry of German-German memory.

In the West, official papers are generally unavailable for at least the canonical thirty years. But individuals can be more open than governments. This book thus draws on the papers of Willy Brandt, on such of the papers of Helmut Schmidt as are deposited in Bonn, on a small selection from those of Egon Bahr, and on those of two notable critics of the social-liberal Ostpolitik, Alois Mertes and Werner Marx, to name only the most important treasure-troves. Such documents, when augmented by other sources and conversations with the survivors, already give some remarkable glimpses into the inner history of the making of Ostpolitik.

This quantity and quality of evidence is still, of course, unsatisfactory. But assessments of Ostpolitik are wanted now. They might even, in a very modest way, help to save tomorrow's policymakers, certainly not from mistakes, but perhaps from some avoidable confusion.

So in what follows we make, on this admittedly unsatisfactory basis of evidence, and from this admittedly awkward distance of time, a deliberately selective analysis of the three intersecting circles of direct German Ostpolitik: *Russlandpolitik*, Deutschlandpolitik and *Osteuropapolitik*. About these we can gather reasonably full and manageable information. In them we can also find the key to the German approach in Western and multilateral fora: to indirect German Ostpolitik. For obvious reasons, this book emphasises what has been peculiar to German approaches, rather than what has been common to all Western ones.

Chapter Three discusses the early development of Ostpolitik, German-Soviet relations, and the overall 'system' of Ostpolitik as it was established by the Eastern treaties of the early 1970s, with that central triangle whose coordinates were Bonn-Moscow-Berlin. Chapter Four looks specifically at policy towards the GDR. Chapter Five begins by looking more closely at Germany's special historical problems in relations with the lands east of the River Oder, and south-east of the Erz mountains. It goes on to examine a few major leitmotifs of Ostpolitik, with special reference to Poland, Czechoslovakia and Hungary. Chapter Six steps outside the governmental frame to look at the so-called 'second Ostpolitik' of the Social Democrats in the 1980s. All these chapters take the story up to, but not systematically beyond, the year of wonders 1989. All try to avoid the fallacies of teleology or retrospective determinism.

Chapter Seven then looks briefly at the European revolution of 1989 and the German unification of 1990. Chapter Eight then looks again at the subject of causality: how far, and in what ways, did Ostpolitik contribute directly or indirectly to the final success? Noting some salient characteristics of this 'German model' of policy, this chapter returns to the question of how far and in what senses this was indeed a policy 'for Europe'. The Epilogue peers into the future.

One should, however, also emphasise what this book is not. This is not a comprehensive, narrative history of the making of Ostpolitik, including all the personal motives and party-political manoeuvres of its makers. A characteristic feature of German Ostpolitik is the wide variety of biographically-determined motives to be found among its leading actors. One cannot begin to understand the subject simply by looking at the rational surface of official speeches, couched in the relatively neutral language of contemporary international relations, and the deliberately low-key vocabulary of German politics after Hitler. The most important facts here are often the simplest biographical data — date of birth, place of birth, religion, war service — and the historian must be able to discern, behind those dry and cautious speeches, the dark or golden shadows of a Thuringian childhood; an East Prussian youth before the Fall; the language of Luther, heard from a pulpit in Halle; a freezing dawn on the Eastern front in 1943; or the echoes of a Frankfurt student demonstration in 1968. We are condemned to generalise when, as Stendhal once remarked, all the truth and all the pleasure lie in the details.

This is not a treatment of the 'political culture' of West Germany, nor of popular attitudes as revealed in opinion polls. Both 'public opinion' and 'published opinion' clearly had a great influence on Ostpolitik, while Ostpolitik in turn influenced them. With the exception of Chapter Six, which treats the policy of the Social Democrats in opposition, we have concentrated on the words and deeds of those in power. Yet this is certainly not a full account even of West Germany's governmental policy. Still less can it be a comprehensive history of East-West or West-West relations in the 1970s and 1980s. What has been called the 'essential triangle' of post-war European politics — USA-Germany-USSR — is essential background to this study, especially when it deals with the Bonn-Moscow-Berlin triangle which was in manifold ways subsidiary to the larger one. Their full geometry must await another Euclid. Issues of security policy, arms and disarmament, are discussed where they impinge directly on Ostpolitik, but in no way treated comprehensively. New global challenges — the risks of nuclear war or accident, threats to the eco-system, the world population explosion, hunger, poverty, the North-South rather than the East-West divide — are considered here only insofar as they figured in debates about Ostpolitik.

In short, the main part of this book looks at the West German approach to reducing or overcoming the 'Yalta' division of Germany and Europe — Ostpolitik — in the light of other Western, East European and Soviet approaches. While it reaches back well before 1969, it nonetheless concentrates on the two decades from the dramatic public proclamation of what came to be known round the world as Ostpolitik, in 1969/70, to the revolution and unification of 1989/90, which marked the end of that Ostpolitik.

III

Bonn-Moscow-Berlin

'Our most important task'

In the introduction to a collection of his speeches, published in 1983 under the memorable title *German History Continues*, Richard von Weizsäcker reflected on Germany's geopolitical situation as the divided centre of Europe. The Federal Republic, wrote its future President and then Governing Mayor of Berlin, was 'not just the East of the West, but also the West of the Centre'. The foreign policy priorities of the western German state derived from this geopolitical situation. 'On the basis of our liberty protected in the alliance [i.e. Nato] we must concentrate our efforts on a good relationship with the Eastern leading power [i.e. the Soviet Union]. This is our most important task.'

The Christian Democrat von Weizsäcker went on to observe that work towards this goal was begun by the Christian Democrat Chancellor Adenauer, and continued by the Christian Democrat Chancellor Kiesinger, before being given a 'treaty framework' by the Social Democrat Chancellor Brandt. And the insight into what Chancellor Kohl would repeatedly call the 'central importance' of the relationship with the Soviet Union was self-evidently not an afflatus of Willy Brandt. It was as old as the Federal Republic, indeed older. Relations with Russia had been a vital interest of the German Reich from 1871 to 1945, and of Prussia before that. Relations with Russia were even more of a vital interest after 1945, when the Red Army had occupied almost half of the former Germany.

The origins of the particular form in which von Weizsäcker formulated this 'most important task' may, however, be traced back, not as far as 1945, nor as near as 1969, but to 1955. Over the decade after 1945, Soviet leaders, like their Western counterparts, played with, and in part attempted, various alternative political 'solutions' for the defeated Germany. So did German politicians, in East and West, albeit with much more limited possibilities of translating desires into deeds.

The history of these plans and attempts is highly complex, and still controversial, but one essential point is clear. In this very confused situation, Konrad Adenauer decisively chose the variant of first creating out of the Western zones of occupation a separate West German state, which would be at once sovereign and firmly bound into a Western alliance. In pursuing this goal, he declined to explore as fully as many of his fellow German politicians — in all parties — would have liked, the possible alternative represented by the so-called Stalin Notes of March and April 1952, and the policy towards Germany of Stalin's successors during the short period between Stalin's death and the 17 June 1953 rising in East Germany. This possible alternative consisted in some variant of a basic deal: unification (of the territories of the Federal Republic and the GDR) in return for neutrality (or some very similar form of 'security guarantee' for the Soviet Union).

Adenauer feared, on the one hand, that he might forfeit the precious confidence of the Western allies by exploring these Soviet offers, and, on the other hand, that the Western allies might themselves be all too interested in exploring them — over his head. As he remarked in 1953, whereas Bismarck had a 'nightmare of coalitions', he, Adenauer, had his own nightmare: 'it's called Potsdam'. As we now know, Churchill did in fact briefly toy with the idea of an arrangement about Germany with the Russians over Adenauer's head: a new Potsdam. With support from the Eisenhower administration, Adenauer ignored all Russian blandishments and steered his part of Germany firmly through the door marked 'Nato' into a room called 'sovereignty'.

This hard-won sovereignty — although still significantly limited by residual allied rights and new obligations to Nato — was finally achieved when the Paris Treaties, signed in October 1954, came into force on 5 May 1955. Adenauer issued a triumphant declaration. 'We are a free and independent state' it said, and concluded 'Our goal is: in a free and united Europe a free and united Germany.' A German flag was hoisted before the Palais Schaumburg in Bonn to mark the occasion. Adenauer placed a photograph of this ceremony at the beginning of the second volume of his memoirs. Subsequently, this date would officially be referred to as the Federal Republic's 'day of sovereignty'.

Scarcely a month after that flag was hoisted, on 7 June, the Soviet Government sent a diplomatic note to the Federal Government (via the West German embassy in Paris) expressing its view that 'the interests of peace and European security, as well as the national interests of the Soviet and German peoples require the normalisation of relations between the Soviet Union and the German Federal Republic'. 'It is known,' said this remarkable missive, 'that in the years in which there were friendly relations and co-operation between our peoples, both countries derived great advantages.' The development of 'normal relations' would also help towards 'the solution of the all-national main problem of the German people — the restoration of the unity of a German democratic state'. After recalling that in the past, trade with Germany had been as much as one fifth of the total foreign trade of the Soviet Union, the note called for the establishment of diplomatic, trade and cultural relations between the two countries.

Within three months of receiving this note, and scarcely four months after the 'day of sovereignty', Adenauer was in Moscow. At the end of tough and dramatic negotiations, the Federal Republic and the Soviet Union agreed to open diplomatic relations. As we have already observed, this visit may be said to be the beginning of an Ostpolitik of the Federal Republic — although not of that particular version of it which came to be known round the world as 'Ostpolitik'.

Yet it was by what he refused to do as much as by what he did that Adenauer set those most basic terms of West German Ostpolitik, which von Weizsäcker summarised in what, by 1983, seemed like a self-evident, passing phrase. For it was far from self-evident to many in the 1950s that the most important task of German statesmanship should be to establish a good relationship with the Eastern leading power '*on the basis of our liberty protected in the alliance*'.

For thirty-five years, from 1955 until 1990, that would continue to be the basic premiss of the Ostpolitik of successive Federal Governments. Yet by the same token, that basic premiss would again and again be questioned in German politics, with arguments that grew out of the logic and achievements of Ostpolitik, yet often uncannily recalled those of earlier periods.

Adenauer certainly did not belong to those 'Easterners' among the German political and intellectual élite who felt some deep affinities with Russia. 'Asia stands on the Elbe' he famously remarked in 1946. And in the 1960s he was still warmly commending to Kennedy and de Gaulle a book called *The Russian Perpetuum Mobile*, which portrayed the Soviet Union as just the latest expression of old Russian expansionism. Yet he got on quite well with the representatives of what he called 'this terrible power'. He even allowed himself to be drawn into one theatrical-emotional gesture of reconciliation, holding hands with Bulganin at the end of a Bolshoi ballet performance of *Romeo and Juliet*. Above all, he saw the overwhelming imperative of national interest.

The first, immediate purpose of his visit was to secure the release of the German prisoners-of-war still held in Soviet camps, whose suffering he had specifically recalled in his declaration on the 'day of sovereignty'. He was also concerned with the position of other ethnic Germans inside the Soviet Union. Their emigration was to be one of the main subjects of a second round of negotiations, in 1957–58. Then there was his constant concern to increase the independence and widen the room for manoeuvre of the Federal Republic, making a 'new Potsdam' ever more difficult. On his return to Bonn, he explained confidentially to his colleagues in the party leadership: 'until now we were like the growing young man, who would be taken along by the other three or left at home at their pleasure. And now we have put ourselves at a stroke in the same row. In Moscow, too, the three Western ambassadors will be compelled to go hand in hand with the ambassador of the Federal Republic . . .'

Finally, Adenauer could see as well as anyone that Moscow held the key — or at least, the most important single key — to German unification. According to a distinguished specialist on German-Soviet relations, Boris Meissner, in the period before the building of the Berlin Wall there were two main tendencies discernible in West German Ostpolitik: one proposing to develop relations with all East European states, paying particular attention to Poland, the other giving clear priority to relations with Moscow. Adenauer belonged to the latter tendency: Moscow First.

The basic vision from which he started was, however, one in which the West's 'policy of strength', and the magnetism of an increasingly prosperous, free and united Western Europe, would so contrast with the growing weakness of the Soviet system and empire (exacerbated by the threat from China, on which he placed great hopes), that the Soviet leadership would sooner or later feel itself compelled to concede — from a position of weakness — the unification of Germany.

Some would maintain that this is precisely what happened in 1989–90. Yet this was not at all what seemed to be happening in the last years of Adenauer's chancellorship, in the late 1950s and early 1960s. On the contrary, the Soviet Union under Khrushchev seemed to be strengthening its position in central Europe, and, worse still from Adenauer's point of view, the Americans seemed increasingly ready to reach a modus vivendi with the Soviet Union on the basis of this strengthened position. The ultimate and shocking confirmation of this tendency was the building of a wall through the centre of Berlin on 13 August 1961, and the lack of anything more than a verbal protest from the United States, Britain and France. 'The hour of great disillusionment,' noted Heinrich Krone, one of the Chancellor's most important political associates, in his diary. 'The German people expected more than just a protest note from the West.' He might have added that many German people — and particularly the Berliners — also expected a stronger reaction from Konrad Adenauer.

Andrei Gromyko wrote in his memoirs, with sour (yet premature) satisfaction, that 'Adenauer probably did not abandon the idea of a united Germany until the night of 13 August 1961, when measures were taken to strengthen the state borders and sovereignty of the German Democratic Republic.' In fact, it is very doubtful whether Adenauer ever abandoned the idea of a united Germany. Indeed, there is some plausibility in the suggestion that he became more rather than less committed to the goal of reunification in the last years of his life, even as that goal seemed to recede rather than grow closer.

The question of the precise nature of Adenauer's commitment to the proclaimed goal of reunification is, however, a source of continuing controversy among historians, and cannot seriously be weighed here. What is clear and material for our purpose is that, in his operative policy after the building of the Wall, Adenauer placed the goal of securing elementary humanitarian improvements and, if possible, increased freedoms for the Germans now 'behind the Wall' before that of reunification in one state.

In a 'word to the Soviet Union' at the end of his government declaration in October 1962 he said: 'the Federal Government is ready to discuss many things, if our brothers in the Zone [sc. the Soviet Occupied Zone, that is, the GDR] can arrange their lives as they wish. Here considerations of humanity play a larger part for us even than national considerations.' If in the early 1950s he had placed the goal of freedom for West Germany before that of reunification, in the early 1960s he placed the goal of freedom for the East Germans before that of unity. Yet he continued to hold that the main addressee of such endeavours should be the Soviet Union and not the GDR — still referred to, if at all, as 'Pankow', after the borough of East Berlin where the leaders of the party-state then lived. One should talk to the landlord, not the housekeeper.

Even before the building of the Berlin Wall, Adenauer and his close associates had been actively considering schemes for reaching some *modus vivendi* with the Soviet Union, on the basis of accepting — albeit for a limited, specified period — the continued existence of a second German state. In early 1958, he tentatively proposed to the Soviet ambassador an 'Austrian solution' for the GDR. After the building of the Wall, he made further tentative advances to the Soviet side, suggesting, for example, a ten-year 'truce' on the German question. Heinrich Krone records him saying, after a conversation with the Soviet Ambassador in December 1961, that 'for the rest of his life he considers the most important thing that he still wants to do is to bring our relationship with Russia into tolerable order'. This, however, he hardly began to achieve in the less than two years remaining to him as Chancellor.

Even if Adenauer had been ready (and able, in terms of domestic political support) to make the crucial concessions that Brandt made eight years later — recognising the GDR and the Oder-Neisse line — it must be doubted whether the overall context of East-West relations at that time would have permitted him to achieve anything like the same results. Since he was not, this must remain forever an open question.

The period between Adenauer's departure as Chancellor, in October 1963, and Brandt's arrival as Chancellor, in October 1969, witnessed a highly complex transition, both in German and in other Western and European approaches to overcoming or reducing the division of Germany and Europe. Agitated and often contradictory movements were to be observed in at least four distinct, yet constantly interacting fields: the West German body politic narrowly defined, that is, the governing and opposition parties; the wider field of public and published opinion, the latter being particularly important in this period of transition; the policies of the Federal Republic's main Western allies, the United States, France and Britain (in that order); and, last but by no means least, those of the Soviet Union and its dependent East European states.

All we can do here is to indicate a few major lines of development. The first of these is Foreign Minister Gerhard Schröder's 'policy of movement', initiated under Adenauer from late 1961, but more fully developed under Chancellor Erhard, from 1963 to 1966. Following the recommendation of an important all-party Bundestag resolution of June 1961 (based on a report by the Sudeten German Social Democrat Wenzel Jaksch), and directly influenced by Kennedy's 'strategy of peace', Johnson's 'bridge-building', and de Gaulle's advocacy of what he called 'détente', Schröder set out very cautiously to develop a more constructive policy towards Eastern Europe. No major party in Bonn was yet prepared publicly to advocate abandoning the so-called 'Hallstein Doctrine', according to which the Federal Republic would not accord full diplomatic recognition to any state which recognised the GDR, since the Federal Republic alone represented Germany. But Schröder was able to establish trade missions in Poland, Hungary, Romania and Bulgaria.

The 'policy of movement' was, however, based on a number of highly contentious premisses. Its first addressees were the East European states, which it emphatically treated as sovereign partners. Yet at the same time it continued demonstratively to ostracise the GDR. Moreover, even the conciliatory 'peace note' of March 1966 — which for the first time formally proposed renunciation-of-force agreements such as would form the core of the Eastern treaties of the early 1970s — even this began and ended with a loud insistence on the German people's right to self-determination and reunification, and declared that 'in international law Germany continues to exist in the frontiers of 31 December 1937, so long as a freely elected all-German government does not recognise other frontiers'. These terms were unacceptable not only to the Soviet Union but also to Poland, Czechoslovakia and, of course, the GDR.

When the Grand Coalition government of Christian and Social Democrats was formed in December 1966, with the Christian Democrat Kurt-Georg Kiesinger as Chancellor and the Social Democrat Willy Brandt as Foreign Minister, it was clear to everyone that Bonn would have to go a step further. Encouraged by a valedictory speech from Konrad Adenauer, in which the elder statesman informed his party conference that 'Soviet Russia has entered the ranks of peoples who want peace', Chancellor Kiesinger immediately struck a number of new notes.

In his first government declaration, he painted his vision of what he now called a 'European peace order'. He repeated the 'peace 'note offer of renunciation-of-force agreements, this time stressing particularly the offer to the Soviet Union, and offered words of historic reconciliation to Czechoslovakia, and to Poland 'whose desire at last to live in a state area with secure frontiers we now understand better than in earlier times, given the present fate of our own partitioned nation'. He advocated the extensive development of 'human, economic and spiritual ties' with 'our compatriots in the other part of Germany'. But the words 'German Democratic Republic' or 'GDR' could still not be spoken. 'Where the establishment of contacts between authorities of the Federal Republic and those in the other part of Germany is necessary, this does not mean a recognition of a second German state.'

In the next year these points were developed in several ways. As we have already noted, the general commitment to work for 'détente', and towards a 'European peace order' in which the division of Germany would also be overcome, was enshrined in Nato's Harmel report. In April 1967, Kiesinger despatched a friend on a secret mission to Moscow, to explain his approach and explore any possible areas of movement or common ground. In an important speech to the Bundestag on 14 June 1967, Kiesinger then publicly emphasised the clear priority that would be given to relations with Moscow, as against that given to relations with other East European states in Schröder's 'policy of movement'.

'We all know,' he said, 'that the overcoming of the division of our people can indeed only be achieved by an arrangement with Moscow, unless we want to wait for one of the scurrilous and dangerous whims of history . . .' One should not think, he continued, 'above all in Moscow', that Bonn would be so foolish as to believe that it could achieve the European peace order and overcome the division of Germany by 'sowing discontent in the East and stirring up the countries there against Moscow'.

Three days later, in the traditional speech to mark the anniversary of the 17 June 1953 East German rising, he expanded on the relationship between the German and the European questions. 'Germany, a reunited Germany,' he declared,

> has a critical size. It is too big to play no role in the balance of forces, and too small to keep the forces around it in balance by itself. It is therefore hard to imagine that, while the present political structure in Europe continues, the whole of Germany could simply join one or other side. Just for this reason one can only see the growing together of the separated parts of Germany bedded into the process of overcoming the East-West conflict in Europe.

Thus Kiesinger already made the fundamental transition from a strategy that might crudely be summarised as 'détente through reunification' to one of 'reunification through détente'. The overcoming of the division of Germany, it was now argued, required first overcoming — or at least, reducing — the division of Europe.

So far as practical policy was concerned, he advocated 'first to seek ground which one can tread together, initially putting to one side the great issues of dispute'. Specifically this translated into a list of proposals for practical co-operation and communication between 'both parts of Germany' which anticipated a large part of the practical agenda of West German policy towards the GDR right up until the end of 1989. There was, Kiesinger told the Bundestag in October 1967, 'a phenomenon' over there, 'a phenomenon, with the representatives of which I have entered into correspondence'.

A great deal of the 'new' Ostpolitik was thus already in place, as a set of premisses and intentions, in 1967. (It was at this point, indeed, that it was christened 'new'.) This policy had been co-conceived, and was, wherever possible, jointly implemented, by Social Democratic members of the Grand Coalition: above all by Brandt as Foreign Minister, by the formidable figure of Herbert Wehner, as Minister for All-German Questions, and by Helmut Schmidt, as parliamentary floor leader of the Social Democrats. Yet it was eloquently and distinctively presented by the Christian Democrat Kurt-Georg Kiesinger, whose early speeches as Chancellor bear re-reading to this day. Ulrich Sahm, a senior Foreign Ministry official at that time, recalls Kiesinger saying emphatically: 'This is *my* Ostpolitik.'

If Kiesinger is a somewhat neglected figure in the history of Ostpolitik, then this is for a simple reason. In politics, as Disraeli observed, nothing succeeds like success — and nothing fails like failure. Although Brandt would say, in a handwritten letter of respect and thanks to the departing Chancellor, that their joint endeavours in the Grand Coalition 'did not do badly by our fatherland', the plain fact is that the Grand Coalition failed to achieve the desired breakthrough to a new relationship with Germany's neighbours to the East.

In January 1967, diplomatic relations were established with Romania. The governments of Hungary, Czechoslovakia, and Bulgaria showed interest in following suit, while Soviet commentaries were initially restrained. Greatly alarmed, the GDR under Walter Ulbricht moved quickly to block this new West German offensive, and soon won support from the Polish party leader, Władysław Gomułka. Yet the decisive voice was, of course, that of the Soviet Union. After a short hesitation, the Soviet leadership backed Ulbricht and Gomułka.

At a Warsaw Pact meeting in February 1967, Romania was sternly criticised for its lack of fraternal solidarity with the GDR, and the other East European states were urged to sign bilateral friendship treaties with the GDR, as the Soviet Union had already done in 1964. Poland and

Czechoslovakia did so at once, thus forming what was christened the 'iron triangle' (East Berlin-Warsaw-Prague) against Bonn's new Ostpolitik. Hungary and Bulgaria followed later. Against the 'Hallstein Doctrine' of the Federal Republic, the GDR placed what journalists would label the 'Ulbricht Doctrine', according to which no other East European state should move faster than East Germany in establishing ties with West Germany. The correspondence that Kiesinger had initiated with 'representatives of the phenomenon' was terminated, by the East German side.

Soviet leaders were themselves in a phase of conservative retrenchment after the overthrow of Khrushchev. They were concerned by signs of growing unruliness amongst their East European satellites — notably Romania's wilfulness in foreign policy, but also domestic developments in Poland, Hungary and Czechoslovakia. They perhaps genuinely misinterpreted this new Ostpolitik as a continuation of Schröder's 'policy of movement', a German revanchist variant of President Johnson's 'bridge-building', designed to split the Warsaw Pact and subvert its individual socialist states. Whatever the precise mixture of motives, the Soviet Union emphatically supported Ulbricht's defensive action, endeavoured to bring not only the Warsaw Pact but all European communist parties behind this line, at a conference in Karlovy Vary (Karlsbad) in April 1967, and launched a propaganda campaign against the new Ostpolitik as alleged West German 'revanchism'. This propaganda campaign only grew in intensity as ideologically 'revisionist' reform movements developed in Czechoslovakia, Poland and (in the economic field) in Hungary.

Although a West German trade mission was established in Prague, and diplomatic relations with bloc-free Yugoslavia (thus further weakening the 'Hallstein Doctrine'), the central thrust of the Grand Coalition's new Ostpolitik was blocked by Moscow. Full recognition of the 'post-war realities' in Europe, including Poland's western frontier on the Oder-Neisse line, the sovereign statehood of the GDR, and West Berlin as an 'autonomous political unit', was made the precondition for negotiations with the Federal Republic.

As we shall see, the social-liberal coalition government formed by Willy Brandt and Walter Scheel in October 1969 came a decisive step closer to this Soviet demand for 'recognition' of the 'Yalta' realities than the Grand Coalition did. Yet it is important to understand that there was also a very significant shift in Moscow's position. Moscow's formal offer to negotiate came in mid-September 1969, before the narrow election victory of the social-liberal coalition. By 1969 Moscow was prepared to do business with the government in Bonn — any government in Bonn — in a way that it was not prepared to in 1967 or 1968.

A number of reasons may be adduced. First, there was the burgeoning of superpower détente. Already in the early 1960s the double climax of the Berlin and Cuba crises, and the growing realisation that neither superpower could hope to win a nuclear war against the other, had pointed both in this direction. In a lecture delivered in 1971, the then State Secretary of the German Foreign Ministry, Paul Frank, would recall how in 1962, at the height of the Cuban missile crisis, he had heard Adlai Stevenson say that in forty-eight hours the world could either be at the start of the third world war or at the beginning of a period of détente between East and West. Frank dryly observed that the nuclear confrontation of 1962 led to a process of rethinking. 'Détente . . . is compelled by the nuclear stalemate', Egon Bahr had pithily noted for Willy Brandt as early as 1963.

Now, at the end of the 1960s, the Soviet Union was seen to be approaching nuclear parity with the United States. In the so-called 'Reykjavik signal' of June 1968, Nato had indicated its readiness to engage in talks about mutual balanced force reductions. The Brezhnev leadership responded favourably to the détente initiatives of the new administration of Richard Nixon and Henry Kissinger, not least because arms control agreements might ease the burden of defence spending on the Soviet economy.

Secondly, the Soviet leadership felt itself to be more secure in its own East European empire after crushing the Czechoslovak reform movement of the 'Prague Spring'. This was directly relevant to Germany. Despite Kiesinger's and Brandt's painstaking and repeated assurances to the contrary, in 1967 and 1968 the Soviet leadership had publicly held the 'revanchist' Federal Republic at least partly responsible for the discontents in East Central Europe, and specifically for the Prague Spring. Czech ideological revisionism was blamed on German territorial revisionism. Indeed, alleged West German interference was one of the main Soviet pretexts for the invasion of Czechoslovakia. After the 'success' of the invasion, however, to which the reaction of West German leaders was as painfully low-key as those of American and French leaders, the Soviet leadership soon signalled a readiness to negotiate, notably in the March 1969 Budapest Declaration of the Warsaw Pact.

The desirability of intensified technological and economic co-operation with the West figured prominently in this document. For after the failure of the 1965 Kosygin economic reforms, the Brezhnev leadership hoped to find salvation in an injection of modernity from the West. Whereas for arms control Moscow's main partner was obviously the United States, for direct inputs of trade and technology it would be Germany. Finally, if the United States was weakened by the conflict in South-East Asia, the Soviet Union was unsettled by the growing independent strength and self-confidence of China, and the possibility that Washington or indeed Bonn might seek a classic *alliance à rebours* with Peking. (So Adenauer's hope was partly fulfilled.) For all these reasons, Moscow gave both public and private indications of greater flexibility. Full recognition of the GDR and the Oder-Neisse line were no longer made preconditions for negotiations.

Although there were powerful figures among the Christian Democrats
— including Franz Josef Strauss — who seriously contemplated responding positively to such Soviet proposals, the Christian Democrats as a whole
could not find it in themselves to go this last kilometre. As the domestic
political fronts hardened in the run-up to the September 1969 federal
election, it became clear that the partners in the Grand Coalition took
different sides on this fundamental issue of German foreign policy. On the
one side, Kiesinger and the Christian Democrats stuck to, indeed retreated
to, their traditional principled insistence on reunification, starting from the
legal position that Germany continued to exist in the frontiers of December 1937, and the non-recognition of the GDR. They feared that the Social
Democratic Foreign Minister was too ready to concede what the Christian
Democrats regarded as fundamental German positions of principle to
communist rulers who had just suppressed the Prague Spring so brutally.

On the other side stood Brandt and the Social Democrats, quite
explicitly since their Nuremberg party congress in March 1968; Walter
Scheel and most of the Free Democrats; and behind them a large part of
the media and the intellectual, cultural, academic, and, not least, ecclesiastical community — 'published opinion' in the widest sense. All pleaded,
some on practical grounds, others more on moral ones, for the recognition
of the realities of 'Yalta' Europe, including the Oder-Neisse line as the
permanent western frontier of Poland, and the existence of a second
German state. This was to be the starting point for a new relationship
between Germany and the East, indeed altogether between East and West
in Europe. Chancellor Kiesinger had sarcastically described this very broad
church as 'the party of recognition'.

In the election of 1969, the Social and Free Democrats between them
won a narrow parliamentary majority, and formed the first social-liberal
coalition government in the history of the Federal Republic. The 'party of
recognition' was — just — in power, and now launched that particular
version of German eastern policy which came to be known round the
world as Ostpolitik.

The road from Berlin

It will be very clear from what has been said so far that many roads led to
the new Ostpolitik personified by Willy Brandt: by his grand, emotive
speeches and symbolic acts. Christian Democrats had started already under
Adenauer, and had gone at least half a step further with Kiesinger. Free
Democrats had made a major contribution, with innovative proposals
associated with the names of Karl Georg Pfleiderer and Wolfgang Scholl-
wer. Other Social Democrats, notably Herbert Wehner and Helmut
Schmidt, had contributed directly to the formulation of Brandt's position.

The influence of 'published opinion' inside Germany should as little be underrated as the international causes: the Western examples, starting with Kennedy and de Gaulle, and the crucial shifts in Eastern positions. All in all, the new Ostpolitik of the early 1970s was much less single-handedly the work of Willy Brandt than the Western integration of the early 1950s was of Konrad Adenauer. Yet Brandt it was who did the thing.

If we were to try fully to understand what moved and informed Willy Brandt's personal conduct of this policy we would also have to go back a long way. He was, after all, fifty-six years of age when he became Chancellor. We would be bound to look at his formative experiences as an illegitimate child in Wilhelmine Germany and as a young revolutionary socialist in the Weimar Republic; at his transition to social democracy in Scandinavian exile; at the hopes of a new, democratic, united Europe — 'left and free' — with which he returned to Germany; at his hard-fought political ascent among the Social Democrats of West Berlin and West Germany; at the arguments among those Social Democrats in the 1950s. But when all that was said we would nonetheless return to one place and one date, the place and date that Brandt himself puts at the opening of both his main volumes of memoirs: Berlin, 13 August 1961.

If the building of the Berlin Wall — in its first days not a wall, just a line of men and barbed wire — was a shock for Adenauer and his associates in Bonn, how much more terrible was the shock for the people of Berlin itself, and for their Governing Mayor, Willy Brandt. 'We consider,' he telexed the next day to the Foreign Minister in Bonn, 'that economic measures are necessary against the initiators of the decrees in East Berlin, as also against the so-called "GDR".' He called, in short, for sanctions against the Soviet Union. 'The barred walls of a concentration camp,' he wrote to Jawaharlal Nehru on 17 August 1961, 'have now been erected inside Berlin.' The horror and the fury come shouting through even the memoirs of the elder statesman, written more than a quarter of century later. Horror, of course, at the human suffering caused by the East German-Soviet action. 'In my Wedding constituency,' Brandt recalls, 'people jumped from houses directly on the sector line into the sheets of the fire brigade. Not all made it.' But fury almost as much at the Western allies, and above all at the Americans, for the weakness of their response.

'Gentlemen,' Brandt told the Western Allied commanders in Berlin, 'last night you let Ulbricht kick you in the arse.' Kennedy, he gathered, had not so much as interrupted his weekend yachting trip. Despite an emotional appeal in a personal letter from Brandt, the American President declined even to take the matter before the United Nations. In a cool response to Brandt's letter, Kennedy promised only to support, with a strengthened garrison, *West* Berlin and the half-city's ties with the West.

'Was it this letter [from Kennedy]', Brandt asks, in his 1989 volume of memoirs, 'which drew back the curtain and revealed the empty stage?' The rather delphic reference is explained in his earlier (1976) memoirs, when, after describing the shock of 13 August, he writes:

> I said later that in August 1961 a curtain was drawn aside to reveal an empty stage. To put it more bluntly, we lost certain illusions that had outlived the hopes underlying them . . . Ulbricht had been allowed to take a swipe at the Western superpower, and the United States merely winced with annoyance. My political deliberations in the years that followed were substantially influenced by this day's experience, and it was against this background that my so-called Ostpolitik — the beginning of détente — took shape.

The conclusion he and his closest associates drew was simple: the Americans are neither all-powerful nor all-willing; if we are to do anything for the inhabitants of our poor divided city (country, continent) we will have to do it ourselves, and we will have to do it by dealing directly with the powers-that-be in the East.

It is interesting to find that Brandt himself makes a connection with 'Yalta'. Discussing what the West might have done to avert the complete division of Germany and Berlin, he comes back to the March 1952 Stalin Note and writes (in his 1976 memoirs): 'I wondered then, not for the first or last time, whether the two superpowers might not, with adamantine consistency, have been pursuing the same principle in Europe since 1945: that, whatever happened, they would respect the spheres of influence broadly agreed at Yalta.' And again: 'The basic principle governing the tacit arrangement between Moscow and Washington remained in force during the construction of the Wall and thereafter.' The real historical process of the division of Europe was a great deal more complicated than this. Yet if one takes 'Yalta' to mean that whole historical process, then one might say that 13 August 1961 was the last day of Yalta and the first of Ostpolitik.

For all the diversity of the German roads that lead to the new Ostpolitik, the single most important road, the historical Autobahn, leads from Berlin. It leads from Berlin in the person of Willy Brandt — first Governing Mayor in Berlin, then Foreign Minister and Chancellor in Bonn. It leads from Berlin in the person of Egon Bahr — first Willy Brandt's press spokesman and close adviser in Berlin, then head of the planning staff in Brandt's Foreign Ministry, then key negotiator of the Eastern treaties. It leads from Berlin in the philosophy and practical policy that these two evolved, together with a tight circle of colleagues in the office of the Governing Mayor, known locally as 'the heavenly family'. Most of them had roots in central or eastern Germany, and all shared a passionate, patriotic concern for the divided city and the divided nation. If one wants to know what makes the West German policy of *Entspannung* different from other versions of détente, Berlin in 1961 is the place to start.

Within months of the building of the Wall, the first, strictly unofficial contact was made between a member of the Brandt team and an emissary of the East German leadership. The latter said, in effect, that a few wives might perhaps be let out through the Wall to rejoin their husbands, a few children to rejoin their parents — if the West Berlin government would pay for those wives and children in hard currency. This it did.

The West Berlin government then tried to negotiate with the East Berlin authorities (but without 'recognising' the GDR) an arrangement by which West Berliners could at least visit their relatives in East Berlin for a day or two over the Christmas holiday. In vain. The emotional pressures they were working under are graphically illustrated by a letter from a doctor (presumably in an East Berlin hospital) that Brandt quoted in a December 1961 speech to the Bundestag:

> Since the total strangulation [i.e. the closing of East Germany's frontiers by the Wall] the desire to get out has taken epidemic form. At least 95 per cent of the escapees are caught and suffer a terrible fate. You should see the bleeding hunks of flesh that are delivered to us here, in ever growing numbers, because the ordinary frontier troops must strike mercilessly with their bayonets . . . otherwise it would be their turn. Give the people here some hope, so that the suicide rate, which grows from week to week, and which leads us to fear the worst for Christmas, will at last begin to fall.

On the 17th of August 1962, an eighteen-year-old building worker, Peter Fechter, was shot by East German border guards while trying to escape over the Wall a short distance from Checkpoint Charlie. He lay amidst the barbed wire at the foot of the Wall for about an hour, bleeding to death, before the guards removed his lifeless body. He cried out for help until he died. A horrified crowd watched from the Western side, just a few metres away. So did American military police. The full implications of what had happened a year before were rammed home to the West Berliners, who responded with angry demonstrations not just against the East but even more against the West, and especially the United States, for its lack of response. Here the 'Yalta' line was drawn in blood, for everyone to see.

Slowly, painfully, Brandt and his team developed what they would call their 'policy of small steps'. For more than two years they struggled, through unconventional, even conspiratorial channels, to restore at least some basic human contacts. On 17 December 1963, Willy Brandt's fiftieth birthday, they finally accomplished that goal. While 'agreeing to differ' about nomenclature, and thus still notionally 'not recognising' the GDR, a representative of the West Berlin city government nonetheless signed with a GDR official — acting 'on the instructions of the deputy chairman of the Council of Ministers of the German Democratic Republic', as the document records — the first so-called 'Permit Agreement'. This enabled West Berliners to visit their relatives in East Berlin for a day at a time over the Christmas and New Year holidays. To the dismay of the East German authorities, and the delighted surprise of Brandt and his team, no less than 790,000 West Berliners — more than one in three — seized the opportunity, many going two or three times.

In interviews, speeches and articles over the next quarter-century, Willy Brandt and Egon Bahr would again and again return to this emotional moment. 'It was then,' declared Bahr in 1987, 'that the foundation-stone was laid for what later became known, also in many foreign languages, as "Ostpolitik".' Nor was it only Brandt and his circle in Berlin who saw the significance of what they had done; and not just with hindsight. Watching suspiciously from Bonn, Adenauer's close associate Heinrich Krone noted in his diary that Brandt and his friends were beginning 'an Ostpolitik of their own'.

But how on earth could a city mayor — in practice, the mayor of just half a city — be developing a foreign policy of his own? The answer lies in the unique significance of Berlin — the divided centre of the divided centre — but also in the unique person of Willy Brandt. Brandt's papers from his time as Governing Mayor reveal a man operating simultaneously on the municipal, federal and world stage. One day Brandt would be dealing with efforts to bring a few children back to their mothers across the Wall. The next he would be discussing the future of the world with Kennedy, Macmillan or de Gaulle. While the elementary human agony of the divided city was sufficient and indeed compelling reason for developing the 'policy of small steps', these two other levels were also vitally important.

At the same time as being Governing Mayor of Berlin, Brandt was the Social Democrats' most popular and attractive national leader, and their candidate for Chancellor. Although he had lost the September 1961 election to Adenauer, his colleagues were still urging him to stand and stand again in order at last to bring the Social Democrats to power in Bonn. 'What you must do, and in this I will gladly try to help you,' Herbert Wehner concluded a seven-page handwritten letter to him at Christmas 1963, 'is a really great political thing for SPD and Germany, for International and Europe-America.' (The order — SPD, Germany, International, Europe-America — is worth noting.) And everything that Brandt and his associates attempted to do in the presentation of their policy for the divided city (country, continent) has also to be seen in the context of this party-political struggle.

In the course of his endeavours in Berlin, Brandt formed the first ever social-liberal coalition in West German politics, a precursor of the federal social-liberal coalition six years later. Just as the 1969 Bonn coalition was forged on the basis of a new, common approach to reducing the division of Germany — and Europe — so this 1963 Berlin coalition was forged on the basis of a new, common approach to reducing the division of Berlin — and Germany. 'Don't believe,' said his Free Democratic partner William Borm, 'that we have gone to such trouble only on account of Berlin. The point is above all to get Deutschlandpolitik on the move again.' And a decade later, after he was triumphantly confirmed in office as the Chancellor of Ostpolitik in the federal election of 19 November 1972, Brandt wrote to the same William Borm: 'What most people don't know or have already forgotten: almost exactly ten years ago we two, by bringing together our two parties in Berlin, set in motion the process that was so emphatically endorsed by the voters of the Federal Republic on 19 November!'

At the same time, Brandt was developing an extraordinary range of international contacts. The most important of these were with the four main victor powers of 1945, who still had theoretically unlimited occupation rights in Berlin and residual rights relating to 'Germany as a whole'. Two planned personal meetings with Khrushchev never happened: one in 1959 met the resistance even of his own party, one in 1963 failed at the last minute because of the opposition of the Christian Democrats in Berlin (at that point still — just — his coalition partners). But he lost no opportunity to take discreet and confidential soundings of the Soviet position, most often through the good offices of Egon Bahr. The Brandt papers contain, for example, a note on the Governing Mayor's 'informal talk' with one Mr Polyanov of *Izvestia* on 16 March 1962. 'The German side,' Bahr records himself as saying in the course of this conversation, 'relied on a certain realism on the part of the Soviet Union, which in the long run could not ignore what 55 million Germans wanted, and that 17 million Germans would not become communists. At this point,' says the minute, 'Mr Polyanov became distinctly emotional.'

Still more stark and dramatic, however, was the message from Moscow to Berlin that Bahr recorded in a confidential memorandum dated 10 July 1962. One 'Herr Eimers ("Kurier")', said this memo, had just returned from Moscow with a message to Brandt from the West German Ambassador, Hans Kroll. The message was: 'Khrushchev wants a Western signature on the frontier of political influence in Europe between East and West. In this, he attaches particular importance to a German signature.' Khrushchev had suggested that Kroll should get together with Semyonov to negotiate on subjects including the withdrawal of American troops from Berlin. 'The Wall had been ordered by him, Khrushchev. This order he could also rescind.'

As a message at fourth hand this is not exactly 'from the horse's mouth'. But the brutal frankness sounds like authentic Khrushchev. In any case this memorandum is a vivid illustration of what Bahr and Brandt understood to be, in a nutshell, the Soviet message. A few years later, shortly before he moved to Bonn as Foreign Minister in 1966, Brandt would have a series of personal meetings with the Soviet ambassador to East Berlin, Piotr Abrassimov.

Most of Brandt's high-level personal contacts at this stage were, however, with Western allies and partners. Meeting with Harold Macmillan in November 1962, Brandt described the tragic human consequences of the Wall. According to the German record, Macmillan replied: 'All this is very stupid.' Rather more helpful, and more important, was General de Gaulle. Even before the building of the Wall, de Gaulle had envisaged the development of practical ties and co-operation between the two halves of Germany: a new Deutschlandpolitik *avant la lettre*. In a series of meetings, de Gaulle now directly encouraged Brandt in his policy of 'alleviation and encouragement for people in the Zone', as he put it in April 1963. 'De Gaulle expressed himself very positively — in German — about the policy of small steps,' says the minute of a conversation in Paris in June 1965.

Most important of all was John F Kennedy. On the one hand, Brandt had clearly resented what he saw as the weakness of the American response to the building of the Wall. On the other hand, American backing for his practical policy was crucially important, both directly in Berlin and in West German politics. Encouraged by his close adviser Klaus Schütz, who had been inspired by the American presidential campaign, Brandt — of the same generation as the American president, young and vigorous by contrast with the 87-year-old Chancellor in Bonn — was also not unhappy to be taken for a German Kennedy.

'Small steps are better than none,' he and his advisers said of their own policy, and: 'small steps are better than big words'. But in fact even the first very small steps of the early 1960s were accompanied by very big words, albeit of a different kind from the reunification rhetoric heard in Bonn. First in Berlin, then with a lecture series at Harvard in the autumn of 1962, subsequently published in German under the title *Co-existence: The Need to Dare*, Brandt began to prepare public opinion for the shift to come. He did so with a kind of inspirational vagueness which was already a hallmark of his political rhetoric. 'Brandt likes to talk a hovering language (*eine schwebende Sprache*)' noted Adenauer's associate, Heinrich Krone, in his diary on 27 December 1959. Willy Brandt, like his fellow journalist Winston Churchill, was a past master of emotive imprecision. In the drafts of his speeches and articles one can follow how, time and again down the years, he substitutes — as any good journalist would — a colourful phrase for a dull one, but also a vague, allusive, delphic formulation for a more precise one. Yet with Brandt, as with Churchill, the private thinking was often much clearer than the public speaking.

In this situation, with even Brandt's close political allies still needing to be persuaded of the wisdom of the new line, President Kennedy suddenly proclaimed his 'strategy of peace' at the American University in Washington in June 1963. The effect of this speech, writes Arthur Schlesinger, was to 'redefine the whole [American] national attitude to the Cold War'. While Brandt and Kennedy had talked about the way forward in the centre of Europe, the President's speech was obviously motivated by larger American concerns. To Brandt and his colleagues in Berlin it came, as Egon Bahr recalls, like 'a gift from heaven'.

Here was the charismatic figure with whom Brandt had politically identified himself, the leader of West Germany's and West Berlin's most important ally, now proclaiming a new direction in East-West relations which magnificently legitimated and, so to speak, covered their own. What is more, later that month Kennedy applied his 'strategy of peace' specifically to Germany in a speech at the Free University in West Berlin. This was the triumphant visit which also saw his famous declaration to a crowd before the city hall: '*Ich bin ein Berliner*' (written phonetically in his notes as 'Ish bin ein Bearleener').

Three weeks after the Kennedy visit, Brandt was scheduled to give a lecture at one of those church academies which played a remarkably important role in the intellectual background of West German politics in general and Ostpolitik in particular — the Protestant Academy in the small Bavarian town of Tutzing. The text of his talk was painstakingly discussed and edited by his close circle of advisers. At the last minute, Egon Bahr was invited by the organisers of the conference to add his own informal presentation. Believing, by his own account, that everything of real importance had been put into Brandt's scrupulously prepared text, he hastily dictated a few remarks. Yet it was Bahr's few informal remarks, not Brandt's finely crafted lecture, which would become famous as 'the Tutzing speech'. And justifiably so. For where Brandt covered the underlying logic of their approach in vague and inspirational rhetoric, Bahr revealed it with brilliant and provocative clarity.

Sketching what he called 'the application of the strategy of peace to Germany', Bahr proclaimed the goal of 'overcoming the status quo, by first not changing the status quo'. Reunification, he argued, would not be a single act but 'a process, with many steps and stops'. He saw no possibility of overthrowing the regime in East Germany, or even changing it against the will of the Soviet Union. Brandt's speech recalled his Harvard plea for 'a policy of transformation' of the other side. Bahr added: 'The Zone [i.e. East Germany] must be transformed with the agreement of the Soviets.' Brandt said: 'The German question can only be solved with the Soviet Union, not against it.' Bahr rammed the message home: 'The preconditions for reunification are only to be created with the Soviet Union. They are not to be had in East Berlin, not against the Soviet Union, not without it.'

The heated discussion about the legal-symbolic importance of not fully 'recognising' the 'GDR' could lead into a cul-de-sac. It was, after all, 'the

Interior Minister of the German Democratic Republic — with no inverted commas –' who on 13 August had forbidden the Western Allies to travel freely into the Eastern sector of the city, and limited them to one crossing at Checkpoint Charlie. No, far more important than the legal-symbolic niceties were the possibilities of practical action, 'beneath the level of juristic recognition', such as had already been ably explored by Dr Kurt Leopold of the Trust Office for Inter-Zonal Trade, the West German agency for trade between the two German states.

And more trade was certainly desirable. An economic blockade would only increase the tensions between the two parts of Germany, and within East Germany: 'Increasing tension strengthens Ulbricht and deepens the division.' Trade and credits, such as the United States had already given to Poland, might help to reduce tensions, both between East and West Germany, and within East Germany. 'A material improvement would be bound to have a tension-relaxing effect in the Zone. A better supply of consumer goods is in our interest.' Some might object that this would lessen popular discontent in East Germany 'but precisely that is desirable' for otherwise there might be 'uncontrolled developments' (like the 17 June 1953 rising or the 1960–61 emigration wave) which would lead to 'inevitable reverses' (such as the crushing of the 17 June rising or the building of the Berlin Wall). No 'practical path' led via attempts to overthrow the regime. 'I see only the narrow path of relief for the people in such homeopathic doses that no danger of a revolutionary turn develops, which would necessarily lead to Soviet intervention out of Soviet interests.'

After citing Adenauer's observation that human considerations should be put before national ones, Bahr summed up his argument.

> We have said that the Wall was a sign of weakness. One could also say, it was a sign of the communist regime's fear and urge for self-preservation. The question is whether there are not possibilities gradually to diminish the regime's quite justified fears, so that the loosening up of the frontiers and the Wall will also become practicable, because the risk will be bearable. This is a policy which one could sum up in the formula: *Wandel durch Annäherung* (change through rapprochement).

This speech, and particularly the formula *Wandel durch Annäherung*, provoked a storm of controversy, in the course of which Brandt made some tactical criticism of his press spokesman — the better to defend him. For in fact, as Brandt later admitted, Bahr was presenting their 'common thoughts'. Bahr himself would say that the strategy outlined in this speech was designed for a specific, transitional phase on the way to reunification, and thus made obsolete already by the 1964 long-term bilateral friendship treaty between the Soviet Union and the GDR. Certainly many elements were added to this conception, not least by Bahr himself, before it went up into the Ostpolitik of a Federal Government.

Yet it is remarkable to observe how many characteristic features of the Ostpolitik of the 1970s are already present here: the courtly, almost exaggerated emphasis on harmony with Western, and especially American policy; the insistence nonetheless on West Germany's need to do more for herself; the premiss that nothing could be achieved against the will of the Soviet Union; the belief in trade and economic co-operation as a means to facilitate political détente, both between East and West and within the East; the rejection of destabilisation; the notion rather of achieving relaxation by reassuring the communist powerholders; the curious combination of bold, dialectical, world-historical theory with the perforce extraordinarily modest, limited, quotidian practice of pursuing the most elementary humanitarian goals (the reunification of mother and child); and all this with an acute and palpable consciousness of the weakness of your own bargaining position. For it is only a slight exaggeration to say that the new Ostpolitik began in Berlin as a negotiation to free hostages from state-terrorists.

Statesmen may work with sophisticated and detailed analyses of complex international situations. They have to trim and adapt their policies to those of allies and adversaries. They also respond constantly to domestic political pressures. In democracies, this means above all the pressure of winning the next election, and in the Federal Republic there are federal or state elections almost all the time. Yet in most statesmen worthy of the name there is an emotional and intellectual core, formed by certain key experiences. Without grasping this biographical core one cannot begin to explain their visions or their actions.

Friedrich Naumann said of Bismarck that he 'thought Europe from Prussia out'. Recalling this comment, Arnulf Baring has argued that Adenauer thought Europe from Cologne out. With all due caveats and qualifications one may say of Willy Brandt: he thought Europe from Berlin out.

Treaty work

The road from Berlin led via Bonn to Moscow. As head of the planning staff in the Foreign Ministry, Bahr worked out his concept for negotiations with the governments in Moscow, East Berlin, and other East European capitals. Because he was personally so close to Brandt, and because other senior officials in the ministry were themselves divided on the way forward in East-West relations, the planning staff also became a clearing-house for proposals in this area. Meanwhile, Brandt and his advisers did not hesitate to use — as they had in Berlin — every available channel to sound out, and send signals to, the other side. These contacts ranged from an official top-level meeting at the UN between Brandt and the Soviet Foreign Minister to confidential mediation by Italian communists or a discreet lunch in a journalist's flat in Vienna. The conspiratorial secrecy of some of these private contacts bred a mistrust shared even by Chancellor Kiesinger. Some Christian Democrats anyway inclined to charge Social Democrats with being too close to the communists ideologically. The Free Democrats' new leader, Walter Scheel, by contrast, commented calmly: 'If one wants to maintain and improve security in Europe, then one must know that one will have to talk to communists.'

After the Soviet Union sent its diplomatic note formally offering to negotiate, on 12 September 1969, and just a week before the federal elections on 28 September, Bahr produced for Brandt a working paper entitled 'Reflections on the foreign policy of a future federal government'. This started by reaffirming the central importance of the United States for West Germany, noting the impact of Vietnam and the strong American interest in détente with the Soviet Union. It went on to give a very realistic assessment of the dilemmas of the Soviet leadership. Torn between the need to preserve their own power and that to increase economic efficiency, Soviet leaders would, Bahr argued, continue to alternate between loosening and tightening the leash on Eastern Europe. Much therefore depended on the skill of the Communist leaderships in the individual East European states. In relation to West Germany, however, the GDR hoped to open the path to international recognition without itself making concessions. 'This hope,' wrote Bahr, 'is not unfounded.' That pessimistic assumption was also crucial to the position he adopted.

The second part of the paper, drawing conclusions from this analysis, also began with the clear statement that 'the Atlantic Alliance and the close relationship to the USA must continue to remain the basis of our policy'. However, the Federal Republic should try to remove as much as possible of the Western Allies' residual occupation rights — those 'last relics of the post-war period'. The attempt should be made to use the Soviet proposal of a European security conference 'as an instrument for the realisation of our interests'. It would be highly desirable to negotiate a mutual balanced reduction of conventional forces in Central Europe, not least because the Americans seemed likely to reduce their troop numbers anyway — another important assumption.

So far as Deutschlandpolitik and *Osteuropapolitik* were concerned, his starting-point was that the division of Germany was getting ever deeper and more permanent. 'We must reckon with it for the foreseeable future. The necessity increases to adapt to this position without abandoning the goal of reunification.' The danger, Bahr repeated, was that the GDR would achieve international recognition even against Bonn's will. The central objective should therefore be a 'framework treaty' with the GDR, which would not need to be revised 'until reunification', and meanwhile would preserve at least elements of 'the unity of the nation'.

This framework treaty should be combined with 'a European renunciation-of-force', the recognition of the Oder-Neisse line and signing up to the nuclear non-proliferation treaty. It would clearly be desirable to establish diplomatic relations with the other East European states. This would give the 'pragmatic and co-operative forces' in those states more possibilities for pursuing a more autonomous policy, and increase the all-round pressure on the GDR to adopt a more co-operative attitude to the Federal Republic. But one would have always to keep in mind that West Germany's relations with Eastern Europe could only be developed to the extent that this was tolerated by the Soviet Union. Therefore an improvement in relations with the Soviet Union must be sought, exploiting, in particular, the obvious Soviet interest in closer economic ties.

A shorter version of this paper was then the starting-point for the foreign policy part of Brandt's discussions with the Free Democrats on forming a social-liberal coalition government in October 1969. But on Ostpolitik there were only small disagreements between them. 'Scheel stated in the debate,' says a note of the coalition talks on 1 October 1969, 'that the negotiating partners' ideas on foreign policy largely coincided.' The Free Democrats had already been thinking along very similar lines. Indeed, in January 1969 they had publicly proposed a general treaty with the GDR. Walter Scheel and a party delegation including Hans-Dietrich Genscher had returned from a trip to Moscow in July 1969 with very similar conclusions to those drawn by Helmut Schmidt and his Social Democratic delegation on their visit to Moscow in August 1969. Ostpolitik was the great common ground between the new coalition partners.

The basis on which the new social-liberal coalition then set about negotiating a new set of relationships with the Federal Republic's eastern neighbours was 'Moscow First'. As a paper written by Bahr in October 1968 makes crystal clear, the Soviet invasion of Czechoslovakia had only reinforced the lesson already drawn from the building of the Berlin Wall. A few members of this new government — notably Ralf Dahrendorf — still pleaded for the alternative line of giving priority to talks with Warsaw. But the negotiation with Moscow was given absolute priority, both in time and in importance, and the task was entrusted — in its crucial phase — to Egon Bahr.

Like a greyhound that has been straining at the leash, Bahr shot off to try out his 'concept' with a speed, *élan*, and secrecy that left Christian Democrats — out of power for the first time since the founding of the Federal Republic — spluttering with shock and indignation. For Bahr's talks with the Soviet Foreign Minister, Andrei Gromyko, in early 1970, were indeed the key to the whole complex of what came to be known as the Eastern treaties. This *Vertragswerk* ('treaty work') was to be the subject of the second most acute and prolonged political controversy in the history of the Federal Republic, comparable only to that which attended the negotiation of Adenauer's Western 'treaty work' in the 1950s. The controversy reached its high-point in 1972, in titanic debates over the ratification of the Moscow and Warsaw treaties, but even in the late 1980s any bold assertions or new 'revelations' about this subject were certain to raise temperatures rapidly, as with an old fever in the bones.

The secrecy of the negotiations, the unavailability (or very partial availability) of important sources, the intrinsic legal-political complexity of the 'treaty work', the memories of controversy and the political sensitivity of the central issues: all make simple generalisations more than usually inadvisable. At the same time, from the perspective of a reunited Germany, many of the points so long and so heatedly debated seem not only arcane — they were always that — but also archaic.

With the benefit of hindsight, and with a nod at the whole library of works written on this subject, we shall therefore concentrate on those few central points about this 'treaty work' which would in fact be most germane to the development of Ostpolitik over the next two decades. What did Bonn give and what did it get? In the foreplay to the Moscow Treaty, the Bonn government gave three major sweeteners. Firstly, it signed the nuclear non-proliferation treaty, thus confirming also to Moscow the renunciation of any claim to nuclear weapons which Adenauer had made to the Western allies in the context of his Western treaty work. Secondly, it indicated that, given a satisfactory outcome to this German-Soviet negotiation, it would support the Soviet Union's long-running goal of a European security conference — intended by Moscow to seal and sanction 'Yalta'.

Last but by no means least, it showed that it would respond favourably to Moscow's desire for increased economic and technological ties. Before the political negotiator Egon Bahr, the banker F Wilhelm Christians was in Moscow. While Bahr and Gromyko were still in a very early phase of their exploratory talks, agreements were signed in Essen providing for a large delivery of German steel pipes in return for subsequent supplies of Soviet natural gas through those pipes, the whole to be financed by a government-guaranteed credit on very favourable terms. A taste of things to come.

In the Moscow Treaty itself, the fundamental concession that Bonn made to Moscow was a comprehensive recognition of what the treaty called 'the existing real situation' in Europe, and a solemn commitment to respect the inviolability of the frontiers of all states in Europe 'including the Oder-Neisse line, which forms the Western frontier of the People's Republic of Poland, and the frontier between the Federal Republic of Germany and the German Democratic Republic'. Days and weeks had been spent by the German side, first by Bahr, then in the official negotiations by Walter Scheel, trying to weaken and complicate these commitments, so as to leave open in the wording just the crack of a possibility of peaceful change of frontiers, and, above all, of the reunification of the two German states.

The Russian negotiators had wanted the frontiers to be described as 'unalterable'; the Germans got them down to 'inviolable'. A reference in the preamble of the treaty to the terms of the opening of diplomatic relations in 1955 was held to include the unilateral letter sent by Adenauer to Bulganin, restating the Federal Republic's legal positions, as well as the hope formally expressed in an exchange of letters between the two leaders that this would contribute to 'solving the main national problem of the whole German people — the re-creation of the unity of a democratic German state'.

Less delphically, a 'letter on German Unity', which accompanied the Moscow Treaty, plainly reaffirmed the Federal Republic's commitment 'to work towards a state of peace in Europe in which the German people regains its unity in free self-determination'. (Twenty years later, controversy would still rumble on in Bonn about who was responsible for conceiving this letter.) The letter was accepted but not formally acknowledged or appended to the treaty by the Soviet side. An exchange of diplomatic notes with the United States, Britain and France also confirmed that the 'rights and responsibilities of the four powers relating to Berlin and Germany as a whole' were not affected.

Months, indeed years, were subsequently spent by the German body politic, debating what had or had not been, what should or might not have been conceded of the Federal Republic's legal-political-symbolic positions on these issues. After fierce internal debates, the Christian Democratic opposition insisted on a Common Resolution of the Bundestag, as the price for its mere abstention on the ratification vote in May 1972. This Common Resolution stressed that while the Moscow and Warsaw treaties were important elements of the '*modus vivendi*' which the Federal Republic sought with its eastern neighbours, they were in no sense part of any final, legally binding peace settlement for Germany. Responding to an appeal from Franz Josef Strauss's Bavarian State Government (formally questioning the constitutionality of the subsequent Basic Treaty with the GDR), the Constitutional Court averred, in a profoundly convoluted judgement, that legally the German Reich continued to exist in the frontiers of December 1937. These legal-symbolic caveats and qualifications, and the important question of how far they served or hindered the national goals of German Ostpolitik over the next two decades, are considered in more detail later on (see pp. 223ff).

In sum, the recognition of the 'existing real situation' contained in the Moscow Treaty — and the whole 'treaty work' that followed, including the Warsaw and Prague treaties and the treaty with the GDR — was not quite so complete and unconditional as the Soviet leadership would have wished, and especially, as the East German leadership would have wished. Yet it was a crucial and decisive step further than any previous Bonn government had been prepared to go.

In the first place, there was the basic recognition of the existence of the other German state. 'Even if two states in Germany exist,' Brandt had declared in his first government declaration as Chancellor, 'they are nonetheless not "foreign countries" (*Ausland*) for each other . . .' This distinctly backhanded acknowledgement of the existence of two states in Germany — after just twenty years of their existence! — was, as Richard von Weizsäcker observed at the time, 'the constitutive political statement on which the government's further measures of Ostpolitik are based'.

Beyond this, however, there was the recognition of the Soviet Union's control over the whole of what had come to be called 'Eastern Europe'. Here was the 'German signature' which Khrushchev had demanded in that confidential message to Brandt back in 1962. As Peter Bender, a knowledgeable and enthusiastic supporter of the new Ostpolitik, plainly puts it: 'When on 12 August 1970 Brandt and Scheel signed the Moscow Treaty, the Soviet Union had achieved what it had been working towards for fifteen years: German recognition of its Central European empire.' Thus it was in a treaty with the Soviet Union, not with the GDR, that the Federal Republic first expressed its recognition of the GDR. It was in a treaty with the Soviet Union, not with Poland, that the Federal Republic first expressed its recognition of Poland's post-1945 Western frontier. That result was, of course, fervently desired by the Poles. But the form in which it was achieved was resented even by the communist leadership of Poland. Germany and Russia agreed Poland's frontiers.

Leaked extracts from the German records of Egon Bahr's conversations with Gromyko note the following contribution from the Bonn government's chief negotiator on 21 February 1970:

We had to make sure that the process which we were now beginning would remain under full control the whole time . . . Here we would have a common interest. The Federal Republic was prepared to do everything it could to help with this. The Minister [i.e. Gromyko] would be informed that the Federal Government had been attacked in the Bundestag with the argument that the policy of the Federal Government would lead to a recognition of the special role — or 'predominance', as it was put there — of the Soviet Union among the socialist states. The Federal Chancellor had said that we would carry on our policy irrespective of these or other attacks. He, State Secretary Bahr, would be pleased if these remarks of his should be understood in their full meaning.

In a further exchange on 10 March, Gromyko showed that he had understood. The minutes record him saying: 'We [i.e. the Germans] should have no particular worry about the behaviour of third states — Poland and the GDR — with which the Soviet Union would talk . . .' And Bahr's response, again according to these leaked and fragmentary protocols: 'He [Bahr] did not have the worry which Minister Gromyko believed oppressed him. Quite the contrary. He [Bahr] would really like to negotiate everything with him [Gromyko].'

At the end of their preliminary talks, on 22 May 1970, Bahr and Gromyko agreed a ten-point working paper, which was soon leaked to the West German press, and dubbed the 'Bahr paper'. Its first four points became, with only relatively minor alterations, the first four points of the Moscow Treaty. The fifth point explicitly stated that this treaty together with 'matching agreements of the Federal Republic of Germany with other socialist countries, especially . . . with the German Democratic Republic (see point 6), the People's Republic of Poland and the Czechoslovak Socialist Republic (see point 8), form a single whole'. The subsequent points spelled out what the Federal Republic would undertake to do in its relationship with the GDR and Czechoslovakia, expressed the intention to expand economic and other ties with the Soviet Union, and committed both states to doing everything they could to advance the Conference on Security and Co-operation in Europe. Although these last six points were not formally incorporated into the treaty, they were solemnly exchanged as joint 'declarations of intent' on the occasion of its signing. The *Ost* in Ostpolitik therefore meant a camp of socialist states dominated by the Soviet Union.

Willy Brandt declared in a memorable television address from Moscow after signing the treaty in August 1970: 'Twenty-five years after the capitulation of the German Reich destroyed by Hitler, and fifteen years after Konrad Adenauer, here in Moscow, agreed the opening of diplomatic relations, the time has come to found our relationship with the East anew — that is, on unconditional mutual renunciation of force, on the basis of the political situation as it exists in Europe.' And, in a phrase that was to become famous, he observed: 'with this treaty nothing is lost that had not long since been gambled away'.

The gambler in this image was Hitler. Without Hitler, Germany might still have had its former territories east of the Oder and Neisse rivers, just as Poland might have had its former territories east of the river Bug. After signing the Warsaw Treaty, Brandt would aver, in another memorable phrase, that his government 'accept[ed] the results of history'. While he might elsewhere suggest that there were missed opportunities in Adenauer's policy towards the East, he left no shadow of doubt that the 'history' at issue here was that of the years before 1945. In his television address from Warsaw, he recalled the image of 'gambled away', and added: 'gambled away by a criminal regime, by National Socialism.' The 'results of history' therefore meant what Hitler had enabled Stalin to take, with a little help — or even, on some interpretations, a lot of help — from Roosevelt and Churchill.

What the Brandt government clearly did not 'accept', however, was that 'the results of history' meant the Germans to the west of the Oder-Neisse line could never be united in one state rather than two. Indeed, in official documents which accompanied the formal proposal for ratification of the Moscow and Warsaw treaties, they took the highly unusual step of publishing (with informal Soviet agreement) their own excerpts from statements made by the Soviet Foreign Minister in his negotiations with Walter Scheel. On the question of peaceful, voluntary changes of frontiers, Gromyko was recorded as saying:

> If two states agree of their own free will to unite, or correct frontiers, as we ourselves have done with Norway, Afghanistan and Poland — there indeed several times — or when two states want, for example, to give up their common frontier and to unite, like Syria and Egypt, it would not occur to us to criticise, for this is an expression of sovereignty and belongs to the inalienable rights of states and peoples.

(The reference — in the course of a German-Soviet negotiation — to Poland's 'voluntary' changes of frontier with the Soviet Union might be taken as a piece of black humour.)

Of course anyone who had suggested at this moment that in just twenty years' time the two German states would be uniting by mutual agreement, with Moscow's assent, would have been laughed out of the room — by German leaders as much as by Soviet ones. Yet the importance attached by the Brandt government to publishing this statement does indicate more than just their desperate desire to get the treaties ratified against furious opposition from Christian Democrats, who accused them of closing the door to German reunification. It also shows, what anyone who examined their earlier record would never doubt, that they cared passionately about bringing the Germans in East and West back together again. In recognising the end of Germany east of the Oder-Neisse line they drew a long-term conclusion from a terrible 'history' — which Brandt had actively opposed. In recognising the second German state, by contrast, they hoped to initiate a long-term process which would lead to fundamental change. While the two 'recognitions' came as one, their quality and thrust differed fundamentally.

Critics said they had conceded too much to Soviet demands, through over-hasty and ill-prepared negotiation by the armchair Metternich, Egon Bahr. Boris Meissner, a leading specialist on German-Soviet relations, described the Moscow Treaty as 'a notable success of Soviet diplomacy'. And while Gromyko at the time suggested the Soviet side had made 'painful' concessions, in his memoirs he writes complacently: 'Consistently in favour of a treaty with the Federal Republic, the USSR was, of course, largely responsible for its character.' There can be no doubt that the explicit recognition of the hard reality of post-Yalta 'Eastern Europe' — where recognition meant not just acknowledgement of *faits accomplis* but also acceptance as the basis for future relations — was profoundly welcome to the Soviet leadership.

Yet to treat this as merely a 'concession' by the German side would be to miss the essential point of what Brandt and Bahr were trying to do. For Bahr's 'concept' was to use this Soviet domination to force the reluctant East German satellite state into closer ties with West Germany, as well as securing vital improvements for West Berlin. As in a judo throw, Bonn would help its much larger opponent to swing in the direction he wanted to go, and then use the Soviet Union's weight for Germany's purpose. Berlin and East Germany were the prizes. Brandt's handwritten notes for his talks with Brezhnev in Moscow on the occasion of signing the treaty start with the question 'Who gets what?' The German side of his list begins: '-*Bln*, -*DDR*'. (Interestingly, the third point is '*Repar. tot*', and he would later note that the annulment of any potential reparations claims was the one and only thing which the Moscow Treaty had in common with Rapallo.)

Bonn insisted that it could not formally negotiate with Moscow over Berlin, since this would tempt the Soviets to resume their old game of trying to undermine the position of the Western Allies in West Berlin. But already in his preliminary talks with Gromyko, Bahr emphasised that Berlin — 'the heart of Europe', as he called it — was a vital German interest. And before signing the Moscow Treaty, the Brandt-Scheel government made an explicit linkage between the ratification of that treaty and the succesful conclusion of a new détente agreement between the four powers over Berlin. In notes scribbled for his response to Brezhnev during their talks in Moscow on 12 August 1970, Brandt listed three 'hopes' '*Ml-Eur* [*Mitteleuropa*], *DDR*, *Berlin*'. From '*Berlin*' he drew an arrow to the lapidary annotation: '*Beding. Ego*'. That is, 'condit[ion] me'.

This so-called *Berlin-Junktim* was, again, a gamble, since it put the fate of West Germany's Ostpolitik in the hands of the three Western allies as well as the Soviet Union. Immensely intricate and delicate negotiations followed, involving, crucially, Henry Kissinger and Egon Bahr — the two Metternichs of détente. But this gamble also paid off, partly because all four powers had a general interest in reducing tensions around Berlin in a period of burgeoning East-West détente, yet more specifically because the Soviet Union faced a hard double linkage: that made by Bonn with the ratification of the Moscow treaty, and that made by Washington with progress in American-Soviet relations, notably over the Strategic Arms Limitation Talks and the arrangement of a Nixon-Brezhnev summit.

The resulting Quadripartite Agreement of September 1971 was, of course, a compromise, which left open or ambiguous a few issues which were to be the source of much diplomatic agony over the next two decades, notably the exact nature and limits of the Federal presence in West Berlin and the inclusion of Berlin in West German treaties or agreements with the Soviet Union and Eastern Europe. Yet the compromise was, on balance, decidedly to the advantage of the West. Looking at the draft agreement worked out through American-German-Soviet back-channels, the American ambassador to Bonn, Kenneth Rush, wrote to Kissinger: 'it is still difficult for me to believe that it is as favorable as it is'.

Brandt's close aide and successor as Governing Mayor of Berlin, Klaus Schütz, had formulated the desiderata for his city as 'three Zs': *Zuordnung* (that is, *assignment* to the Federal Republic, including the right for Federal institutions to be present in West Berlin, and for West Berlin to be represented in and by Federal bodies), *Zugang* (that is, *access* from West Germany to West Berlin, and vice versa), and *Zutritt* (that is, the right of West Berliners to *entry* into East Berlin and the rest of East Germany). On the first point there was some improvement on the status quo, since the Soviet side accepted a formulation in the treaty whereby the 'ties' between West Berlin and West Germany would be 'maintained and developed'. Clear progress was made on the second and third points, since the Soviet Union formally resumed overall responsibility for securing Western civilian access through East Germany to West Berlin, and for ensuring that 'communications' between West Berlin and the surrounding territory (i.e. East Berlin and East Germany) would be 'improved'.

The practical realisation of these commitments of course depended on agreements between what the Quadripartite Agreement called 'the competent German authorities'. Reaching *West* Berlin via Moscow was thus only half the diplomatic journey on which Brandt, Bahr and Scheel had embarked at the end of 1969. The other, and in the longer-term the more important half, was to reach *East* Berlin via Moscow. Brandt mentioned one further anniversary in his television speech from Moscow, beside the twenty-five years since 1945, and the fifteen years since Adenauer's visit. 'Tomorrow [i.e. 13 August 1970],' he said, 'it will be nine years since the Wall was built. Today we have, so I confidently hope, made a beginning, so that the fracturing can be worked against, so that people no longer need to die on barbed wire, until the division of our people can hopefully one day be overcome.' Would Moscow now, as Gromyko had promised Bahr, 'talk to' the leaders of the GDR, pressuring them to open up to the Federal Republic? Here was the vital third side of the Bonn-Moscow-Berlin triangle.

From the Brandt papers we get glimpses of the Chancellor trying to, as it were, work the triangle. Thus, following the signature of the Quadripartite Agreement on Berlin and his controversial summit meeting with

Brezhnev at Oreanda in the Crimea in September 1971, where Berlin and the GDR had been top of his personal agenda, Brandt emphatically informs Brezhnev — in a letter dated 9 February 1972 — that he 'regards the creation of a *modus vivendi* with the GDR . . . as [a? the?] central task of our policy'. And in a message sent with Egon Bahr to Moscow in October 1972 he discreetly appeals for Soviet help in pushing the GDR to conclude negotiations on the Basic Treaty with the Federal Republic, *before* the federal election in November. He links this appeal, in the most delicate way, to the prospect of the GDR entering the United Nations, progress towards a Conference on Security and Cooperation in Europe, improved relations between the Soviet Union and the European Economic Community and, not least, the strengthening of German–Soviet economic ties. *Quid pro quo*. Armed with this letter, Bahr spent four hours talking to Brezhnev.

To see precisely what direct effect such appeals had on the East German position — whether Brezhnev, as it were, picked up the telephone or dashed off a note to Erich Honecker — we will, of course, need to study the top-level documents from the third side of the triangle. A few of these documents are, in fact, already accessible, and we may hope that more will follow. What appear to be Honecker's own notes of two sets of talks between the East German leadership and Brezhnev in December 1969 and May 1970 suggest a deep Soviet suspicion of the West German leader's intentions — 'one must unmask him' — but also a determination to press ahead with negotiations.

Most revealing in this connection are the notes on a one-to-one conversation between Brezhnev and Honecker on 28 July 1970, at the very moment when Walter Scheel was also in Moscow negotiating the last small amendments to the (West) German–Soviet treaty. The main subject of this conversation was the unacceptable arrogance and pig-headedness of the veteran East German Party leader, Walter Ulbricht, and the possibility of Brezhnev's replacing him with the younger and more flexible Erich Honecker. '*I tell you quite openly,*' the German record has Brezhnev saying, '*it will not be possible for him [Ulbricht] to rule without us, to take ill-considered steps against you [Honecker] or other comrades in the Politburo. After all, we have troops in your country.*' (Emphasis in original, presumably by Honecker). In the midst of this frank, comradely exchange, Brezhnev mentions that Scheel is in Moscow, and that a treaty will be signed. 'This will not solve all problems, *but the conclusion of this treaty will be a success for us, for the SU, the socialist countries. The GDR will gain from this treaty*. Its international authority will be increased. Its frontiers, its existence will be confirmed for all the world to see, its inviolability. This will consolidate the position inside the GDR.'

'To be sure,' Brezhnev went on, 'Brandt also expects advantages. He wants to penetrate you. But with time he will find that ever harder.' And in what seems to be an earlier rough note of the same conversation, Brezhnev is recorded as saying: 'Brandt is under double pressure. He must come to agreements with us. He hopes in this way to realise his goals in relation to the GDR. Socialdemocratisation [of the] GDR.' In the course of the conversation, Brezhnev urges Honecker to do everything to resist these influences: 'It . . . must not come to a process of rapprochement between the FRG and the GDR.' So, he says, 'concentrate everything on the all-sided strengthening of the GDR, as you call it.'

The mistrust of, and even hostility to Brandt which speaks from the records of 1969–70 was obviously moderated, at the very least, by their subsequent encounters. Talking to Honecker in Moscow in June 1974, shortly after Brandt's resignation, Brezhnev said 'objectively one must pay him tribute'. The tribute was nonetheless double-edged: 'For thirty years we have fought to realise our political goals in Europe. This man has risked pursuing such an Ostpolitik. Have we lost by it? No. The socialist countries and in the first place the GDR have won by it.'

Altogether, these documents show, in an uncommonly direct and vivid way, that Brezhnev had a quite shrewd idea of what Brandt was up to; that he felt the Soviet Union had the upper hand in the initial negotiations with the Federal Republic; and that — although not without considerable misgivings — he judged that a new East German leader, more flexible but also more closely tied to Moscow, should be able to control the effects of West German influence inside the GDR.

How far that was in fact the case — whether Brandt's gamble or Brezhnev's paid off — we shall examine in the next chapter. But it is a matter of chronological record that the opening of negotiations between Egon Bahr, for the Federal Republic, and Michael Kohl, for the GDR, followed three and a half months after the signature of the Moscow Treaty; that only following the removal of the recalcitrant Walter Ulbricht and the appointment of Erich Honecker as Party leader in May 1971 did these negotiations bear fruit, first in two minor agreements (made necessary by the Quadripartite Agreement on Berlin), then in a Traffic Treaty, then in the full Treaty on the Bases of Relations, which was initialled, as Brandt had requested, before the federal election of November 1972; and that, in these early years as Party leader, Honecker both publicly and privately emphasised the unbreakable and exemplary closeness of his relations with Moscow.

So Brandt, Bahr and Scheel did indeed make concessions, or diplomatic down payments, to the 'Eastern leading power'. But what they gave in Moscow was intrinsically and, so to speak, umbilically linked to what they hoped to get in the centre of Germany and Europe. Their long-term aim was not to cement the existing reality in Central Europe, but to transform it. As they themselves averred, a shade dialectically: one had to recognise the status quo in order to overcome it.

It is, however, equally important to note what they did not give. What they did not give was any immediate weakening of the Federal Republic's ties with, indeed its Adenauerian anchoring in, the West. Publicly and privately, Brandt and Scheel never tired of repeating the message that Ostpolitik did not diminish their commitment to further steps of economic-political integration in the (West) European Community, on the one hand, and to continued military-political integration in Nato on the other. They devoted considerable diplomatic efforts to reassuring their Western partners on this point. Nor did Brandt omit to mention it in his talks in the East. His scribbled notes for his response to Brezhnev in Moscow in August 1970 say: 'Alliances, us: Rome, loyal'. (There had been an important Nato meeting in Rome in May 1970.) And in his notes for their Crimean summit he writes 'Basic principle: in loyalty to allies and not at the cost of others.' In his Nobel Peace Prize lecture, Brandt said he did not like the very term 'Ostpolitik' not only because it was poisoned by earlier usage but also because it suggested that foreign policy was like a chest of drawers, in which one could pull out now one and now the other drawer. 'In reality it is thus: our détente policy began in the West and remains anchored in the West.'

Yet, as we have indicated already, this profound harmony was far from self-evident, not only to West Germany's Western partners, not just to the social-liberal government's Christian Democratic critics, but also to at least one of the main architects of the Ostpolitik. In his time as head of the planning staff in the Foreign Ministry, Egon Bahr produced two working papers which he considered to be of fundamental importance. As we have seen, the second of these, dating from September 1969, sketched the overall concept of 'normalising' West Germany's bilateral relations with the East: a concept that he himself put into practice in the crucial negotiations with Moscow and the GDR.

The first working paper attempted, in June 1968, to 'analyse German interests in the discussion about the shaping of European security'. The goal of the Federal Republic was here defined as 'the overcoming of the status quo through a European peace order', at the centre of which it clearly placed 'the overcoming of the division of Germany'. Sketching three different 'conceptions' of European security, the paper argued that German interests, thus defined, would best be served by 'Conception C': an entirely new European security system, replacing Nato and the Warsaw Pact. (The suggestion had been made in the 1966 Bucharest declaration of the Warsaw Pact.)

This entirely new European security system, whose headquarters were to be in Berlin, would consist of a central zone of non-nuclear states, including the two German states, the Benelux countries, Poland and Czechoslovakia. They would have no foreign troops on their soil, but their collective security would be guaranteed by the nuclear-armed superpowers.

This system would 'to be sure, concede Soviet demands (recognition of the GDR and the Oder-Neisse line, probably also weakening of our ties to Berlin), but only uses them to create the preconditions for reunification'. The communist leadership of the GDR would fear for its own survival without the presence of Soviet troops, but 'higher Soviet interests' would compel them to accept it. Judo again.

The paper conceded, however, that such a system did not seem achievable for the foreseeable future. In the meantime, it argued, the best variant for Germany would be to continue to work for the greatest possible détente between the existing alliances ('Conception A'), and, in particular, to press for substantial reductions of conventional forces in Central Europe. The clear implication was, nonetheless, that if it ever became possible, Germany should attempt to move from Conception A to Conception C. The notion of a dynamic sequence — from A to C — was spelled out even more clearly in a conversation which Bahr had with an American political scientist, Walter Hahn, in January 1969.

Conception C was more sophisticated than the crude deal proposed in the early 1950s: unity in return for neutrality. But it was still, in its basic premisses, closer to that than it was to the Adenauerian commitment, in which the political-military alliance with the United States was as important as the political-economic integration in the European Community. The result would be Germany between East and West rather than Germany as part of the West. This was, of course, precisely what the Federal Republic's Western allies feared.

Now one should not make too much of a single planning staff paper. Planners are there to think the unthinkable. Yet this was more than a mere *jeu d'esprit*. There was a hard and powerful logic of national interest to these arguments, a logic that had persuaded many national-minded Christian and Free Democrats as well as Social Democrats in the early years of the Federal Republic. As we shall see, the Social Democrats returned to these ideas, and developed them further, while in opposition in the 1980s. The other working paper of Bahr's planning staff was largely put into practice in the foreign policy of the Federal Republic. And in a letter to Brandt dated 14 November 1972, anticipating the social-liberal coalition's return to office for another term, Bahr wrote:

> in foreign policy the government can ensure that until the end of the next term the first steps of troop reductions are implemented. I would happily take on this task, neglecting the CSCE. The sainted planning staff has, as you know, already for this term too its papers, which, by the way, in the last three years have proved to be quite workable.

In the event, however, the Brandt government in its second term did no more that attempt to put into practice the — for Germany — most desirable variant of Conception A. In particular, they pressed hard, but unsuccess-fully, for rapid progress on conventional troop reductions in Central Europe. 'We deflected the German initiative,' writes Henry Kissinger in his memoirs, 'by supporting a Canadian set of general MBFR [Mutual Balanced Force Reductions] principles of inspired vagueness.' Bahr him-self would clearly have liked to do more, but, as he recalls, for the first half of 1973 he was simply exhausted after the huge endeavour of negotiating the treaty work. By the time he recovered, the government was already shaking under other problems. Moreover, in this first phase of the new Ostpolitik, most policymakers agreed that it would be disastrous to be seen in the West to put in question the basic lines of Nato strategy and policy. It is far from certain that even Willy Brandt would at this time have fully endorsed Bahr's analysis of where long-term German interests lay. Walter Scheel and the then Defence Minister, Helmut Schmidt, certainly did not. As we have noted before, the motives and attitudes of the main architects of social-liberal Ostpolitik were quite diverse.

There were three main arguments for making the Nato connection non-negotiable. The first was, so to speak, existential. After the erratic course it had steered in the past, Germany required this heavy anchor in the West to prevent it straying once again between East and West, and losing its balance, as the post-Bismarckian Reich had lost its balance, in the tangle of competing ties, aspirations and demands.

The second was strategic. So long as Germany (West) was threatened by a nuclear-armed superpower in the East, it required the protection of a nuclear-armed superpower in the West. This 'balance of power' argu-ment was urged most forcefully by Helmut Schmidt, who was much less inclined than Bahr or Brandt to believe that the relaxation of tensions, and the development of new forms of political, economic, cultural and other ties with the Soviet Union and its allies, could be a substitute for military defences against what he saw as an historically expansionist Russia.

Finally, there was the tactical argument: in order to gain and retain the support of Germany's Western partners, Bonn could not be seen to put those Western ties in question. On the contrary, she must redouble her insistence on their importance.

The existential argument was probably accepted by only a minority of those who made Ostpolitik. Most of them thought Germany was now big enough and wise enough to do more looking after herself. That was, indeed, a leitmotif of the new policy. The strategic argument was probably accepted by most, albeit with some reluctance. The tactical argument was endorsed by all without exception.

As a result, the diplomatic 'system' which Brandt, Bahr and Scheel built in the years 1970–73 contained no new security components — a fact which Bahr would subsequently regard as a crucial omission (see Chapter Six). It was also erected on the clear understanding that the Federal Republic would not diminish, but would rather redouble, its efforts to push ahead with political integration of the (West) European Community. Following the important Hague summit of December 1969, the EC — enlarged to include Britain, Ireland and Denmark — began the practice of regular consultation on foreign policy, later formalised as European Political Cooperation. 'I think it is no exaggeration to say that the European ship has only set sail again following the Hague conference', Willy Brandt wrote in an eloquent personal letter to the sceptical former US High Commissioner in Germany, John McCloy, pleading for acceptance of the Ostpolitik. Like the commitment to the Atlantic Alliance, this commitment to the European Community was tactical for some, but strategic or existential for most.

The last year and a half of Brandt's Chancellorship, after the double triumph of his re-election and the signature of the Basic Treaty with the GDR at the end of 1972, saw the installation of the last bilateral components of Ostpolitik, and the beginnings of what was always meant to be its multilateral development. Bilaterally, Brezhnev's successful state visit to Bonn in 1973 confirmed the new quality of German-Soviet relations, while placing particular emphasis, predictably enough, on economic ties. In his thank-you letter, Brezhnev wrote: 'After public opinion in our country has made itself thoroughly acquainted with the work done together with you during the visit, I can now tell you with absolute certainty that the Party and the Soviet people fully endorse and support the course of improvement and development of relations between the USSR and the Federal Republic.' Handing over this letter, the Soviet ambassador to Bonn, Valentin Falin, said he had the impression that a 'remarkable personal contact' had developed between the Chancellor and the Soviet leader.

Responding, a few months later, to Brezhnev's message of greetings on his sixtieth birthday, Brandt passed in review the development of German-Soviet relations, emphasised particularly the tripling of trade, touched on problems connected with West Berlin, and then, once again, appealed directly to Brezhnev to make the GDR more co-operative with the Federal Republic. He was particularly concerned, he wrote, about the doubling of the minimum amount that visitors from West Germany and West Berlin were compelled to exchange on every visit to the GDR: 'The Soviet side may not realise how negative is the impression made by this and other measures taken by the GDR on our public opinion.' (If Brezhnev could cite his 'public opinion' so, with considerably more justification, could Brandt.)

> The situation which has emerged compels me to draw your attention to the danger that such a negative development could significantly endanger the efforts of my government to widen the policy of détente. I should be most

grateful, dear General Secretary, if you could also turn your attention to this problem. It must surely be possible that, for example, the GDR finds a way to compensate the negative effects of its order on the minimum exchange.

Working the triangle again.

At the same time, the bilateral East European network was completed with the relatively easy establishment of diplomatic relations with Hungary and Bulgaria, and the much more difficult conclusion of a treaty with Czechoslovakia. Negotiated with Husák's 'normalising' regime in the shadow of the Soviet invasion, and plagued by legal arguments about whether the 1938 Munich Agreement should be considered invalid from the outset (*ex tunc*) or merely from now on (*ex nunc*), the Prague Treaty of 1973 left unclarities which would return to trouble relations between Prague and Bonn in the early 1990s. Meanwhile, both German states finally became full members of the UN. Multilaterally, both the talks of Mutual Balanced Force Reductions (MBFR) in Vienna and the Conference on Security and Co-operation in Europe (CSCE) got under way, with active German participation. Public statements and private papers make it clear that Brandt regarded the two sets of talks as intimately linked, and that he looked for the completion of those on conventional troop reductions in a time-scale of five years. But these plans were to remain on paper.

Already drained by the Herculean effort of putting this system into place, and much less effective in domestic than in foreign policy, Willy Brandt was toppled, ironically enough by the exposure of one of his aides as an East German spy. Walter Scheel became Federal President. It therefore fell to Brandt's successor as Social Democratic Chancellor, Helmut Schmidt, and Scheel's successor as Free Democratic Foreign Minister, Hans-Dietrich Genscher, to try and 'make work' the complex and delicate diplomatic system that Brandt, Bahr and Scheel had built.

System and crisis

At the time, an outstanding historian of German foreign policy, Waldemar Besson, commented that two fundamentally different traditions had now to be combined: the Adenauerian tradition of unambiguous commitment to Western Europe, and the Bismarckian tradition of standing free in the centre of Europe while attempting to keep a balance with and between the states around Germany. Adenauer met Bismarck.

It was not to Besson alone that the comparison with Bismarck occurred. Henry Kissinger, in his memoirs, compared Bahr's approach to that of Bismarck. When the comparison was put by an interviewer to Bahr himself, he said: 'I have been fascinated, really for as long as I can remember, by Bismarck's foreign policy, and I consider him to have been one of the real greats that we had.' Yet as that interviewer observed, Bismarck had begun a juggling act with many balls, a game which was very complicated, indeed 'too complicated'. Yes, agreed Bahr, 'the real mastery is showed when one has a system that continues to work even without its inventors'. Spoke the latter-day Bismarck.

It is also interesting to find that in a statement to mark the centenary of the proclamation of the German Reich, on 18 January 1971, Chancellor Brandt described Bismarck as 'one of the great statesmen of our nation'. 'The solution of 100 years ago,' he wrote, 'reflected the insights and possibilities of the time. The world-political situation today requires new forms of the Germans' political living and working together . . .', and hence 'the event of 1871 can be no model today'. But 'the work and achievements of Bismarck are nonetheless a lasting illustration of the fact that only skilful and courageous action, not passive waiting, bring us closer to the given goals' — a side-swipe, of course, at the Christian Democratic opposition.

Plainly the analogy can be pushed too far. But with all due caveats, the diplomatic system that Schmidt and Genscher inherited did have elements of a neo-Bismarckian juggling act. Indeed, in one vital respect it was even more complicated. For at its centre was not a static but a dynamic task: not the defence of the state unity already achieved in Bismarck's Reich, but the business of trying to keep alive a cultural and human unity of the nation in two opposed states, and, in the longer term, even of working towards some kind of political unity, albeit in constitutional forms and geographical boundaries quite different from those of the Bismarckian Reich.

To achieve this, the system demanded — or was thought to demand — what might be called horizontal synchronisation of the whole Ostpolitik. The failure of Foreign Minister Schröder's 'policy of movement' was held to have shown that Bonn could not hope to develop closer ties with East European states without Moscow's assent. Moscow's assent depended on recognition of the GDR, and Moscow's weight was at first needed to bring the GDR itself to the negotiating table — the Bahr-judo. But as relations with the GDR warmed up, so it was felt that relations with East European states and with the Soviet Union itself must also be enhanced, so that neither Moscow nor its East European allies (who might then complain to Moscow) would feel threatened by the German-German rapprochement. Whereas the United States' Ostpolitik was based on the principle of 'differentiation' — rewarding those Soviet bloc states that 'behaved well' in domestic or foreign policy, punishing those that behaved badly — the Federal Republic's Ostpolitik was thus based on a principle of synchronisation.

Yet this horizontal or eastward synchronisation, complicated enough in itself, was only half the juggling act. For given the continued, Adenauerian, commitments to the West, a complementary, westward or vertical synchronisation was needed. If the Federal Republic was to carry on integrating into Western Europe as well as thickening its ties with Eastern Europe, then the rest of Western Europe must also go on thickening its ties with Eastern Europe. Otherwise the tension between the two, between Ostpolitik and Europapolitik (a term used in Bonn essentially to describe EC-policy), would become unbearable. An untoward development in any one East European country, or Soviet reaction to such a development, would be threatening to Bonn's policy not only because it might impel Moscow to tighten the imperial leash on the GDR, but also because it might incline Bonn's West European partners to retaliate against Moscow.

Similarly, but *a fortiori*, Bonn could only develop its relations with Moscow (the key to Berlin and the GDR) and maintain its intimate political-military integration in the US-led alliance, if the United States and the Soviet Union continued to have 'détente' relations as good or preferably better than they had when the system was erected. If US-Soviet relations worsened, then Bonn would be torn between the two. The system thus demanded vertical as well as horizontal synchronisation. The national, regional and global levels of détente had somehow all to be kept in harmony. This was a very tall order for what was still only a medium-sized European power, economically stronger than France or Britain, to be sure, but also with unique historical and diplomatic handicaps.

Moreover, this complex task had to be attempted at a time when the Federal Republic faced other major challenges in its external relations. Brandt, Bahr and Scheel had concentrated on Ostpolitik, and to a lesser degree on Europapolitik, to the disadvantage of, indeed even to the neglect of, other areas. One of these was the turbulence in the world economy following the collapse of the Bretton Woods international monetary order and the shock of drastically increased oil prices. For the Federal Republic, a 'trading state' *par excellence*, this was a challenge of the first order. Here was, without question, the first external preoccupation of the new Chancellor, Helmut Schmidt.

In a long, confidential *tour d'horizon* drafted during his Christmas holiday at the end of 1976, and hence known internally as the 'Marbella paper', Schmidt wrote: 'Never since the world economic crisis of the thirties have domestic political, foreign political, and political-economic actions of the rulers (and of parliament) in Germany had such a strong mutual dependency . . . as in the last years. That would seem to be no less true, indeed perhaps more so, for *the year 1977, which will again stand under the primacy of economic policy*' (italics in original). And it is perhaps for his achievements in organising world economic crisis management, and European economic co-operation, that Schmidt will be remembered. Meanwhile his new Foreign Minister, the Free Democratic Hans-Dietrich Genscher, although deeply committed to increasing contacts with the part of Germany from which he himself came, 'profiled' himself (and his party) in this period above all by cultivating the relationship with the United States.

The relative importance of Ostpolitik in the foreign policy of the Federal Republic under Chancellor Schmidt was therefore less than it had been under Brandt. But it would be wrong to suggest that Schmidt neglected or did not care about it. To argue, as did his sometime private archivist, Hans Georg Lehmann, that Schmidt had actually been the true architect of the Social Democratic concept of Ostpolitik which Brandt and Bahr implemented, would be, to put it mildly, an overstatement. But Schmidt had been actively involved in the Social Democrats' public discussion of Ostpolitik since an important speech he delivered at the Dortmund party conference in 1966, a year in which he also travelled privately to Eastern Europe. As parliamentary floor leader, he had been intimately involved in the formulation of Ostpolitik in the late 1960s. As we have noted already, he led a parliamentary delegation on an important trip to Moscow in 1969.

If childhood and family ties gave Hans-Dietrich Genscher a very special interest in East Germany, Helmut Schmidt shared with many of his generation a very specific and complex emotional involvement in relations with the East that derived from having fought as a soldier on the Eastern front in the Second World War. He was, typically, almost archetypically, a representative of this *Frontgeneration*, combining a sombre intellectual and emotional reading of the lessons of that terrible experience ('never again') with a strong residual liking for the methods and manners of a General Staff.

Like all his predecessors, Schmidt also saw very clearly the intimate link between the relationship to the East and the Federal Republic's real freedom of action as a sovereign state. 'We seek,' he wrote in the 1970 Preface to the English edition of his book *The Balance of Power*, 'to use Germany's present scope for taking action. If that attempt is successful it will change and improve the part of the world we live in. If it should fail the partition of Europe will become more permanent. . . . This book basically deals with the scope of action of German foreign policy.' As Chancellor, he self-consciously and self-confidently used the enlarged room for manoeuvre, the greater *de facto* sovereignty, that the Eastern treaty work gave to the Federal Republic. Yet, as with all his predecessors, there were two sides to this coin.

On the one hand, he could on occasion quite directly and even aggressively assert German interests, and German views of European, Western or global interests, notably in his bilateral discussions with the United States and above all with President Jimmy Carter. On the other hand, he was concerned to enmesh German interests, policies and perspectives in the increasingly multilateral frameworks of Western foreign policy-making. Indeed, he was very active in promoting this multilateral co-ordination, whether in the EC, Nato, or the new Group of Seven (G7) top industrial states which held a notable summit in Bonn in 1978. Partly, of course, this was because he thought such multilateral co-ordination was good in itself, good for the world. But there was also, as with his predecessors, a special German motive.

In his confidential Marbella paper he argued that the Federal Republic had become 'in the eyes of the world *de facto* economically the second world power of the West'. This 'unwanted and dangerous rise to second world power of the West in the consciousness of other governments — including especially the Soviet leadership! –' would arouse concerns, and could have negative effects, notably for Berlin. There could be 'a revival of memories not only of Auschwitz and Hitler but also of Wilhelm II and Bismarck . . . perhaps as much in the West as in the East.' It was therefore, he went on, 'necessary for us, so far as at all possible, to operate not nationally and independently but in the framework of the European Community and of the Alliance. This *attempt to cover [abdecken] our actions multilaterally will only partially* succeed, because we will (necessarily and against our own will) become a leadership factor in both systems' [italics in original]. One could write a small essay on the nuances of the word *abdecken* in this sentence. For multilateralism was to 'cover' the growth of German power in many senses: to camouflage, but also to control; to manage, but also to permit; to facilitate, but also to palliate.

In relations with the East, too, the period of Schmidt's Chancellorship, from 1974 to 1982, was one of burgeoning multilateralism. There were the multilateral talks on Mutual Balanced Force Reductions. There were, increasingly, multilateral consultations about economic relations with the East, in the Group of Seven, the International Monetary Fund, the World Bank, the so-called CoCom, controlling the export of Western high technology to the East, and later in the Paris and London 'clubs' of the Western governments and banks to whom Eastern states were increasingly indebted. There was the growth of the EC member states' European Political Cooperation, particularly in connection with the preparations for, and then the follow-up to, the Helsinki Conference on Security and Cooperation in Europe. Above all, there was that whole 'Helsinki process' itself. Yet beside this novel style of institutionalised, ongoing multilateralism there was some quite old-fashioned bilateralism as well.

For Schmidt had in many ways a very old-fashioned view of history being made by what history teachers used to call 'great men'. He regarded summit meetings between those whom he described as *Staatslenker* (rough-ly: state-pilots) as the key to the development of bilateral relations between states. Accordingly, he systematically went down the list of East European leaders, organising visits from and to Bonn. Plainly, these meetings had an importance of their own. Thus he established a particularly close rapport with the Polish Party leader Edward Gierek: a friendship that combined the profound desire of a member of the *Frontgeneration* for 'reconciliation' with personal liking, but resulted in economic, political and even moral misjudgement (see Chapter Six). Yet all these East European ties were clearly subordinated to those with Moscow, Schmidt's first Eastern port of call in 1974.

On a return visit to Bonn, in May 1978, Brezhnev cannily observed that (as the interpreter's protocol records) 'the role of the Federal Republic of Germany as a state which pursues a distinct and independent policy had begun when the door had been opened to a rapprochement (*Annäherung*) with the Soviet Union and the other socialist states: when what in the Federal Republic was called Ostpolitik had begun.' West Germany, he implied, had its own very special interest in the continuation of détente. In his response, Schmidt said (again according to the interpreter's record) that 'the General Secretary was right when he said that the international weight of the Federal Republic had grown since the Moscow Treaty. This weight had been used to further détente. . . . Visits and the exchange of visits had taken place with Gierek, Kádár, Zhivkov, Ceauşescu. Dr Husák had visited his country as the first Western country [i.e. to give Husák that opportunity].' (The favour was more warmly appreciated by the rulers in Moscow than by the ruled in Prague.) But, Schmidt went on, 'naturally German-Soviet relations stood at the centre of Ostpolitik. This would be so for the next 30 years.'

Schmidt established a good and even sentimental relationship with Brezhnev, based, as more than once between Germans and Russians of their generation, on the experience of having fought each other on the Eastern Front. When they first met, during Brezhnev's first visit to Bonn in May 1973, Schmidt responded to Brezhnev's remarks about the suffering of the Soviet people in the Great Patriotic War with a long and very personal explanation of the schizophrenia of those young soldiers who had fought for Germany by day, yet at night privately wished for Hitler to fail. Willy Brandt, with the exile's quite different perspective on that war, comments drily that 'when war reminiscences are exchanged, the false and the genuine lie very close together'. Yet though Schmidt also recognises the element of calculation in Brezhnev's regular vodka-and-tears turns, he records that he felt genuine sorrow on receiving news of Brezhnev's death. Indeed, he sometimes believed himself better understood by Leonid Brezhnev than by Jimmy Carter.

Like Brandt and Bahr, Schmidt tried to work the Bonn-Moscow-Berlin triangle for the benefit of West Berlin and West German policy towards the GDR. Thus, for example, in the record of a conversation with the Soviet Ambassador to Bonn, Valentin Falin, in the run-up to Schmidt's visit to Moscow in October 1974, we find the Chancellor once again raising the subject of the increased compulsory minimum exchange of hard currency for Western visitors to the GDR. Three days before Schmidt flew to Moscow, the GDR announced a reduction of the minimum exchange. A purely sovereign East German decision, of course.

A more explicit subject of debate between Bonn and Moscow was the interpretation of the Quadripartite Agreement on Berlin, which occupied a great deal of time in German-Soviet talks. In a conversation with the Chancellor in 1974, Gromyko spoke dismissively of the idea that Berlin could be a 'barometer' for the state of East-West relations, since the Soviet Union 'wanted détente and peace for the whole world. For this, Berlin was hardly an impressive quantity.' Berlin might not be a barometer, Schmidt replied, but the ties to Berlin were a 'central interest' of the Federal Republic, which was — he modestly observed — 'a power of middling importance, limited to Central Europe, and thus the [Berlin] problem was much more significant for us.'

In the event, Schmidt, Genscher and their diplomats would have to argue again and again and again for what Brezhnev and Brandt had agreed to call the 'strict observance and full application' of the Quadripartite Agreement. In a personal letter to Brezhnev in April 1975, Schmidt wrote that relations between the Federal Republic and the Soviet Union could not be better than the state of affairs around Berlin. However, Schmidt subsequently concluded — somewhat at odds with the Foreign Ministry — that the interests of Berlin would best be served in the long-term by an indirect strategy of all-round improvement of relations with the Soviet Union, and above all of economic relations, rather than by tactics of constant, direct confrontation on issues such as the presence of Federal Government institutions in West Berlin.

The key-word that recurs constantly in the public statements and private papers of his Chancellorship is 'stability'. As we shall see, this key-word had many meanings, but in this context the primary meaning was: stability of the overall diplomatic system of Ostpolitik, with its dual imperative of vertical and horizontal synchronisation. Thus he was, for example, openly and contemptuously dismissive of Jimmy Carter's missionary campaign to secure more respect for human rights in the Soviet Union and Eastern Europe. As he himself observed retrospectively in a lecture in 1991, he — or, as he put it, 'we Europeans' — had in the 1970s placed the principle of stability before human rights. His book, published in 1969, was called *The Balance of Power. German peace policy and the superpowers*. That, in a nutshell, was what he was about. Like Henry Kissinger (and partly influenced by him) he regarded the balance of power as the key to preserving peace in Europe, and international order more generally. At the same time, he saw détente at the superpower and European levels as the necessary condition for working incrementally to reduce (or at the very least, to prevent the deepening of) the division of Berlin and Germany.

In pursuing these twin goals, he gave priority to two classical instruments. The foreign policy of a state, a French president is reported to have said, consists of arms and then money. In the relationship with the Soviet Union, at least, Schmidt acted pretty much in line with that classical dictum, concentrating heavily on the economic-political and the military-political aspects of the German-Soviet relationship. As a former Defence and then Finance and Economics Minister these were, of course, his own personal specialities. Yet it would be superficial to suggest that he considered them to be crucial because they were his own specialities. It was rather that he had made them his specialities because he considered them to be crucial.

As we have noted already, the hope of modernising the Soviet economy through imports of technology, joint projects and expanded trade had been a major Soviet motive for détente with the West in general, and West Germany in particular. It was, in fact, a key element in that Westpolitik of Brezhnev without which the Ostpolitik of Brandt could never have succeeded. In one of the lighter symbolic moments of Brezhnev's first visit to Bonn, in 1973, the Soviet leader jumped into a gleaming new Mercedes sports car presented to him by the Chancellor and roared off down the road, to the consternation of his security guards. He spoke to his German partners in glowing terms of the prospects for great co-operative ventures and joint exploitation of the Soviet Union's natural resources.

Schmidt took up this ball and ran with it. Already, in a conversation with Gromyko in September 1974, he observed that two motives were especially important for the German side: 'the political motive of stabilisation in Europe and the economic motive of expanding economic co-operation with the Soviet Union'. To describe the latter as an 'economic motive' was a diplomatic simplification. Certainly, the Federal Republic had some economic motives. Its expanding economy had growing energy requirements and, especially following the sharp increases in the price of oil from the Middle East, it seemed attractive to supply more of these from Soviet sources. There was a clear complementarity between a Soviet Union rich in raw materials but poor in quality manufactured goods, and a Federal Republic poor in the former but rich in the latter. The Soviet Union was a genuinely important market for a few particular sectors of German industry. In the 1976 election, the government claimed that trade with the East overall secured some 300,000 jobs, although that number was cut in three by more sober analysis.

Yet private papers and even public statements make it clear that Schmidt's primary motive for expanding economic ties was political. He saw, as he writes in his memoirs, that this Soviet economic interest could be used for advancing German national interests. A memorandum in preparation for a 1977 brainstorming session with leading bankers and industrialists dealing with the East observed that the political aim was 'the long-term securing of détente-policy: increasing Soviet interest in good relations with the West'.

Accordingly, Schmidt was prepared to countenance the barter deals frowned upon by sober-minded industrialists, and the low interest rates deplored by sober-minded bankers. With Brezhnev he discussed grandiose projects such as a state-of-the-art nuclear power station in Kaliningrad (formerly Königsberg), and a huge steel mill at Kursk. Where the Germans and Russians of Schmidt and Brezhnev's generation had fought one of the greatest tank-battles of the Second World War, they would now work peacefully together turning crude Russian ore into shining German steel.

Schmidt himself produced the grandest idea of all: an economic co-opera-tion agreement to run for no less than twenty-five years. The Soviet Union, he told the industrialists and bankers assembled in the 'Chancellor bungalow' for that 1977 brainstorming session, must be convinced that Germany was a peaceful neighbour in the long-term. The point was to create trust 'into the third millennium'. So when Brezhnev came to Bonn in May 1978, he and Schmidt signed a very broadly framed agreement on economic and industrial co-operation with a term (*Laufzeit*) of twenty-five years — although its 'initial period of validity' (*Geltungsdauer*) was only ten years, after which it was to be 'continued' by mutual agreement for five years at a time. According to a government spokesman, the Chancellor saw this as a 'political act without parallel in the recent history of the world'. The businessmen were noticeably more reticent. Otto Wolff von Amerongen, the Nestor of West Germany's eastern trade, observed drily: 'It is not a historic accord.'

Nonetheless, the results of Schmidt's efforts in this area were signifi-cant. The total volume of German-Soviet trade in 1979 was six times that of 1969. At the beginning of the decade the Soviet Union accounted for thirty-two per cent of the Federal Republic's eastern trade; by the end of the decade it accounted for forty-five per cent. German policymakers never tired of pointing out that West German exports to the Soviet Union were still much less than those to Austria or Switzerland. Yet some important specialist firms and branches of German heavy industry were very dependent on this trade, while under the commitments entered into during the Schmidt period, Soviet natural gas was to provide nearly thirty per cent of West Germany's natural gas supplies (up to five per cent of its total energy imports) by the end of the 1980s. The Soviet Union was altogether much less dependent on foreign trade than West Germany. But West Germany had become by the end of the decade both quantitatively and qualitatively its most important Western trading partner.

There can be little doubt that these burgeoning economic ties, and the perspective of their grandiose expansion, contributed to the goodwill that is apparent in confidential personal letters from Brezhnev to Schmidt, and that the already seriously ill Soviet leader publicly displayed on his May 1978 visit to Bonn. Indeed, this summer of 1978 was arguably the foreign policy high-point of Schmidt's Chancellorship, with the G7 summit in Bonn following two months after the Soviet leader's visit. Yet even as he and Brezhnev publicly celebrated the achievements of détente, in a Joint Declaration liberally studded with the word, Schmidt knew that the overarching 'stability' of the permissive framework of détente was under serious threat.

Now the reasons for what would be called (prematurely) the 'end of détente' and (overdramatically) the 'second Cold War' were, of course, many and controversial. Indeed, at the time there was a sharp polarisation of opinion in the West, with some portraying Brezhnev's Soviet Union as pursuing Stalinist expansionism under the cloak of 'peaceful co-existence', while others placed the blame equally on both superpowers or mainly on the United States. Yet the new makers of Soviet foreign policy under Gorbachev would themselves subject the Brezhnevite version of détente to withering criticism. No doubt their criticism was in some points exaggerated, as that of political successors and historical revisionists tends to be. Nonetheless, when Soviet policymakers said that certain faults lay with Soviet policy, they surely knew what they were talking about.

First of all, and despite repeated American warnings, the Brezhnev leadership continued to treat détente as divisible. It actively extended its influence in the Third World, using the military and security forces of such close allies as Cuba and East Germany. In itself, this did not worry the Bonn government half so much as it worried the United States. For the Federal Republic was, as Schmidt told Gromyko, a power confined to Central Europe. Indeed, in one of his confidential private letters to Brezhnev, in February 1976, Schmidt had gone so far as to remark that 'in my view the quarrel of both world-powers over Angola is not so important that the confidence of other peoples in the durability of détente should be allowed to suffer from it'. But even if Bonn policymakers thought that American concerns were exaggerated, they had to be worried about the increasingly negative effect of those concerns on American-Soviet relations, and hence on their own Ostpolitik. This was the imperative of vertical synchronisation.

Secondly, the Brezhnev leadership continued its formidable arms build-up, and in particular brought on a new middle-range nuclear missile, known in the West as the SS-20. Whereas Schmidt saw the extension of Soviet power and influence in the Third World only as an indirect challenge, this he saw as a direct threat to vital German interests. There is a deep irony in the military-political story of the German-Soviet relationship in the Schmidt era. 'Altogether, the political part of détente must be complemented by a comprehensive military part', Schmidt told Brezhnev in 1978, and that had been a central tenet of his personal approach to East-West relations for nearly twenty years. As he told Gromyko in their private talks in 1974: 'he liked to think that he was one of the inventors of the principle that was today called MBFR. In 1959 he [had] published a carefully prepared book the central subject of which was mutual balanced arms limitations.' That book, *Defence or Retaliation*, was actually first published in 1961, but Schmidt could justly claim that this had been one of his leitmotifs since 1959, when he delivered a memorable speech to the Bundestag on the need for regional arms control in Central Europe. When Bahr wrote in his 1968 planning staff working paper on European security that 'no account [would be] given of the military aspects', Schmidt underlined the sentence and scribbled in the margin: 'Why?'

It was, therefore, precisely because he attached such importance to balanced arms reductions that Schmidt was so exercised by unbalanced arms increases. That the MBFR talks on conventional forces actually made so little progress, since Nato and the Warsaw Pact could not even agree how many arms and men each side had, was certainly no fault of his. On the other hand, when the superpowers did make slow progress towards a second treaty on strategic arms limitation, the SALT II treaty finally signed by Carter and Brezhnev in June 1979, the West German leader had serious concerns about the weapons it did not cover. In the 'grey area' between SALT and MBFR, containing what Schmidt liked to call 'Eurostrategic weapons', he believed both that German interests were directly affected and that German policy could have some effect.

By his own account, Schmidt first raised this problem on his visit to Moscow in October 1974. When the Soviet Union began to build up its arsenal of SS-20 missiles at considerable speed; Schmidt was increasingly alarmed by this development, as well as being infuriated by what he saw as the inconsistency of Jimmy Carter's leadership. In what was to become a famous speech at the International Institute of Strategic Studies in London in 1977 — and even more in conversation over dinner following the speech — he suggested, among many other points about the economic and political aspects of security, that the West would have to consider restoring the military balance in this area too. There followed what one of the guests at the dinner, the historian Michael Howard, would describe as a transatlantic comedy of errors, with American leaders thinking 'the Europeans' needed more American weapons to reassure them of the American commitment, while 'the Europeans' — and above all the West Germans — felt they should accept these weapons to reassure the Americans, although in fact aiming all the time at arms reductions to be negotiated with the Soviet Union.

In any case, as the culmination of this complex transatlantic conversation, the leaders of the United States, West Germany, France and Britain, meeting on the island of Guadeloupe in January 1979, agreed to produce a 'two-track' proposal according to which, if satisfactory reductions in this area could not be negotiated with the Soviet Union by a given date, Nato would deploy new, modernised American Pershing II and land-based Cruise missiles in Western Europe. This decision was then formalised in Nato's 'double-track' resolution of December 1979, with the date for deployment if negotiations failed set for 1983. In Schmidt's view this was still intended as a contribution to creating the vital military component of détente. It was to be a step towards a SALT III. In the event, however, the SS-20s and the double-track decision proved to be, at least in the short term — and the qualification is an important one — a major blow to what Schmidt had understood to be, and what, from the point of view of German Ostpolitik, was most important about, the thing called détente.

The next blow followed within weeks, although no direct causal connection between the two has credibly been established. This was the Soviet invasion of Afghanistan. Schmidt's reaction was cautious to a fault. With his close political ally and friend Valéry Giscard d'Estaing he issued a declaration which said that 'détente could not survive another blow' such as this. By implication, détente could survive this blow. Yet given the quite different reaction in the United States, and to some extent also in Britain, the whole permissive framework of global détente was actually shaken to its foundations. The Carter administration suspended the ratification process for the SALT II Treaty and imposed sanctions on the Soviet Union, including a boycott of the Moscow Olympics which it called on its allies to join. From this time forward, Schmidt and Genscher looked increasingly like jugglers whose balls were beginning to wobble. Now they travelled tirelessly between Washington and Moscow, attempting to persuade both sides to behave more 'reasonably': that is, to negotiate on arms control and not to allow their extra-European conflicts to interfere with the continuation of intra-European détente.

At the end of June 1980, Schmidt became the first Western head of government to visit Moscow after the Soviet invasion of Afghanistan, although Giscard d'Estaing had, independently — and without prior consultation with his allies in Bonn or anywhere else — gone to meet Brezhnev in Warsaw six weeks before. Schmidt's was a high-risk visit which brought Soviet agreement in principle to negotiate with the United States about intermediate nuclear forces. In his last hours in the Chancellery, in the autumn of 1982, he would look back to this as one of the high points of his Chancellorship. 'The dialogue on nuclear disarmament could continue,' noted his close associate Klaus Bölling. 'There [in Moscow in summer 1980] the first lieutenant of the Greater German Wehrmacht, who in 1941 had come close to Moscow, had undertaken a highly successful reconnaissance mission for the West.'

But then came the emergence of Solidarity in Poland in August 1980. The Polish revolution directly threatened both the horizontal and the vertical synchronisation of Ostpolitik. It made the GDR clamp down not only on any stirrings of dissent at home (it was doing that anyway) but also on the developing relationship between the Germans in East and West. Already in August, Schmidt felt obliged to cancel his planned visit to East Germany because of the strikes in Poland. Then, in October, the GDR increased that compulsory minimum exchange of hard currency which both Brandt and Schmidt had devoted so much diplomatic effort to reducing in the 1970s. The challenge of Solidarity, of the 'Polish disease' as they saw it, clearly frightened all the other East European communist leaderships. Above all, it brought heavy Soviet pressure and the real threat of an armed intervention, such as had ended the Prague Spring.

Even if some in Germany might have wanted to continue the détente with the Soviet Union — in the national interest — even after such an intervention, this could only have been done at the cost of untold damage to Germany's Western ties, both those with her West European neighbours and those with the United States. 'If the Russians invade, everything is *kaputt*' was the succinct analysis of a Schmidt confidant. The imperatives of horizontal and vertical synchronisation therefore demanded that Bonn should, first, do everything in its power to persuade the Soviet Union not to intervene directly; second, do everything it could to limit the damage done by the Polish crisis, both to its own relations with the Soviet Union and the rest of Eastern Europe, and to the permissive environment of regional and global détente; and, third, do what little it could to help towards a 'peaceful' solution in Poland. When General Jaruzelski declared a 'state of war' in Poland on 13 December 1981 — while Schmidt was actually making his long-delayed visit to East Germany, and urging Erich Honecker to use his influence in Moscow — the Bonn government was not entirely clear whether it had failed or succeeded.

The government in Washington, by contrast, had no such doubts: this was neither a peaceful nor an internal Polish solution; it was another August 1968; the thing called détente had failed. For this Washington government was that of Ronald Reagan, which came into office in January 1981 with a strong ideological commitment to stop what it saw as the expansion of the Soviet 'evil empire' by a decisive build-up of American military force. The crisis of the East therefore also became a crisis of the West, with the fiercest argument running between Bonn and Washington. This was the last straw. At the end of Schmidt's Chancellorship, in the autumn of 1982, it looked very much as if the diplomatic house that Brandt, Scheel and Bahr had built, the 'system' of West German Ostpolitik, was, if not in ruins, then at least seriously damaged.

In the gathering storm, the Bonn government tried desperately to keep the lines of communication open between the superpowers, and more generally between East and West. When Giscard d'Estaing went to Warsaw in 1980 to meet Brezhnev, François Mitterrand memorably described him as '*le petit télégraphiste de Varsovie*'. Though a scorching insult in the terms of the *grande nation*, Schmidt would probably have had no great problem with such a description. Indeed, in his talks in Moscow in the summer of 1980 he reportedly described himself as 'only a postman'.

He was not, he insists in retrospect, attempting to be a mediator or broker, just an interpreter in the elementary sense of helping the American and Soviet leaders to understand each other when 'the one was talking Eskimo, the other Japanese'. Where Bismarck had described his own and Germany's role as that of an 'honest broker' between the great powers to East and West, Schmidt modestly described his own and the Federal Republic's role as that of 'honest interpreters', but honest interpreters '*of Western policy*' [author's italics]. Yet to make the self-description exact one would have to add 'and of German interests'. Perhaps also: 'in Europe's name'.

At the same time, the German adoption of this role clearly had a special significance. No other Western state's vital interests were so directly involved. Other Western states, starting with the United States, had policies of 'bridge-building'. Only Germany might itself be the bridge — a traditional self-image of late nineteenth- and early twentieth-century German policy, revived by Chancellor Kiesinger in 1966, and on occasion used by Schmidt himself.

The pressures on, and temptations for, German policy in these last years of the Schmidt Chancellorship were very great. For beside this woeful external constellation, there were all the associated domestic pressures. All over Protestant north-west Europe the proposed deployment of new Nato missiles provoked a wave of fear and protest, but nowhere was the fear and the protest more extreme than in Germany. It reached deep into Schmidt's own party. Leading Social Democrats took part in a demonstration of more than a quarter of a million people in Bonn in October 1981 — a demonstration against the new American missiles.

The Soviet Union and East Germany tried both overtly and covertly to encourage these protests. The Social Democrat, Horst Ehmke, wryly remarked to a senior East German functionary in 1981 that the peace movement was growing apace 'with God's and your help'. Yet the more important causal connection went in the other direction. For these essentially indigenous protests encouraged the key foreign-policy decision-makers in Moscow — which now meant Gromyko, Ustinov, Andropov and Suslov as much as the terminally sick Brezhnev — to believe that if they played their cards right they might be able to prevent the new Nato deployment, and thus drive a deep wedge between the United States and West Germany.

At the Social Democrats' party conference in April 1982, the leadership could not be sure of getting a majority for the deployment of American missiles if negotiations failed. Instead, this decision was put off to a special conference in 1983. At the same time the Schmidt government was racked by deepening economic and financial difficulties, and by the increasing fragility of the coalition with the Free Democrats. The way in which all these internal and external concerns came together in the formulation of foreign policy positions is vividly illustrated by an internal Chancellery planning staff paper, leaked in the spring of 1982.

This paper proposed 'for substantive, electoral and coalition-political reasons' that the Chancellor should 'set new and controversial accents' in the discussion of foreign policy. The intended controversy was not with the East but with the West: to be precise, with the new right-wing governments of the United States and Great Britain. Public opinion polls, argued the paper, showed that the majority of the population — and particularly of Social and Free Democratic voters — was for a continuation of détente, for increased economic co-operation with the Soviet Union, and 'for a mediator-role of Europe/the Federal Republic between the United States and the Soviet Union, even if this could lead to dissonance with the United States'. (Note the conflation of 'Europe' and 'Federal Republic', even in an internal analysis.) A forcefully expressed claim for 'more autonomy for Europe/the Federal Republic . . . and thereby conflicts with the neo-conservative ideology and the Reagan-Thatcher administrations' would divert public attention from domestic problems and put the Free Democrats on the spot.

The paper went on to spell out elements of the proposed 'controversial' argument. For example: 'Large groups in the USA and GB are in the process of turning away from the common policy and the common values of the West. They endanger the social-political attractiveness of the West in competitition with the communists. They endanger détente (*Entspannungspolitik*).' So far as the Soviet Union was concerned, there had also to be a clear ideological argument: 'clear distance to Soviet bureaucratism; this is not what socialism looks like,' and furthermore: 'clear distance to overarmament; clear distance to imperialist elements in Soviet policy (Afghanistan)'. Yet at the same time there should be a continuation of the long-term policy of economic and political co-operation and 'careful handling of the Polish crisis with the protection of special German interests'. 'To count on the collapse of the Eastern bloc makes no sense for a number of reasons.' 'Altogether,' the paper went on, 'the impression of equidistance should be avoided; however the impression of a "third way" is important.' But a 'third way' for whom? For Germany? For Eastern Europe? For Central Europe? For Europe altogether?

Now clearly this was just one think-piece from one section of the Chancellery, and a deliberately provocative one at that. As in the case of Egon Bahr's planning staff paper on European security, one has to emphasise that planners are there to think the unthinkable. And all political leaders in democracies do mix party, domestic and foreign policy.

Nonetheless, the fact that such an option in public policy could seriously be contemplated at a high level in the Chancellery indicates both the pressures and temptations of the period and — as important for our theme — the possibilities for German policy which more than a decade of Ostpolitik had, or seemed to have, opened up.

Chancellor Schmidt, it must plainly be stated, did not adopt the proposed public posture. He would do all he could to contribute to an arms control agreement between the superpowers, although all that was strictly limited by his disagreements with the American leadership on the one side, and by the senility and miscalculated inflexibility of the Soviet leadership on the other. He would do everything in his power to preserve the developing relationship with the GDR against pressures from both East and West. He would accept and even encourage 'stabilisation' in the rest of Eastern Europe. He would not allow Germany's economic, political or cultural ties with the East to be cut, and certainly not from across the Atlantic. But if it came to the crunch, he would cleave to the West. To be more precise: he would hold to a particular idea of the West which, in the conditions of Yalta Europe, involved shared weapons as well as common values, Pershing missiles and Popperian open societies, Kant but also Cruise.

He told Brezhnev on the latter's last, painful visit to Bonn in November 1981: 'if an agreement cannot be reached, despite all efforts, then my country will certainly meet its obligations from the other half of the two-track decision, in the security interest of my country and of the Western alliance'. On this position he stood, and on this position he fell. Not just or even mainly for this reason, to be sure: there were other, more direct causes of his fall from power. Yet ironically, given the attitudes now prevalent in his own party and even, as we have seen, in his own Chancellery, to lose power was perhaps the best thing he could have done for the basic 'two-track' approach to German foreign policy which he had so long and so consistently represented. Although no one can ever prove 'what would have happened if' — in this case, what would have happened if a social-liberal coalition had remained in power in the autumn of 1982 — there are strong grounds for arguing that the larger continuity of German foreign policy was in fact only assured by the discontinuity in domestic politics. There is a real sense in which Schmidt won by losing.

A new book

When discussing the period of centre-right coalition government which began in the autumn of 1982 the temptations of retrospective determinism are particularly strong. Since this period culminated in a breakthrough in German-Soviet relations more significant even than that of 1970, it is tempting — above all for the politicians and policymakers involved — to read developments in German-Soviet relations and the overall system of German Ostpolitik as somehow leading logically and even inexorably towards that outcome.

We are, of course, bound to examine Western policy and East-West relations more generally for putative causes, or at least contributing causes, of the spectacular events of 1989–91, from the revolution in Eastern Europe through German unification to the end of the Soviet Union. At the same time, it is important to recapture the sense of what people did not know, to note the guesses that were proved wrong, the visions that turned out to be illusions, and to chart those paths of real policy that led either to nowhere or to somewhere quite different from the place the driver thought he was heading.

The search for both sides of this history — the unexpected that happened and the expected that did not — is hampered by the paucity of high-quality unpublished sources for such a recent period, although some very revealing individual items can already be found. It is made doubly difficult by the internal and the external complexity of the context in which German Ostpolitik was made.

The internal complexity of coalition politics and inter-agency rivalry had, of course, been there already under Schmidt and under Brandt. But it was arguably more important in the Kohl-Genscher years. This was a coalition not just of two but of three parties. Not only did the Free Democrats have elaborate coalition talks with the Christian Democrats. The Christian Democrats — that is, Helmut Kohl's Christian Democratic Union and Franz Josef Strauss's Christian Social Union — had first to agree among themselves. Even after their coalition agreements were written down, in considerable detail, Franz Josef Strauss continued to be a significant individual — often highly individual — actor in the field of Ostpolitik.

Meanwhile Hans-Dietrich Genscher, by now beginning to earn the sobriquet of 'veteran' Foreign Minister, had a much more distinctive position in the making of Ostpolitik under Chancellor Kohl than he had under Chancellor Schmidt. While Schmidt had taken the leading part in attempting to develop Germany's relations with the East, and above all with Moscow, Genscher had, partly for substantive, partly for party-political reasons, established himself as the high-priest and guardian of Germany's relations with the West, and above all with Washington. When Kohl set out to re-emphasise West Germany's vital relationship with the West, Genscher presented himself as the high-priest and guardian of Germany's relations with the East.

He did so with growing confidence through the 1980s, skilfully deploying his experience, connections and prestige as Foreign Minister, and the leverage power of his small party, so that German Ostpolitik in the late 1980s came to be known as 'Genscherism', not 'Kohlism'. This in turn was misleading, since it underrated both the strategic and the direct operative contribution of the Chancellor and his foreign policy advisers, notably Horst Teltschik. In short, the changing shape of German Ostpolitik in these years was the product of a complex internal interaction between, as it were, Kohlism and Genscherism, with a rich dash of Strausserie.

The external complexity was also, self-evidently, there in earlier years. We have seen already how the system of German Ostpolitik was always, to put it somewhat mechanistically, a sub-system of the larger system of East-West relations, with its regional and above all its superpower levels. What happened in the triangle Bonn-Moscow-Berlin always depended crucially on what was happening along the Soviet-American side of the larger triangle America-Germany-Soviet Union. And these were years of truly unprecedented movement in American-Soviet relations, from the depths of what was described in the early 1980s as a 'new Cold War', with Ronald Reagan's 'evil empire' speech, his Strategic Defence Initiative and the bitter polemics around the Soviet shooting down of a Korean airliner, to the heights of summitry in the second half of the decade. From the Geneva summit in 1985 to that in Washington (and Camp David) in 1990, the United States and the Soviet Union finally went beyond even the most optimistic versions of détente to a mutual celebration of the end of the Cold War. At the same time, these changes in East-West relations were to a large extent driven by internal developments inside the Soviet Union and in Eastern Europe, which have their own separate and intricate history. It is impossible to explain the evolution of German-Soviet relations without frequent reference to this larger context.

At the outset, while affirming the continuity of German foreign policy — from Genscher to Genscher — the Kohl government made three clear, strong, central commitments. First, it reaffirmed the central importance of the relationship with the United States, and the Federal Republic's full commitment to Nato's double-track resolution, including, if need be, the deployment of Cruise and Pershing II missiles on German soil. 'The Alliance,' said Kohl in his government declaration of October 1982, 'is the core of German *raison d'état*.' The Bundestag protocols record restlessness and heckling from Social Democrats. Second, it reaffirmed West Germany's commitment to move towards what it called 'European Union' inside the existing (that is, West) European Community.

Finally, it roundly reasserted the Federal Republic's commitment to the goal of German unity. This meant, in the words of the Spring 1983 coalition agreement between the Christian Social and Christian Democratic Union, 'not only to keep the German question theoretically open, but also to be actively engaged for the German right to unity in freedom'. What such an active engagement would look like in practice was another question, but the emphatic reassertion of the goal was itself a political act.

These three basic positions could be described, with some oversimplification, as the short, the medium and the long-term foreign policy priorities of the Kohl government. All three reflected long-held convictions of Helmut Kohl. All three would displease Moscow. There is a certain irony — but also a certain logic — in the fact that the Chancellor under whom Germany's breakthrough with the East was achieved was the one who had the least experience of, and personal relationship to, the East. Helmut Kohl, the Catholic from the Rhineland-Palatinate, too young to have fought on the Eastern front (as Schmidt, Weizsäcker and Strauss had done), inspired as a young man by the lifting of frontier barriers between France and Germany, deeply and simply committed to an increasingly united, federal (that is, German-style federal) Europe built around the Franco-German axis, was an archetypal 'Westerner' in West German politics.

Yet of course this did not mean he was blind to the importance of the Soviet Union for German foreign policy. The politician from Germany's western borders had first visited Moscow as a still inexperienced party leader in September 1975, armed with some cautionary notes from a colleague who was at once protégé and mentor, Richard von Weizsäcker. The record of his meeting with Alexei Kosygin reveals a slightly chaotic conversation, in which Kohl emphasised that, being Konrad Adenauer's 'great-grandson in office', he had learned from the old man that after the Nazi period 'the most important thing is that after this period the Germans win back trust'. In this connection he stressed that the Christian Democrats would adhere to the treaties signed, including the Helsinki Final Act, which they had just voted against. As Weizsäcker sophistically suggested in his notes: 'We wouldn't dream of regarding the Final Act as questionable and dubious just because we criticised its negotiation and signature'!

Earlier in the conversation, recalling that Kosygin had enquired after Strauss at the very beginning of their talk, Kohl observed 'he [Strauss] had with good reason said, and I am wholly of his opinion, "*Pacta sunt servanda*" . . .' To which Kosygin rather surprisingly replied: 'I didn't specially put it first. My concern is not Herr Strauss. But I looked at you and thought that you look in very good health. That reminded me of Strauss. You have a similar figure.' Kohl replied that he was 'fully in agreement with this interpretation'. Thus, almost in burlesque, began Helmut Kohl's dealings with the Kremlin. (Yet in a curious way, Kosygin had surely identified one of Helmut Kohl's real political strengths: his sheer physical bulk and stamina.) It is however worth noting that in this first conversation with a Soviet leader, as in many subsequent ones, Kohl spoke clearly and with personal conviction about 'the wish of the German people once again to be united', albeit 'in [a] historical perspective, which may last generations'.

We cannot trace here all the stages in the evolution of his own and his party's understanding of Ostpolitik over the eight years until he became Chancellor. But the general direction was plain: towards acceptance of the basic lines of social-liberal Ostpolitik, but only on the foundations of unqualified adherence to the West (in values and in security policy), full commitment to European Union, and the long-term goal of German unity. Horst Teltschik, already Kohl's key foreign policy adviser, was a specialist on Soviet foreign policy and East-West relations, who had studied and taught in Berlin under Richard Löwenthal, the outstanding Social Democratic authority on international relations. With more detailed knowledge and analytical refinement than Kohl, Teltschik both understood, accepted and wished to develop the overall system of Ostpolitik they inherited from Brandt and Schmidt, with the central triangle (Bonn-Moscow-Berlin) inside a larger triangle (America-Germany-Soviet Union), the priority for relations with Moscow, and the imperative of synchronisation.

While Genscher and Strauss might squabble, the Free Democrats' own record of the coalition talks on foreign policy in March 1983 record none other than Strauss declaring that 'the object in East-West relations was a realistic détente policy' (thus using Gencher's own phrase from 1975). In his own unconventional way, Strauss was to be almost as active as Genscher in advancing Bonn's double-track strategy over the next four years. The idea of an overall double-track Western strategy towards the East, resolute in deterrence but also in détente, was of course embodied already in Nato's Harmel report, to which Chancellor Kohl referred as reverently as his predecessor had done. The specific version of the double-track strategy in Nato's December 1979 resolution was: negotiation about reducing intermediate-range nuclear forces, but also readiness to deploy them by a stated date if no agreement could be reached. Now, as it became apparent that the Soviet-American negotiations would not succeed before the deadline for deployment, the Bonn government pursued its own particular double-track.

On the one hand, despite massive and emotional domestic opposition, and the heaviest intimidation from Moscow, it steeled itself to go ahead with deployment of the new American missiles on German soil, starting in the autumn of 1983. On the other hand, like the Schmidt government before it, it did everything in its power to continue the détente track with the Soviet Union, Eastern Europe and, above all, East Germany, in political, social, cultural and — its strongest card — economic relations. Thus, for example, it paid the most solicitous attention to the development of German-Soviet economic ties, despite heavy pressure from the Reagan administration to curb them. Meanwhile, in the most spectacular single move, Strauss negotiated the first government-guaranteed billion DM credit for East Germany in the summer of 1983, at a stroke restoring the GDR's international creditworthiness.

In July 1983, while Strauss prepared for meetings with Honecker and Jaruzelski on a 'private' East European tour, Kohl and Genscher visited Moscow. The confidential note on these talks sent from the Soviet to the East German Party leaderships plainly records how the Soviet side, now led by the dying Andropov instead of the dying Brezhnev, threatened the West Germans with negative consequences for their relationship with East Germany: 'The Germans in the FRG and the GDR would have to look at each other through a thick fence of missiles.' The note records how the Bonn duo stuck to the American position, although the Soviet side claimed to detect a lack of deep conviction. At the same time, 'Kohl and Genscher assured us in every register of the loyalty of the FRG government to a policy of peace, of détente and of stability'.

While the Chancellor once again presented what the Soviet note called 'the FRG's well-known revanchist concept of the "unity of the German nation" ', he also emphasised the need for practical co-operation between the two German states, notably in increasing contacts "between people on both sides of the frontier" (quotation marks in the original). Further: 'noteworthy is the Chancellor's statement that the FRG's decision to give a bn. Mark credit to the GDR was to some extent a signal "to our compatriots, that we don't want to have any missileatomicweapon(sic)-fence between us".'

The conclusion of this Soviet interpretative missive was revealing: 'Although the present government, as the visit showed once again, takes a more strongly pro-American position than the Schmidt cabinet, the possibilities of continuing to work with it, in order to pin it down to the basic principles of the treaties signed in the 1970s, continue to exist. We believe it is important to continue actively to work on Bonn on the question of the intermediate-range missiles and to make clear how the "*Nachrüstung*" of Nato can affect the interests of the FRG itself, including also its bilateral relations to individual socialist countries.' A veiled threat to the GDR! Thus a report on the Bonn-Moscow line of the Ostpolitik triangle, sent down the Moscow-East Berlin line, ends with a clear hint for action on the East Berlin-Bonn line.

Yet at the same time, Kohl, like Schmidt before him, was also trying to work the triangle the other way. Bonn tried to encourage and give incentives to Honecker both to influence Moscow (insofar as that was at all possible) to be more conciliatory in relations with the West, and (more realistically) to maintain good relations with West Germany, despite heavy breathing down the line from Moscow. In the latter, much more than the former, it had some success. While the geriatric progression from the dying Brezhnev to the dying Andropov to the dying Chernenko produced a mixture of stubbornness and irresolution in Soviet policy, the increasingly self-confident East German leader risked a cautious public dissonance with Moscow.

Following the Bundestag's vote in November 1983 to deploy the Cruise and Pershing II missiles, Honecker, instead of freezing relations with West Germany, immediately proclaimed the need to 'limit the damage' done by this deplorable decision, and to pursue a 'coalition of reason' with the West. While Soviet negotiators walked out of the Geneva arms control talks and Soviet propaganda stormed, the GDR (joined in this by Hungary) continued to urge the need for dialogue and practical (above all, economic!) co-operation with the West. Honecker also resolved to take up the invitation to visit West Germany, extended by Schmidt in 1981 and explicitly renewed by Helmut Kohl. As Honecker himself recalled in a retrospective conversation with the author, he was particularly encouraged in this by his first personal meeting with Kohl, in a guesthouse in Moscow's Lenin Hills on the occasion of Andropov's funeral. Only after a stormy meeting with the Soviet leadership in the Kremlin in August 1984 did he decide to call off the planned visit, although continuing in practice to develop the relationship with the Federal Republic. (This remarkable episode, and its significance for German-German relations, are considered in more detail in Chapter Four.)

After the cancellation of Honecker's visit, Willy Brandt read Helmut Kohl a public lesson, in the Bundestag, about the laws of Ostpolitik geometry. You could not, he said, expect to improve relations with the GDR without simultaneously improving relations with the Soviet Union, nor while playing one East European state against the other. Ostpolitik could not merely be a series of bilateral relations but had to be based on an overall concept of a systematic, synchronised approach to West-East relations: a *Gesamtkonzept*. Rejecting the criticism, Kohl nonetheless took Brandt's point. 'The Soviet Union is our most important and most powerful neighbour in Central and Eastern Europe,' he observed, using the word neighbour in an imprecise yet revealing way. 'We know very well that all conceivable bilateral possibilities, whether in talks with the GDR, whether with Poland, Hungary, with Romania or with whoever, can ultimately only be successful if they are bound in to the overall conversation (*Gesamtgespräch*) with the Soviet Union.' Horst Teltschik, playing Bahr to Kohl's Brandt, would spell the lesson out even more clearly: Moscow First.

Yet, as Ronald Reagan remarked, it took two to tango. The dying Konstantin Chernenko, and the obdurate Gromykos and Ustinovs, were plainly not ready for the dance. Kohl, Genscher, Strauss and Weizsäcker, were all eager to start, if not perhaps a vulgar American tango, then certainly an old European waltz. All that was needed were the partners in Moscow. Now with hindsight it is apparent that the new Soviet Party leader who emerged in March 1985, Mikhail Gorbachev, and the colleague he appointed as Foreign Minister in July of that year, Eduard Shevardnadze, were those partners. But hindsight can mislead, and actually the waltz was very slow to begin. For this there were general and specific reasons.

The general reason was that Soviet foreign policy in Gorbachev's first years was concentrated on the relationship with the United States and issues of arms and disarmament. From Geneva in November 1985, through the extraordinary Reykjavik summit/non-summit of October 1986, down to the signature of the treaty agreeing not only to reduce but to destroy intermediate-range nuclear forces, at the Washington summit in December 1987, the superpower relationship and hard security issues headed the new Soviet leaders' agenda. For all Gorbachev's visionary talk of the 'common European home', for all the genuine identification with Europe among many who were close to him, Europe remained a subsidiary theatre.

Within that theatre, moreover, Moscow initially concentrated on improving relations with France, Britain and Italy, rather than with West Germany. This was the price that the Kohl government paid for its combination of demonstrative loyalty to the West, above all in the Nato deployment, and forceful reassertion of the German claim to unity, including easily misunderstood statements about the continued legal existence of the German Reich in the frontiers of 1937. Such statements were grist to the Soviet propaganda mill. In the run-up to the fortieth anniversary of the end of the Second World War, the Soviet Union whipped up a gale of propaganda against the alleged threat of German 'revanchism', with a line being drawn from Hitler's *Wehrmacht* to Helmut Kohl. This was clearly meant to win domestic support in both the Soviet Union and Eastern Europe, and to bring back into line those wilful East European regimes which were trying to save their own ties with Western Europe, and above all with West Germany. Even if this propaganda campaign did not reflect the real convictions of the younger generation of Soviet leaders, it was, for reasons of domestic as well as foreign policy, difficult to change overnight.

German-Soviet economic relations continued despite the rhetorical storm raging overhead, and within weeks of becoming Party leader, Gorbachev summoned F Wilhelm Christians of the Deutsche Bank for a long conversation. Two months later he received Willy Brandt. Altogether, the Soviet leadership continued to cherish and nourish its ties to the German Social Democrats. Gorbachev twice met the Social Democrats' candidate for Chancellor, Johannes Rau, before the January 1987 federal elections. For the Bonn government this was a distinctly ambiguous development. On the one hand, in such difficult times it was helpful to have any high-level German-Soviet contacts. On the other hand, the Social Democrats could score domestic political points by being seen as the people with whom Moscow would talk. There are some indications that Moscow did drag its feet in relations with the centre-right government in the hope of having more congenial partners — say a Rau-Genscher government — in Bonn after the elections. Arguably, it was only after the Kohl-Genscher government was clearly confirmed in office for another four years that Moscow sat down to deal with it in earnest.

If so, this was not for want of trying by the Bonn government. For example, in a ten-page letter to Gorbachev dated 30 January 1986, opening with the slightly unusual greeting 'Highly esteemed (*Hochverehrter*) Mr General Secretary', Kohl started by welcoming the Geneva summit and the progress of talks on reducing intermediate-range nuclear forces. 'In the course and results of the Geneva meeting,' he wrote, 'the Federal Government sees confirmation of the rightness of its own policy. For years it has urged a continuation and intensification of the dialogue between the United States and the Soviet Union at the highest level. It has deliberately worked in this direction in the framework of the North Atlantic Alliance and with the Government of the United States of America.' It is, in fact, questionable what the real impact of West German representations in Washington had been, but in claiming credit in Moscow for services as what Schmidt had called the 'honest interpreter', Kohl stood in the clear continuity of Ostpolitik.

After going on to interpret SDI as a response to existing Soviet defence systems, and making a clear connection between security and human rights, Kohl carefully pressed the special German interests. Picking up Gorbachev's image of the common European home, he wrote: 'I am convinced that life in a common European home with fewer tensions will only be possible when relations between the two German states, too, are constantly stimulated as a stabilising element in the context of the overall process of development between West and East.' A very cautious formulation, showing clearly that he respected the imperative of synchronisation. After pointing to the prospects for improved economic relations he returned to special German interests in connection with the forthcoming Helsinki follow-up meeting in Bern. 'Important subjects there must be particularly the humanitarian aspects of relations between the two German states and the quantitative reduction in the field of family reunification and the possibilities for Soviet citizens of German nationality to emigrate.'

After referring back to an earlier letter, in which he had proposed a Helsinki follow-up conference on economic co-operation — the German carrot again! — he concluded: 'The Federal Republic of Germany wishes, and this goes for all political forces, a deepening and widening of relations with the Soviet Union. If the Soviet side shares this wish, nothing should prevent us from going down the path of a more intensive political dialogue and the consolidation of co-operation.'

Six months later, in July 1986, Genscher was able to visit Moscow. He recalls that Gorbachev began by giving him a long lecture about the wrongness of West Germany's Nato deployment. But then, putting that argument aside, Gorbachev spoke for even longer about his vision of the common European home and the possibilities for East-West, and specifically German-Soviet co-operation. At the end, they agreed that the two states should 'open a new page' in their relations.

This page was, however, then almost torn by an extraordinary gaffe. In an interview with journalists from *Newsweek*, before a visit to the United States, Helmut Kohl compared Gorbachev's public relations skills to those of Joseph Goebbels. Instead of deleting this passage from the version sent for authorisation, the Government spokesman merely edited it so the published version read: 'He [Gorbachev] is a modern communist leader who understands public relations. Goebbels, one of those responsible for the crimes of the Hitler era, was an expert in public relations, too.' This comparison so infuriated the Soviet leadership that the Politburo actually decided to freeze all political contacts with the Federal Republic for a time. The January 1987 federal election results showed that if they wanted to deal with West Germany they would have to deal with Kohl, but for at least a year the leading role in developing relations with the Soviet Union was played by others.

The first of these was Hans-Dietrich Genscher. Having come through the January 1987 election with an improved vote for his party, and successfully fended off a challenge to his position as Foreign Minister from Franz Josef Strauss, almost the first thing Genscher did was to deliver a widely reported speech to the annual meeting of the World Economic Forum at Davos. Warning against the danger of being lamed by 'worst case analysis' — such as could still often be heard in Washington, Paris and London — he concluded with a ringing appeal for the West to 'take Gorbachev seriously, take him at his word!' The two key areas in which the West should 'take Gorbachev at his word' were, of course, disarmament and economic co-operation.

Following the Davos speech, Genscher played a part which was sometimes described as that of 'pacemaker' between East and West. This vanguard role, actually one of relatively few exposed positions that Genscher took in his political career, earned him much criticism, and the initially sceptical tag of 'Genscherism'. Yet his optimistic working hypothesis, inspired by his first long conversation with Gorbachev, was, in the event, triumphantly vindicated.

Secondly, Richard von Weizsäcker, once Kohl's protégé in domestic politics and mentor in foreign policy, now as much a rival as anything else, stepped into the breach. Even before he actually became President, Weizsäcker had emphatically informed two members of the East German Politburo, in a meeting in the summer of 1984, that he wished to visit Moscow. 'However,' as one of his hosts recorded him saying, 'he would need to know whether he was welcome there.' In the summer of 1987 he finally was welcome there — although preceded two months earlier by another German visitor, a young man called Matthias Rust, who piloted his Cessna airplane undetected through Soviet air defences to land on Red Square, thus giving Gorbachev a marvellous pretext to purge and establish full control over his military. Weizsäcker's more conventional visit in July 1987 was important less for his encounters with his formal counterpart and host, President Andrei Gromyko, than for his meeting with Gorbachev.

Greeting Weizsäcker, and Genscher who accompanied him, Gorbachev recalled his agreement with Genscher a year before to 'open a new page' in German-Soviet relations: 'for the time being, however, it had remained unwritten, and for a time there was even a danger that it would be closed. Fortunately this had not happened'. As in his conversations with Brandt, Gorbachev stressed that he had always distinguished between the German people and the Nazi regime. He then spoke at length about the 'realistic' possibilities for an all-round improvement of relations between the two states. At one point in the conversation, Richard von Weizsäcker raised — 'almost just for the record', as he later explained to the author — the question of German unity. He elicited an unexpected response that was rapidly to become famous. The political reality, said Gorbachev, was the existence of two German states with different social orders. Both had learned lessons from history and each could make its own contribution to Europe and the world. And — in the wording of the published Soviet report — history would decide what would happen in a hundred years . . .

Weizsäcker recalls at this point interjecting 'or perhaps fifty?', and receiving an indication of assent from Gorbachev, thus, as Weizsäcker wryly observes, negotiating a fifty per cent cut. But the significant point was less the time period than the fact that Gorbachev did not say 'never'. This requires a little exploration. Whatever the innermost thoughts of the Brezhnev generation of Soviet leaders, whatever the earlier experiments in Soviet policy which they had witnessed or participated in, their public position from the mid-1960s to the mid-1980s had been unequivocal. The division of Germany and Europe into two groups of states with different 'social systems' was permanent. Yalta was for ever. As in the old Soviet bloc joke, the past might be unpredictable but the future was certain. So the mere public acknowledgment that the future was open, that 'history', 'time' or 'life itself', to use three of Gorbachev's favourite philosophical terms, might have other plans than those scientifically discovered by the Communist Party of the Soviet Union, was a significant departure.

But was there not more to it than that? In his memoirs, Eduard Shevardnadze recalls being asked by Genscher — after Germany was united — when he had first come to view German unification as inevitable, and records his own very surprising answer: 'Already in 1986.' In discussion with a leading Soviet expert on Germany, he had then expressed the view that this issue would soon come centre stage in Europe. Asked about this by the author in 1992, Shevardnadze not only repeated his version, with circumstantial detail, but averred that by 1987 both he and Gorbachev had come to the conclusion that German unification was inevitable. Of course the time-scale was unknown but, said Shevardnadze, Gorbachev's formula of 'a hundred years' was a tranquilliser for domestic public opinion, which was not ready for the radicalism of the top leaders' private thinking.

Talking in 1992, Anatoly Chernyaev, one of Gorbachev's closest aides, also averred that 'in his heart' Gorbachev was already convinced at the time of the Weizsäcker visit that 'without a resolution of the German question and without the establishment of historically conditioned normal relations between the two great peoples, no recovery would occur in Europe or the world'. In a separate conversation, another very senior figure close to Gorbachev, Alexander Yakovlev, made the even more surprising statement that Gorbachev probably reckoned with German unification from the very outset, from 1985. But the exigencies of politics did not allow Gorbachev to say what he thought.

These retrospective claims are remarkable. They cannot simply be ignored. There are certainly more to come. But one has with them the same problem as with the West German Ostpolitiker's retrospective claims of deep foresight. In the absence of precise documentary corroboration from records made at the time (which may yet be forthcoming) these tantalising statements are simply what policymakers say now that they thought then.

It is, however, fairly well established that Vyacheslav Dashitschev, a privileged maverick policy intellectual in the important institute headed by Oleg Bogomolov, made a presentation to an advisory council of the Foreign Ministry in November 1987, in which he argued that it was in the vital interest of the Soviet Union to go beyond the Cold War to a fully co-operative relationship with the West — and that the price for this might even eventually include the sacrifice of the separate East German state. Moreover, in obviously embittered recollections, Erich Honecker remembered the East German ambassador to the Soviet Union reporting serious discussions in Moscow about 'overcoming Germany's dual statehood' in 1987. In a television interview, Honecker further claimed that he had raised this issue with Gorbachev, and received firm contrary assurances.

And there's the rub. There is enough retrospective and circumstantial evidence to suggest that by 1987, in the context of a general questioning and rethinking of all the basic positions of Soviet foreign policy, even the question of eventually overcoming the division of Germany into two states was privately discussed at a high and even at the highest level in Moscow. But there is no evidence whatsoever that this was translated into operative policy. Quite the contrary. Dashitschev himself says that his speculative proposals were roundly repudiated by virtually the whole foreign policy apparatus of the Soviet party-state. On a day-to-day basis that apparatus continued to make Soviet foreign policy. When detailed German-Soviet negotiations began in earnest in 1988, the West German negotiators found themselves, like their predecessors in the 1970s, spending weeks and months wrangling over the inclusion of West Berlin in German-Soviet agreements.

As for the Moscow-East Berlin side of the triangle, political relations might be sour, but comprehensive assurances of fraternal solidarity were still repeatedly given. Thus the East German record of a top-level consultation in July 1987 between Hermann Axen, Honecker's Central Committee Secretary for international relations, and the new heads of the Soviet Central Committee departments for international relations and relations with Socialist countries, Anatoly Dobrynin and Vadim Medvedev, has Dobrynin glossing the Weizsäcker-Gorbachev conversation thus: 'Weizsäcker raised the question of the German nation. Comrade M Gorbachev reacted as is known. The USSR would allow no speculation about the "German nation". The defence of the interests of the GDR was a cornerstone of Soviet policy.'

Dobrynin also emphasised that the Soviet Union would continue to look critically at Kohl and the Christian Democrats. 'The policy of the USSR towards Kohl would depend on what policy he pursued towards the Soviet Union. This was the Politburo's opinion.' Kohl therefore still had his work cut out. Not only did the Soviet Union turn to West Germany last among the major powers of Western Europe. Among West German leaders, Gorbachev turned last of all to Kohl.

At the end of December 1987 he received Franz Josef Strauss in Moscow. Strauss, who — like Matthias Rust — had piloted himself to Moscow, and landed perilously in a storm, was euphoric. He came away, he said, 'with the most agreeable feelings', having concluded that East and West might be standing 'on the eve of a new age'. Strauss's visit was actually quite useful for Kohl, securing his right (or southern) flank at home, but it left the Chancellor as almost the only top West German politician who had not had a summit meeing with Gorbachev.

While the evidence is fragmentary, it appears that it was only after the Washington summit and the signature of the INF Treaty in December 1987 that Gorbachev and Shevardnadze turned their full attention to what was clearly their most important potential partner in Western Europe. In January 1988 Shevardnadze visited Bonn, the first time he had done so, and the first visit of a Soviet Foreign Minister for five years. He warmly congratulated the Bonn government on its contribution to the INF treaty. Apart from the 'honest interpreting' and 'pacemaking', this contribution consisted concretely in the Chancellor's decision to sacrifice West Germany's own little stock of 72 Pershing 1A missiles, very much against the better judgement of some of the Christian Democrats' leading defence experts.

Shevardnadze went on to plead for a 'third zero' in arms reductions —

that is, for the removal from Central Europe of those short-range nuclear missiles which, in practice, could only be fired from West Central Europe to hit East Central Europe or vice versa. At the same time, he signed a protocol on bilateral consultation, such as Britain and France had long had with the Soviet Union, and an extension of the 1978 Schmidt-Brezhnev economic co-operation agreement for a further five years.

In February, the Christian Democrat premier of Baden-Württemberg, Lothar Späth, visited Moscow and was received by Gorbachev. The Soviet information note sent to the party leadership in East Berlin records that Späth was told 'that the Soviet Union wishes to bring about a decisive turn for the better in relations with the FRG'. However, it was still concerned that the Federal Republic was dragging its feet. According to the Soviet note (clearly not a wholly reliable record) Späth attempted to explain this by referring to the West Germans' problems with their 'national identity and national consciousness'; to the fact that West Germany belonged to Nato, 'a bloc in which a state which lies on the other side of the Atlantic Ocean takes the leading position'; and to Bonn's fears of arousing the suspicions of its Western partners. But Chancellor Kohl was personally determined to open a new page in relations with Moscow, and 'for many important reasons,' Späth continued, 'the West Germans could not live calmly without good relations with the Soviet Union'.

'At Kohl's request,' the Soviet note reports, 'Späth addressed the question of a meeting between the Chancellor and the General Secretary of the CC of the CPSU . . . In this connection he observed that the Chancellor would react very sensitively if Mikhail Gorbachev, who had already been in France and Great Britain, would leave the FRG to one side. It was agreed that Helmut Kohl would visit the Soviet Union this year. A visit by Mikhail Gorbachev to the FRG would take place next year [i.e. 1989].' This laconic statement concealed the fact that in protocol terms Gorbachev should first have visited Bonn, since Kohl had come to Moscow in 1983 (as well as to the 'working funerals' of Andropov in 1984 and Chernenko in 1985). The Bonn government only agreed to this double visit on condition that it was treated as one whole. 'For our part,' the Soviet note continued, 'it was emphasised that the forthcoming encounter should have the political importance worthy of this level. It should be concluded by a weighty common document, which would clearly express the will of both sides to achieve a qualitative renewal of their relations as well as their responsibility for the future of their peoples and for the whole world.'

With that characteristically deep note, the long-sought, long-delayed, German-Russian waltz could begin in earnest. But while the negotiators got down to the painstaking preparatory work, there was one more move to be made on the West German home front. Nikolai Portugalov, an important messenger and interpreter of Soviet policy towards Germany in these years, had in late 1987 summed up Soviet concerns about the Christian Democrats in a striking phrase. 'The CDU,' he said, 'lacks its Ostpolitik Bad Godesberg.' As the Social Democrats had signalled their acceptance of the basic elements of the Adenauerian integration in the West in their Bad Godesberg programme of 1959, so now the Christian Democrats should signal their acceptance of the basic elements of Brandtian Ostpolitik, in a programmatic statement. And this was exactly what the Christian Democrats did. As we have noted already, at their Wiesbaden party conference in June 1988, the Christian Democratic Union agreed a programmatic foreign policy statement which went farther than the party had ever gone before to codify its practical acceptance of the main lines of Ostpolitik.

Thus it was by no means only the Soviet side that moved in the six years between Kohl's accession in Bonn and his October 1988 visit to Moscow. The centre-right government had began by defiantly restating the Federal Republic's attachment to the West, with Nato missiles and common values, to West European integration, and to the long-term goal of German unity. But while sticking to these three fundamentals, it had come a very long way to meet Soviet concerns and to woo the new Soviet leaders with all the charms at its disposal. As we shall see, the Social Democrats were by now prepared to go several steps further (see Chapter Six). But it is probably true to say that by 1988 leading Christian Democrats had come close to the positions taken up by leading Social Democrats twenty years before. With all their firmly restated Western, European and national principles, Kohl and Teltschik, like Brandt and Bahr two decades before, found themselves accepting the status quo — in order to overcome it.

It was on this basis, then, that Kohl at last visited Moscow. The Chancellor was accompanied by a huge party of ministers, officials, businessmen and bankers. The latter, led as usual by the Deutsche Bank, arranged a credit of DM 3 billion, earmarked for the purchase of machinery for Soviet light industry. Six inter-governmental agreements were signed, covering such subjects as nuclear safety, co-operation in environmental protection, food production and the first formal programme of cultural exchanges between the two states. 'Now,' said Gorbachev, 'we have very many German friends,' referring to the GDR as well as West Germany. Kohl had some ten hours of talks with the Soviet leader. The atmosphere was somewhat frigid at first, but Gorbachev later said that the ice had been broken. In fact, according to Anatoly Chernyaev, Teltschik's counterpart as notetaker at these talks, there were already the beginnings of a strong personal rapport. At the concluding press conference, Kohl ventured to suggest that this was not merely a new page but the beginning of a 'new chapter' in German-Soviet relations.

This important visit was as nothing, however, compared with the Soviet leader's visit to West Germany in June 1989. 'Gorbymania' was not peculiar to Germany. Great popular enthusiasm was manifested on the streets of Washington, London and Paris. But even by those standards, the reception given to Gorbachev by the crowds, the media, the politicians and the business community in West Germany was extraordinary.

One former government spokesman described it, crudely but not innacurately, as a 'Gorbasm'. The tabloid daily *Bild* ran a cover photo of a schoolgirl being embraced by the Soviet leader with the headline: 'A kiss for Annette, a kiss for Germany'. The alternative daily *taz* wryly described Gorbachev as 'the object of desire'. German commentators compared his visit to that of John F Kennedy. High-level Soviet commentators, working the German media with great smoothness, compared it to the historic reconciliation between France and Germany under Adenauer and de Gaulle. West German policymakers reasonably asked to be judged by their own words and deeds, not those of schoolgirls and tabloids. Yet this emotional charge, amounting almost to euphoria, reached to the very top, and should not be underrated.

'After a good sowing in the autumn,' said Chancellor Kohl, 'we can now bring in the harvest.' And what a harvest it was. This time there were no less than eleven agreements, ranging from such major economic items as investment protection and management training, through school and youth training to an agreement on the establishment of a 'hot line' between Bonn and Moscow. A government spokesman pointed to similar connections with Washington and East Berlin.

'We are drawing the line under the post-war period' said Gorbachev in his formal response to Chancellor Kohl. Referring to the Joint Declaration that they were to sign, he observed: 'This must be the first document of such a character and such dimensions in which two great European states belonging to different systems and alliances make an attempt to reflect philosophically upon the meaning of the moment presently being experienced by the world community, and together to lay down the goals of their policy.'

This remarkable document, informally known as the Bonn Declaration, started with the grandiose statement that the two states 'agree that humanity stands before new challenges on the eve of the third millennium', and proceeded to spell out the common principles on which the two states would respond to those challenges. 'The Federal Republic and the Soviet Union,' it said, 'consider it a paramount objective of their policy to continue Europe's historical traditions and thus to contribute to overcoming the division of Europe. They are determined to work together on concepts of achieving this goal through the building of a Europe of peace and co-operation — of a European order of peace or of a common European home — in which the USA and Canada also have a place.'

It then listed a number of 'building bricks' for this Europe of peace and co-operation, including further steps of disarmament, intensified dialogue at all levels, economic, technological and ecological 'co-operation', and exchanges of all possible kinds. In a section devoted specifically to security policy, the declaration said, amongst other things: 'The Federal Republic of Germany and the Soviet Union advocate

– a fifty per cent reduction of the strategic nuclear offensive weapons of the USA and the Soviet Union

– agreed American-Soviet solutions at the nuclear and space talks; this also applies to observance of the ABM Treaty . . .'

The Bonn Declaration thus explicitly equated the overarching long-term goal of Ostpolitik, a 'European order of peace', with Gorbachev's vision of a 'common European home'. It spoke of West Germany and the Soviet Union, each in its alliance, having a common policy ('their policy') for working towards this goal or vision, albeit one in which the United States would 'also' have a place. It went on to list vital steps of disarmament which the Soviet Union and the Federal Republic agreed the Soviet Union should take with the United States.

It therefore ascribed an extraordinary place to the Federal Republic in European and world affairs. 'The Federal Republic of Germany,' it said, 'and the Soviet Union realise, in view of Europe's history and its position in the world as well as the weight that each side has in its alliance, that a positive development of their relationship has central importance for the situation in Europe and East-West relations as a whole.' The two states therefore wished to build on the 'good traditions of their centuries-long history'. (The Federal Republic was founded in 1949, the Soviet Union in 1922.) In one of his keynote speeches, Gorbachev averred that the co-operation between Moscow and Bonn could serve as 'a catalyst for new relations between East and West altogether'.

Bonn had come a very long way since Adenauer's first trip to Moscow in 1955, after which he proudly explained to his Christian Democratic colleagues that the 'growing young man' Federal Republic had put itself 'in the same row' as the 'other three' — meaning the United States, France and Britain. Now the Federal Republic was in the middle of a new and even more exclusive row, which might be described as the new 'Big Three': the United States, (West) Germany, the Soviet Union. Adenauer's 'nightmare called Potsdam' was but a distant memory. In 1945, the United States and the Soviet Union had decided what should happen to Germany. Now West Germany and the Soviet Union were making a joint statement about what the United States should do! The implicit change in Bonn's relationship with the United States was quite as dramatic as the explicit change in its relationship with the Soviet Union. In fact, President Bush had already acknowledged the (re)emergence of (West) Germany as a major, even a leading power in (not just Western) Europe. In a speech at Mainz just two weeks earlier, he declared that the United States and the Federal Republic should now be 'partners in leadership'.

This new position for (West) Germany was not just a matter of the changing balance of power between states. It also concerned what Gorbachev called the 'philosophical' approach to East-West relations. West German officials were at pains to stress the Western values and West German positions that they had persuaded the Soviet leader to endorse: for example, the references to 'the human person with his dignity and rights . . . stand[ing] at the centre of policy', to the cultural value of national minorities, to the supremacy of international law in domestic and international affairs and above all to the right of self-determination. Connoisseurs pointed out the significance of a change of one letter in the Russian-language text. For decades, the Soviet side had described the Federal Republic as the *Federativnaya Respublika Germanyii* (i.e. the German Federal Republic) while the West German Foreign Ministry had tried to persuade them to call it the *Federativnaya Respublika Germaniya* (i.e. the Federal Republic of Germany). Now, at long last, the Russians had changed the 'i' to 'a'.

If one looks closely, however, the 'philosophical' balance of the document was a little more complicated. It certainly incorporated those elements of Western thinking about international relations which had already been adopted as part of Soviet 'new thinking'. Unlike the only comparable bilateral document — the 1972 Soviet-American Agreement on Basic Principles of Relations — it did not contain the compromised Soviet notion of 'peaceful co-existence'. On the other hand, it also included crucial Soviet reservations. For example, the reference to self-determination as a 'building brick' of the new Europe read as follows: 'The unlimited respect for the integrity and security of each state. Each [i.e. state] has the right freely to choose its own political and social system. The unlimited respect for the principles and norms of international law, especially respect for the right to self-determination of peoples (*Völker*).'

Two crucially different notions were thus conflated: the right of peoples to self-determination and the right of states to choose their own political system without outside interference. Thus, applied to Germany, it could be taken to mean two diametrically opposed things: (1) the GDR — as a state — has the right to choose its own political system, and to demand umlimited respect for the integrity and security of the state built on that system, or (2) the Germans — as a people — have the right to choose unity in freedom, thus spelling the end of the GDR as a state!

The commitment to self-determination in the Bonn Declaration was further qualified by two references to the continued existence of different systems. 'Continuing differences in values and in political and social orders are no obstacle to future-shaping policy across the system-frontiers', it said. And again: 'Europe, which suffered most from two World Wars, must give the world an example of stable peace, good neighbourliness and constructive co-operation, which brings together the productive abilities of all states, *irrespective of different social systems*' (author's italics). This was of course one of the crucial premisses of the original social-liberal vision of a 'European order of peace', as articulated by Brandt, Scheel and Bahr in 1969 — but here it was being underwritten by a Christian Democratic Chancellor in the year 1989. Small wonder that Egon Bahr said he could not have formulated it better himself. 'I must admit,' Bahr observed, 'that I am immensely taken with this Bonn Declaration.'

Now it may be recalled that the Soviet-American Agreement on Basic Principles contained an almost identical formula: 'Differences in ideology and in the social systems of the USA and the USSR,' it said, 'are not obstacles to the bilateral development of normal relations based on the principles of sovereignty, equality, non-interference in internal affairs and mutual advantage.' But that was May 1972, not June 1989.

In June 1989 the peoples of two East European states were already well on the way to changing their systems. Just one week before Gorbachev arrived in Bonn, the Poles had, following the Round Table talks between Solidarity and the authorities, voted in the first half-free election in Eastern Europe since the imposition of the Soviet-type 'social system'. The result was a landslide victory for Solidarity which led, within three months, to the appointment of a non-communist prime minister. As Gorbachev was feted in Bonn, another set of round table talks was beginning, in Budapest. The day after he left, the Hungarians gave a ceremonial reburial to the leader of the 1956 revolution, Imre Nagy, thus putting the last nail in the coffin of the ruling Hungarian Socialist Workers' Party. Responding to these developments, the American President had proposed in his Mainz speech that the Helsinki process should be strengthened and broadened 'to promote free elections and political pluralism in Eastern Europe', a message that he subsequently took to Warsaw and Budapest.

This is the context in which the German-Soviet commitment to shaping together a new Europe 'across the system-frontiers', 'irrespective of the differences between social systems' must be seen. Of course all such documents contain ambiguities and compromises. (This is one argument against producing such documents.) And Chancellor Kohl articulated Western values and specific German interests much more clearly in his keynote speech to the Soviet leader. The continuing division of Germany, he said, was 'an open wound'. The Berlin Wall should be pulled down. West Germany's ties with the European Community and Nato were non-negotiable. 'From the decision for freedom and democracy followed the decision to ally ourselves in Nato with the states which recognise the same values.'

Yet at the same time he observed that this Bonn Declaration should 'set the course' for German-Soviet relations 'in the perspective of the year 2000'. His adviser on foreign affairs, Horst Teltschik, one of the architects of the Bonn Declaration, would subsequently write that it might be regarded as 'guidelines for the course of European politics in the coming decades'. So it was certainly not meant to be taken lightly.

Not just in power-political terms but also 'philosophically' Bonn had taken a public position between Washington and Moscow: incomparably closer to Washington as regards the fundamentals of the internal political, economic and social system, but less so in the vision and the priorities of East-West relations. In fact, between Kohl's visit to Moscow and Gorbachev's visit to Bonn, Bonn had been involved in a major controversy with Washington. It concerned Nato's front-line, short-range nuclear missile system, known as Lance. The United States and Britain wanted to modernise this, seeing it as the last surviving link in the Nato chain from conventional to nuclear weaponry. The Soviet Union wanted it removed altogether, as part of the 'third zero' solution.

True to form, Kohl had initially accepted the American argument. But Genscher strongly opposed it. In the spring of 1989 he succeeded in bringing the Federal Government on to his line, with two main arguments. First, these missiles could only be fired from Germany (West) to hit Germany (East). 'The shorter the range the deader the Germans', as West German politicians pithily put it. Second, it might jeopardise the unique chance of a dramatic improvement in East-West, and specifically German-Soviet relations. This was a major row, with even the Federal President talking loftily of the superior wisdom of 'the continental Europeans', while American congressmen muttered the old refrain 'no nukes, no troops'. And it was a row which Genscherist Bonn effectively won, with a compromise hastily patched together for Nato's fortieth anniversary summit in May. When Bush said 'partners in leadership', he was talking from hard experience.

The Bonn Declaration with Gorbachev was not, of course, a pure summary of Bonn's real position. But nor was Nato's fortieth anniversary declaration. Both were compromises. The former spoke of building a new Europe based on the different social systems, but not as unambiguously as Moscow (let alone East Berlin) would have liked. The latter spoke of support for 'the opening of Eastern societies' and encouragement of 'reforms that aim at positive political, economic and human rights developments' — but not as forcefully as Washington (and many East Europeans) would have desired. In both, there was a large element of Bonn's own distinctive approach to East-West relations, with its vision of spinning a web of dialogue, exchange and co-operation across a divided continent (see p. 258f).

But was this all? Were there not private understandings which went beyond the public statements and impressions? Chancellor Kohl suggests that there were. He recalls, in particular, a conversation with Mikhail Gorbachev one evening, in the garden of the Chancellor's bungalow, overlooking the Rhine. After a heart-to-heart talk about their childhood experiences of the war, and after discussing what Germany and the Soviet Union might do together in a better future, Helmut Kohl raised the subject of German unity. The river of history, he said, was flowing towards German unity, as the Rhine before them flowed down to the sea. You could try to dam the Rhine, but the mighty river would flood its banks and find a way round the dam. So also with German unity. Gorbachev could of course stop it for many years, in which case he, Helmut Kohl, would not live to see the day. But the day of German unity — and that of European unity! — would surely come, as the Rhine flowed down to the sea.

In Kohl's recollection, Gorbachev silently registered this weighty statement, expressing neither assent nor contradiction. Then he spoke of the Soviet Union's economic difficulties. If he had, at some point, to request urgent economic help, he asked, would the Chancellor be able and willing to give it? Kohl said yes. This conversation in the garden of the Chancellor's bungalow, looking over the Rhine, was, says Kohl, 'the decisive moment' on the road to German unity.

Now of course this account must be treated critically. Before making a serious judgement one would want to read the interpreters' records in both Moscow and Bonn. But it does seem that Kohl and Gorbachev, despite or perhaps partly because of earlier slights and outright insults ('Goebbels'), established a remarkable rapport. Almost exactly the same age, provincial politicians both, they displayed a rather similar mixture of toughness and sentimentality, and a shared taste for rambling discourse on history, time and life itself. They would subsequently go over to the familiar '*Du*' form, at a time when Kohl was still using the more formal '*Sie*' with George Bush. It is credible that Kohl would have talked with real conviction — and not 'just for the record' — about the rightness and inevitability of German unification, because he had a long track-record of doing just that in all his conversations with Soviet leaders.

The gist of Gorbachev's response, as recalled by Kohl, is also both plausible and revealing. It suggests that even in Bonn he was still overwhelmingly preoccupied with his problems back home, and that he was looking to Germany above all, with something now amounting almost to desperation, for economic help. In looking to Germany for long-term help in tackling the Herculean task of modernising Russia, he stood in a tradition that stretched back at least to Peter the Great. But he was also looking for short-term help to alleviate the deepening economic crisis which had arisen precisely from his own attempt to modernise the Soviet Union, after seventy years of a command economy, with half-measures of perestroika.

It, is course, quite impossible to summarise here the whole story of developments in the Soviet Union, in Eastern Europe and in East-West relations over the previous four years. But to avoid tunnel vision and retrospective determinism it is important to try and work out what point Gorbachev himself had reached in the summer of 1989, and to ask what larger factors — beyond the specific history of German-Soviet relations — had brought him to that memorable moment on the Rhine.

Willy Brandt, in his 1989 volume of memoirs, poured gentle scorn on the idea that a Western policy of military strength brought Gorbachev to power. In the same volume, he highlighted the influence of the Olof Palme commission, and of his own Brandt commission, on Gorbachev's 'new thinking' in foreign and security policy. He thus touched on two opposite claims for the impact of Western policy on Soviet politics in the 1980s. On the one side, a straight line is drawn from Palme to Gorbachev, on the other, from Pershing to Gorbachev. On a larger canvas, there are those who argue that it was Reagan's new-old policy of Cold War, rearmament and, yes, the Strategic Defence Initiative — 'star wars' — that compelled the decisive turn in Soviet foreign policy. And there are those who argue that, on the contrary, the true sources of 'new thinking' are to be found in Western détente policies, in impulses that came from the peace movement and the parties gathered in the Socialist International. So was it SDI or SI?

Evidence and testimony for each partisan claim is sought, and can be found, from Soviet sources. Thus it is demonstrably the case that some of the concepts and terms of Soviet 'new thinking' — especially in security policy — came from left-wing or left-liberal foreign policy debate in Western Europe and North America. Brandt and Bahr can trace a direct line from the Palme commission via Georgi Arbatov to Gorbachev. And they quote Valentin Falin: 'without Ostpolitik no Gorbachev!' Yet this same Falin could say, in an interview with *Die Zeit* in 1992, that the Americans had arms-raced the Soviets to death. Did that mean, came the alarmed question of *Die Zeit*'s publisher and chief editor, that Reagan was right? 'In this sense, yes', Falin replied, although he went on to observe that the deeper cause was not just Reagan but American policy since the war (in other words, containment).

So far as Germany was concerned, Schmidt, Kohl and Genscher all stressed, in retrospective conversations with the author, the crucial part which they now believe their resolve to go ahead with the deployment of Pershing and Cruise missiles had played in compelling a revision of Soviet policy. Had anyone from the Soviet side endorsed this interpretation? Yes, said Chancellor Kohl, Gorbachev had. But had anyone on the Soviet side endorsed Willy Brandt's contrary interpretation? Yes, said ex-Chancellor Brandt, Gorbachev!

At the risk of sounding more harmonisingly dialectical than the most seasoned Ostpolitiker, one is bound to say that there are probably two realistic answers to the simplistic and partisan question of whether it was Cold War or détente that led to the fundamental change in Soviet policy. The first answer is: both. The second is: neither.

The manifestation of the West's military strength, political solidarity and economic and technological superiority, the hallmark of Reagan's and to a lesser extent of Kohl's first term(s) in office, may have convinced the new Soviet leadership that they could neither out-arm nor split the West. The Soviet Union's achievement of rough nuclear-strategic parity in the 1960s had been a fundamental precondition for the first main period of détente, in which — to paint with a very broad brush — the West moved towards the East. Now the West's demonstration that it could, if it wanted, not only match but beat anything the Soviet Union could do — however large a proportion of public spending the Kremlin devoted to defence — was, arguably at least, a precondition for this second period of détente, in which the East moved towards the West. Yet in this painful and contested realignment of Soviet policy, it was important for Gorbachev and his always small group of firm allies in Soviet politics to be able to show that there were partners in the West, people ready to co-operate without compelling the Soviet Union utterly to lose face. To recall the simplistic dichotomy: if Pershing and SDI showed the impasse, perhaps Palme and SI pointed to a possible way out.

This may be too harmonic an interpretation. It is, as we have seen, also possible to argue that hopes of dealing with the Social Democrats in power in West Germany, and thereby also of driving wedges between Western Europe and the United States, actually retarded the rapprochement between Moscow and Bonn in 1985 and 1986. One might go further and say that the people who showed Gorbachev the way out of the impasse were not the opponents of Reagan and Kohl, but Reagan and Kohl themselves, each in their second terms. It was, after all, the Reagan of the Reykjavik summit who underwrote the most sweeping proposals for nuclear disarmament, to the dismay of many in Western Europe, and especially in West Germany. And was not the Kohl of the Bonn summit a very paragon of détente? Yet the line taken by the opposition, and supported by much of public and published opinion, had helped to modify that government policy, not least through that high-performance semi-conductor called Hans-Dietrich Genscher.

The fact is that, both within the Western alliance and within West Germany itself, the two tracks of the overall Harmel strategy were sustained through argument as much as though consensus: argument within the government coalition, argument between government and opposition, argument between Bonn and Washington. It is therefore impossible to give any clear answer to the question 'who was right?' because both sides ended up doing both. With many alarums and diversions, the Western alliance as a whole pursued both Cold War and détente. Within that overall double-track, the Bonn government had developed a particular double-track of its own.

It challenged the Soviet Union with its allegiance to Nato, and the deployment of missiles that threatened the Soviet Union directly. It challenged the Soviet Union with the development of the Franco-German relationship and the European Community's project of a single market ('1992') and political union, all of which alarmed and goaded the Gorbachev leadership. It defied the Soviet Union by upholding the claim to German unity, which threatened the cornerstone of Moscow's external empire in Eastern Europe. But for each of these sticks, brandished most visibly in the Kohl-Genscher government's first term, it held up a matching carrot, waved most alluringly in the Kohl-Genscher government's second term.

Just because it was so firmly in Nato, it could plead forcefully and successfully for further arms reductions based on an optimistic hypothesis about Soviet policy. Just because it was such a strong player in the EC and other structures of Western economic and political co-operation, it could become the most important advocate in the West of 'helping Gorbachev to succeed', arguing forcefully for the shortening of the Cocom list restricting West-East technology transfer and for expanded economic ties between the EC and Comecon countries. As Kohl remarked in Moscow in October 1988, 'our firm anchoring in the West increases the value of our offer of fair partnership'. Finally, just because it had a major potential to destabilise East Germany, its restraint in operative policy towards East Germany, its reception of Honecker, its anxious solicitude not to 'destabilise' the rest of Eastern Europe, was of real importance to Moscow. The Federal Government spokesman summarised Kohl and Gorbachev's discussions of Eastern Europe at the Bonn summit in two words: 'no destabilisation'.

This double-track could also be described as a balancing act: between Cold War and détente, between Moscow and Washington, between Eastern and Western Europe, between preserving the favourable and changing the unfavourable parts of the status quo. Taken all in all, Bonn governments had not seriously lost their balance in walking this tightrope over the twenty years since 1969, although they had wobbled more than once. With Gorbachev in Bonn, they could congratulate themselves on a success for the combination of Westpolitik and Ostpolitik.

Yet there is a danger of retrospective *hubris* here, especially since unjustified self-congratulation is part of the politician's stock in trade. It is time to remember the other answer to the crude question whether Cold War or détente had brought Gorbachev to this point. That answer is: neither! The primary causes of the changes that led to the end, first of the Soviet Union's external empire in Eastern Europe, then of the Soviet Union, are to be found inside the Soviet Union, in Eastern Europe, and in the nature of Communism. The fundamental contribution of the West was simply to be, and to enhance, what it was: the West. Compared with this, everything it did in direct policy towards the East was of secondary importance.

Writing in 1975, Boris Meissner observed that the strategy of the social-liberal coalition marked a profound change in German Ostpolitik, and then cautiously speculated thus: 'a commensurate change on the Soviet side over a longer period cannot be excluded. It could be the result of a process of development in the Soviet Union which gives domestic renewal the priority over the unfolding of external power.' Was not that, in a nutshell, what happened ten years later? Arguably the evolution of Soviet foreign policy under Gorbachev is a classic example of what in German historiography has been called the *Primat der Innenpolitik*, the primacy of domestic political imperatives.

Gorbachev and his associates, with the pent-up frustration of what many of them saw as ten, some even as twenty lost years of Soviet policy, grasped what they felt was their last chance to modernise the Soviet Union. As they proceeded, they realised that the task was much larger, the problems much deeper, than they had feared. To address this Herculean task, they needed to cut defence spending and establish a co-operative relationship with the West. We have noted already some of the steps they took to achieve this. It also required a fundamental revision of the ideological bases of Soviet foreign policy.

In the Soviet system, such an ideological revision had an autonomous importance which should by no means be underrated. By the time of Gorbachev's speech to the United Nations in December 1988, the main components of 'new thinking' were firmly in place. The 'all-human' replaced the class-based interpretation of international relations. The common problems of humankind should take priority over systemic differences. Most important, the principles of renunciation of force, non-interference and 'freedom of choice' should apply to relations between all states. There was no longer to be a special set of rules governing relations between socialist states. Yet more than a shadow of doubt still remained, especially when it came to Germany.

Domestically, Gorbachev, having become President in the autumn of 1988, was by the summer of 1989 more clearly in command of the partly reformed structure of the Soviet party-state than before. At the same time, however, the half-measures of perestroika had first revealed and then exacerbated the disastrous condition of the economy. As his evening conversation with Kohl indicated, this economic crisis preyed on his mind. Meanwhile, the progress of glasnost strengthened demands for democratic participation and, more threateningly still, fanned the flames of national-ism in what Seweryn Bialer has called the 'internal empire' — that is, the non-Russian republics of the Soviet Union itself. Gorbachev came to Bonn hot foot from a stormy session of the Congress of People's Deputies. From Bonn, he had to keep in daily touch with developments at home, not least because of an acute nationality conflict in Uzbekistan. A small taste of things to come. The quest for a new quality of relations with the

West was thus also, increasingly, a 'flight forward' from mounting problems at home.

Mid-way between the revision of external policy and the ructions of internal politics, and directly affected by both, was Eastern Europe. A new line of more permissive Soviet policy towards Eastern Europe was formally enshrined in a short memorandum to the Politburo in the autumn of 1986, and privately communicated in general terms to East European leaders at that time. But the practice of Soviet policy towards Eastern Europe lagged a long way behind the theory. Gorbachev himself was extremely cautious about undermining the position of East European leaders by unambiguous public articulation of what in the West would be called the 'renunciation of the Brezhnev Doctrine'.

By early 1989, however, Gorbachev had two concrete proposals from East European leaders for changes which went farther than anything he was publicly advocating at home. General Jaruzelski, probably his most trusted East European partner, initiated the Round Table talks with Solidarity. A little later, in March, the new Party leadership in Hungary told him they were preparing to move towards a multi-party system. Gorbachev gave his assent to both experiments. By June, with Solidarity's election triumph and the reburial of Imre Nagy, he was beginning to see where they might lead.

So was the United States. After taking several months in a comprehensive policy review, President Bush had launched his proposals to go 'beyond containment' in a series of speeches leading up to Nato's fortieth anniversary. Fascinated by these developments in Poland (where he had paid a moving visit in 1987) and in Hungary, he went on to make trips to those two countries and to encourage them down the road from Communism to democracy. While his Secretary of State, James Baker, had assured Shevardnadze that 'this isn't meant to create problems for you' he also warned that if the Soviet Union tried to stop these changes it would endanger the new co-operative relationship. Thus, at this crucial juncture, the United States linked the development of its relationship with the Soviet Union to Soviet conduct in East Central Europe.

So in the summer of 1989 Gorbachev was, for all the sunny appearances and the adulation, a politician under immense pressure with very limited options. If Kohl was walking a tightrope, Gorbachev was riding a tiger along a tightrope. What, then, did the Soviet leadership anticipate at this crucial juncture? Defending the loss of Eastern Europe against furious criticism a year later, at the twenty-eighth (and last) congress of the Soviet Communist Party, Shevardnadze said: 'Yes, we had in principle predicted this . . . In principle, we sensed this, we knew this. We felt that if serious changes did not take place, then tragic events would follow.' In his memoirs, he recalls a report from the Soviet ambassador to Bonn as early as April saying that East Germany could collapse within days.

Similar warnings were made by other specialists in the spring and early summer.

Sergei Tarasenko, one of Shevardnadze's closest aides in the Foreign Ministry, recalls a confidential discussion in a small circle around the Foreign Minister, after the dramatic outcome of the Polish elections in June 1989. The conclusion, as he recalls it, was that Eastern Europe would probably 'go'. Although they foresaw grave repercussions, not least inside the Soviet Union, they felt Moscow had no serious alternative to letting it go. For to intervene to prevent this would be to ruin everything they had worked for over the previous four years, at home as well as abroad. And Shevardnadze reportedly told Baker, in a meeting in late July, that for the Soviet Union to use force to stop the changes in Eastern Europe 'would be the end of perestroika'. There are thus significant indications, to put it no stronger, of a pessimistic realism — or realistic pessimism — at a very high level in Moscow.

On the other hand there are also indications of an optimistic idealism which would prove to be unrealistic. After all, the basic starting point of Gorbachev and his closest associates was that the Soviet Union could be modernised while remaining the Soviet Union, and that socialism could be reformed while remaining socialism — that is, a system qualitatively distinct from even the social democratic variant of capitalism. Many of them had been strongly influenced by the Prague Spring. Asked what was the difference between what was happening in Moscow and what had happened in Prague in 1968, the Foreign Ministry spokesman, Gennady Gerasimov, had memorably replied 'nineteen years'. Gorbachev himself said in early 1989 that the aim of perestroika was to 'reveal the human face of socialism', thus taking up the key phrase of 1968. As we have noted already, in his speech to the Council of Europe in July 1989 Gorbachev clearly envisaged the continued existence of two distinct 'social systems' in East and West.

So he probably still hoped that reformed communist leaders — little Gorbachevs, so to speak — could continue to play the leading role in states that would continue to be in some sense socialist. In Czechoslovakia's velvet revolution a few months later, home-made posters would appear showing '89' as '68' upside down. But the people who really believed that '89 might be another '68 were, arguably, the middle-aged reformers in Moscow. These were illusions. But they were, for Eastern Europe, helpful illusions. For if Soviet leaders had foreseen exactly what would happen in Eastern Europe, they might after all have been tempted to draw back. The people of Eastern Europe were thus the beneficiaries not just of the Soviet leaders' realism but also of their illusions — which were, in one of history's nicer ironies, in some measure the East Europeans' own illusions of twenty years before.

If we are right — and such a reconstruction is of course speculative —

then Gorbachev, Shevardnadze and their closest associates were, in that early summer of 1989, hovering between illusory hopes and realistic fears. And what of Kohl, Genscher and their closest associates? Everyone could see that relations between Bonn and Moscow were now better than they had ever been in the history of the Bonn republic. After a long, painful prologue the new page had became a new chapter, and the new chapter now looked like a new book. In economics, at least, Bonn was now Moscow's single most important partner in the West. It was equally plain that what Bonn wanted in return was progress in Deutschlandpolitik. For Kohl and Genscher, as for all their predecessors, the end of the road from Bonn to Moscow was Berlin. For a time, in the mid-1980s, they had got farther along the German-German side of the triangle than along the German-Soviet side. But now they were almost back to the original Brandt-Bahr geometry, working through Moscow to put pressure on a recalcitrant East Berlin.

Reflecting on the significance of the Gorbachev visit, Horst Teltschik wrote that the Bonn Declaration took on 'a particular significance, and in a certain sense even political explosiveness' against the background of Gorbachev's reforms at home. 'If German unification is principally understood to be the means to realise human rights and the right of self-determination for all Germans,' he wrote, 'it can only have a chance if such rights are also realised in the Soviet Union *and if this development then spreads to its allies*' (author's italics). Like Bahr, Teltschik saw change coming from the centre of the Soviet empire and from above. The 1989 version of Bahr-judo was: Moscow must help bring reforms to East Berlin. This was perhaps not so far from what Gorbachev himself envisaged.

However, the time-scale Teltschik then imagined for such changes was still one of many years, probably of decades. If anything, Gorbachev, Shevardnadze and their closest advisers may have had a slightly more realistic idea of how quickly East Germany might collapse than Kohl, Genscher and their colleagues in Bonn. Policymakers in Bonn had worked for so long with Soviet power in Central Europe as a fact almost of physical geography that to anticipate its collapse was almost like anticipating the dissolution of the Alps. Soviet policymakers, by contrast, knew from inside just how rotten the mountains were. What is more, they could sense — even if they did not positively know, let alone publicly admit — how they themselves would react to an avalanche.

The Chancellor and his Foreign Minister had a sense — perhaps scarcely more than a hope against hope — that the German question really might be coming 'open' again, in a way that it had not been for decades. Like any good politician, they were ready to seize the main chance if it came. But nobody knew exactly when or how it would come. That now depended on the workings of what Gorbachev rather mystically described as 'history' or 'life itself', in a state called the GDR.

IV

Germany and Germany

Foundations

In a sense, all Ostpolitik was Deutschlandpolitik. Reducing and eventually overcoming the division of Berlin and Germany was not the only objective of Bonn's new opening to the Soviet Union and Eastern Europe, but it was the single most important one. Increasing the Federal Republic's freedom of action was an end in itself, but also a means to this larger end. Relations with Moscow, above all, but also, to a lesser degree, with Warsaw, Prague or Budapest, were seen to have a crucial permissive function for the pursuit of Deutschlandpolitik. The affairs of Berlin still directly involved the four powers. However, that involvement became less intense, and West Germany's dependence on the Western Allies accordingly less acute, as a result both of the calming effect of the Quadripartite Agreement and of the development of direct relations between the two states in Germany.

It was these direct relations which after 1969 became the central stuff of Deutschlandpolitik. As part of the initial 'recognition' of the GDR, the Brandt government renamed the Ministry for All-German Questions the Ministry for Intra-German Relations, and that deliberately awkward term henceforth became official parlance. A description more widely used, with conscious paradox, was 'German-German relations'. Whatever the label, they were relations and no longer merely questions.

Egon Bahr memorably commented, after signing the Basic Treaty with the GDR in December 1972, that whereas previously the two German states had had no relations they would now at least have bad ones. To say that the two states had previously had no relations was of course a characteristic overstatement. So far as trade was concerned, the two states in Germany had recognised each other from the very beginning. With only minor amendments, the Berlin Agreement of September 1951 remained the contractual basis of what the Federal Republic referred to as 'intra-German trade', right up until 1990. In the crucial area of humanitarian help for political prisoners in the GDR and families divided by the Wall, the efforts not just of the West Berlin city government but also of the West German federal government went back to the early 1960s. Starting in 1963, under the Christian Democrat Rainer Barzel, the All-German and then Intra-German Ministry oversaw these secret and extraordinary humanitarian actions for twenty-seven years.

Moreover, Chancellor Kiesinger's April 1967 declaration on the principles of the government's Deutschlandpolitik, a declaration shaped both by the Social Democrat Herbert Wehner, as Minister for All-German Questions, and by his predecessor Rainer Barzel, reads almost like a check list for the operative Deutschlandpolitik of the 1970s and 1980s. Among the possibilities of 'alleviating the burden of the division of our people (*Volk*)', in order 'to create the preconditions for a détente inside Germany', this listed 'I. Measures to alleviate everyday life for the people (*die Menschen*) in both parts of Germany, such as (a): improved travel opportunities, above all for relatives, with the goal of developing normal communications'. I(b) was 'permit agreements' for Berlin and areas along the frontier, and I(e) the reunification of families (*Familienzusammenführung*), especially the return of children separated from their parents by the division (*Kinderrückführung*).

Sections II and III then listed diverse measures of economic co-operation, improved transport connections, post and telephone links, academic, cultural, youth and sporting exchanges. In proposing the 'creation of a rational electricity network economy' it even anticipated arrangements for the exchange of surplus electricity between East and West Germany which were finally agreed twenty-one years later: if not a *Zollverein*, then at least a *Stromverbund*. (The first part of this cross-border power grid was finished just a month before the opening of the Berlin Wall.)

Yet as we have seen, the Kiesinger government did not manage even to begin the realisation of this practical agenda. It was only after further change in the positions of Moscow, Washington and Bonn, only after the government declaration of October 1969, recognising the existence of 'two states in Germany', that Willy Brandt and the East German Prime Minister Willi Stoph would meet, in two fraught and deeply emotional encounters, first in the East German town of Erfurt and then in the West German town of Kassel. It was only after the Moscow Treaty was signed and the Warsaw Treaty initialled that Egon Bahr could sit down formally to negotiate with State Secretary Michael Kohl of the GDR. It was only after Walter Ulbricht was replaced by Erich Honecker, with a little brotherly help from Moscow, that these negotiations began to bear fruit.

It was only following the Quadripartite Agreement on Berlin that the first, very modest, German-German agreements, on post and telephone links, and transit to and from West Berlin, would be signed. It was only after the ratification of the Moscow and Warsaw treaties, and the blossoming of American-Soviet détente with President Nixon's visit to Moscow and the signing of the SALT I arms control treaty, that Bahr and Michael Kohl could sign the first formal bilateral treaty between the two German states; modestly enough, a treaty about traffic (albeit in a broad sense). And it was only after all this, and some heavy use of the Bonn-Moscow-Berlin triangle, that Bahr and Michael Kohl could, at long last, reach agreement on 'A Treaty on the Bases of Relations between the Federal Republic of Germany and the German Democratic Republic'.

These three pioneering years of German-German relations saw one of the most awkward and yet deeply emotional *pas de deux* in diplomatic history; or rather, a *pas de deux* inside a foursome reel, for the Soviet Union, the United States, Britain and France were intimately involved at every stage; and everyone was dancing on a minefield. The summit meetings in Erfurt, where Willy Brandt was greeted by crowds chanting 'Willy to the window!', and in Kassel, where Willi Stoph was greeted by right-wing extremists, were the great symbolic moments. 'The day of Erfurt,' wrote Brandt, looking back from old age, 'was there any in my life that was more laden with emotion?' Both sides made extraordinary preparations. Reckoning with listening devices in the hotel at Erfurt, the West German delegation had a briefing book with numbered alternative formulations and in their internal discussions merely exchanged numbers. The Politburo briefing book for Stoph's trip to Kassel runs to more than one hundred pages, with detailed arguments for every eventuality.

Quite as remarkable, in a less public and dramatic way, were the long drawn-out negotiations between Bahr and Kohl. Here too every tiny detail was prescribed and analysed to exhaustion. When an East German official forgot to remove his hat as he greeted Egon Bahr on a wet and windy day at the airport, West German analysts speculated that this was a deliberate affront. But when that same official waited to receive Bahr inside the foyer of the Council of Ministers, instead of stepping out to greet him, it actually was a deliberate gesture. And so on and so forth. Only if one recalls the fantastic hypersensitivity of these early years, and the years of megaphone diplomacy that preceded them, can one understand the standards by which West German policymakers judged the progress of later years. It should also soon be possible, drawing on the wealth of documents which are just becoming available, to make a serious assessment of the achievement of Egon Bahr in his negotiations for Germany. What was in many ways the high-point of Bahr's personal diplomacy can only be the starting-point of our analysis here.

The Treaty on the Bases of Relations (*Grundlagenvertrag*), sometimes loosely referred to as the Basic Treaty, was at once wholly unique and supremely typical of the Ostpolitik as conceived and implemented by Willy Brandt and Egon Bahr. It was, more directly than all the rest, the culmination of the work they had begun in cruelly divided Berlin a decade before. We have suggested that the hallmarks of that embryonic Ostpolitik were not, as they put it, 'small steps instead of big words', but rather small steps *and* big words, though of a different kind from Adenauer's. Nowhere were the steps smaller, or the words bigger, than in German-German relations.

Thus the '20 points' which Willy Brandt presented to Willi Stoph in Kassel as the basis for negotiating a treaty still included such elementary humanitarian demands as: 'the problems which result from the division of families should be brought to a solution' (point 15). Yet they also included such high-flown, pathos-laden affirmations as: 'the treaty parties declare that never again may war go out from German soil' (point 7). This phrase, over which Brandt and Stoph had already agreed in Erfurt, was not actually included in the treaty, but it was to play a crucial part in German-German relations over the next twenty years.

The treaty itself was the most extreme example of the approach which the other Eastern treaties exemplified to a lesser degree: putting to one side all the irreconcilable differences of principle so as to open the door for the development of a practical *modus vivendi*, under the general headings of 'détente', 'co-operation' and 'normalisation'. Thus the Preamble declared this treaty to be 'without prejudice to the different views of the Federal Republic of Germany and the German Democratic Republic on fundamental questions, including the national question'. The Federal Republic made explicit its different view by handing over, at the point of signature, the same 'Letter on German Unity' that it had handed over on signing the Moscow Treaty.

Concessions made by the West German side included, beyond the basic — yet not, the Bonn government insisted, full — diplomatic recognition of the GDR, a fairly strong statement in Article 6 that the two states 'proceed on the principle that the sovereign jurisdiction of each of the two states is confined to its own territory. They respect the independence and autonomy of each of the two states in their internal and external affairs.' In a laconic accompanying exchange, however, the Federal Republic declared that 'questions of citizenship have not been regulated by the treaty' — meaning that it would continue to regard citizens of the GDR as citizens of the Federal Republic, and hence automatically to give them West German passports, if they got to the West and wanted to take up that distinctly attractive offer.

Article 1 of the treaty said the two states would develop 'normal, good neighbourly relations' although no-one could say exactly what 'normal, good neighbourly' relations would be between two halves of a divided nation, let alone of a divided city. In a statement to mark the initialling of the treaty, Brandt recalled a central passage from his October 1969 government declaration. 'Twenty years after the foundation of the Federal Republic and the GDR,' he had said, 'we must prevent a further drifting apart of the German nation, that is, try to move via a *geregeltes Neben-einander* [roughly: a regulated next-to-each-other] to a *Miteinander* [with-each-other]'. The treaty, Brandt now commented, 'is the instrument to organise the *Miteinander* under the given circumstances'.

Here was another classic piece of Brandtian inspirational vagueness. For who precisely was to be 'next to' whom? Who was 'regulating' what? When, how, by what criteria would who decide that they (the states? their leaders? the people?) were 'with' rather than just 'next to' each other? Clear, unambiguous meanings were precisely what these big words were not to have.

Meanwhile, Brandt and Bahr pointed to the small steps. Beyond the contorted compromise formulae of the agreements, and the vague emotive glosses, what the Bonn government would stress above all was the possibilities the treaty opened up for practical improvements for 'the people' (*die Menschen*) in the two states. Humanitarian improvements that were achieved in direct connection with the treaty included an explicit formal acceptance by the GDR, albeit only in a letter accompanying the treaty, of the need to reunite families, and detailed provision for easier travel into East Germany for West Germans from areas immediately adjoining the borders of the GDR. Article 7 of the treaty said that the two sides 'will make agreements so as to develop . . . co-operation in the areas of the economy, science and technology, transport, legal relations, post and telecommunications, health, culture, sport, environmental protection, and in other fields.'

So the proof of the pudding was to be in the eating. After the Basic Treaty was ratified, against the opposition of the Christian Democrats, and found by the constitutional court to be in accordance with West Germany's Basic Law, Egon Bahr delivered a lecture at the Tutzing Academy, to mark the tenth anniversary of his 1963 'Tutzing speech'. '*Wandel durch Annäherung* (change through rapprochement),' he said, recalling his famous formula of ten years before, 'is the concept for the conduct of the nation, so long as it is divided. It is a concept which, from this summer, having become an effective treaty, has begun its probation.'

However, it took yet another year, until the summer of 1974, before the so-called Permanent Representations — embassies in all but name — were installed at what were carefully described as 'the respective seats of government', for of course neither West Germany nor the Western Allies would ever refer to East Berlin as the 'capital' of the GDR. The West German Permanent Representative reported directly to the Chancellor. The East German Permanent Representative reported formally to his Ministry for Foreign Affairs — for was not West Germany a quite foreign country?

Behind this formal construction, itself anything but simple, there was on both sides a complex politics — and bureaucratic politics — of German-

German relations. In West Germany, leaders of all the main parties — in the government coalition and in opposition — would, as we shall see, get their oar in, while within the bureaucracy the policy had to be co-ordinated between senior officials from at least three departments, and more would be involved in many individual decisions.

In East Germany, the Chancellor's real counterpart, the man who took the key decisions, was clearly the East German party leader, Erich Honecker. But the party-state's economic chief Günter Mittag was also an important actor, while the State Security Service under Erich Mielke had both an active operational interest and a formidable passive *droit de regard*. The unique nature of the relationship to West Germany, combined with Honecker's — and Mittag's — desire to keep control of it to themselves, led to unusual politbureaucratic devices, such as the Politburo's 'Working Group FRG', chaired by Mittag. Most unusual, too, was the lack of any direct control of the Foreign Ministry's 'FRG Department' by a department of the Central Committee. These factors also favoured a heavy use of unconventional emissaries such as the lawyer Wolfgang Vogel and, above all, Alexander Schalck-Golodkowski — or plain Schalck, as he was known in the GDR.

From 1976 on, Schalck was the single most important East German intermediary in German-German relations. After unification, a Bundestag special committee struggled valiantly to disentangle the web of his politbureaucratic subordination. Was he answerable to Honecker directly? To Honecker via Mittag? To Mielke? But this was to try to disentangle the undisentangleable. For the ambiguous, murky, duplicated and duplici-tous lines of reporting and command reflected not merely the character of Schalck but the reality of his position, and the reality of the party-and police-state he served.

On many issues, above all in relation to Berlin, West Germany had still to consult with its Western Allies. The so-called Bonn Group (or 'Group of Four'), which for many years had regularly brought together senior officials from the American, British and French embassies and the West German Foreign Ministry, remained an important co-ordinating body. This was as nothing, however, compared to the minute consultations which the East Germany Foreign Ministry, Central Committee apparatus and Polit-buro leadership had with Moscow. As the East German party documents now definitely show, even in the 1980s these consultations sometimes still took the form of taking orders. On the other hand, just because of this exacting requirement, the satellite state went to considerable lengths to establish its own discreet channels to Bonn, if only to test the water before putting the issue to Moscow — and especially to Moscow's long-time Ambassador in East Berlin, the high-handed and suspicious Piotr Abrassimov.

Wolfgang Mischnick, then parliamentary leader of the Free Democrats, recalls a conversation with Erich Honecker in 1973 during which, in the course of a walk in the woods(!), the East German leader suggested that some things could be done between the two German states 'without the big brother'. (Mischnick insists that Honecker himself used the phrase 'big brother'.) Direct correspondence and the despatch of informal emissaries, not only to the Chancellor or Chancellery Minister but also to Wehner or Strauss, all served not only to take measures quietly without consulting Moscow but also to prepare the ground before making a case to Moscow.

Wolfgang Schäuble, responsible for relations with the GDR as Chancellery Minister from 1984 until 1989, suggests a further reason for the sometimes secretive and even conspiratorial style of German-German relations. This, he argues, enabled the GDR to discuss subjects that it was not even prepared to discuss in official talks. More important still, it allowed West Germany to raise and East Germany to accept linkages — for example, between hard currency payments and the easing of travel restrictions — that the GDR would never countenance officially. Since these were precisely the subjects and linkages in which the Bonn government was most interested, it had to accept the conspiratorial terms of business.

Looking back in 1992, the East German party leader himself emphasised the particular importance of his personal telephone conversations with Chancellors Schmidt and Kohl. Talking to the author in the hospital of Berlin's Moabit prison, the former General Secretary of the SED and Chairman of the Council of State of the GDR pulled out of the pocket of his prison pyjamas a slightly dog-eared card on which his (former) secretary had once typed for him the direct telephone number to the Chancellor's office in Bonn. They used to call each other quite often, he said. On occasion he had even dialled the number himself. Hence the little card.

Thoughts, words and deeds

The first Permanent Representative of the Federal Republic in the GDR, Günter Gaus, subsequently described the policy conducted through these diverse and curious channels not as Deutschlandpolitik but as *DDR-Politik*. The term was much criticised in West Germany, because it was taken to imply a too substantial recognition of the GDR, at the expense of an operative commitment to working towards unity. Gaus himself would indeed later plead, explicitly and passionately, for what he called an 'inner' recognition of the GDR. At the same time there is no doubt that the primary meaning of 'Deutschlandpolitik' in Bonn over the next fifteen years, until 1989, was dealings with the GDR, a state which was assumed by virtually all policymakers and responsible politicians to be there for the foreseeable future. In this sense, if one can separate the term from the specific implications of the Gausian view, one may usefully describe this policy as *DDR-Politik*.

Yet can one thus separate it? Can one detach what West German policymakers did from what they said or thought they were doing? In what they actually did in policy towards the GDR there was an overwhelming continuity through the 1970s and 1980s. In what they said, there was near-total consensus on the short-term, operative goals. The diversity of publicly stated views grew as one looked to the medium-term, and became even more pronounced in respect of long-term objectives. And what they thought? This is most difficult of all to pin down, especially given the remarkable transformative effect of unification on so many German memories.

In the wake of unification, the immediate West German (party-) political debate concentrated on this issue of long-term goals. Who, it was severely asked, somewhat in the tones of the Spanish Inquisition, had continued through all these years to 'believe in' German unity? Had not Willy Brandt, the symbol of Ostpolitik and now the father-figure of German unification, declared in 1988 that reunification was the *Lebenslüge* (literally: life-lie) of the Federal Republic? Why yes, came the somewhat strained reply, but the term 'life-lie' referred only to the prefix '*re-*', which, please note, was carefully put in italics in the original speech. A new unification was a quite different matter. Had not Helmut Kohl, by contrast, constantly and loudly insisted that reunification was the ultimate goal? Why yes, but at roughly the same time as Brandt spoke of the 'life-lie' Kohl had confessed that he probably would not see German unity in his lifetime. And so on and so forth.

It is a prudent assumption in all human affairs that people do not always think what they say or say what they think. This assumption is particularly prudent in politics, and nowhere more so than in the politics of East-West relations in Germany. Granted this premiss, one has, logically speaking, four possible categories of person: those who both spoke and thought about German unity, those who neither spoke nor thought about it, those who spoke about it without thinking about it, and those who thought about it without speaking about it. One can state with some confidence that in West Germany in the 1980s the first class was very small and the second very large. There were very few people who both spoke and thought about the unification of Germany in one state as a serious objective in the foreseeable future. The few who did thus speak or write were often regarded, even among the Christian Democrats, as somewhat marginal and even slightly irresponsible.

There were, on the other hand, a very great many people who, although if asked in an opinion poll whether they were in favour of German unity would naturally say 'yes', neither spoke nor thought about it otherwise. A leading analyst of public opinion data on this subject records that whereas in the 1950s and 1960s between thirty-five and forty-five per cent of those asked considered reunification to be 'the most important question with which one should generally concern oneself in the Federal Republic today', from the mid-1970s the figure was never more than one per cent.

Most of West Germany's political class, however, fell into the other two, more problematic categories. The problem of defining attitudes is further exacerbated by the party-political divide. There is no doubt that leading Christian Democrats, in opposition and in government, more constantly and loudly reiterated their formal commitment to work towards German unity. Leading Social Democrats accused them of merely paying 'lip-service' to the commitment to unification in the preamble to the Basic Law, of making 'Sunday speeches' for the benefit of their expellee nationalist voters, without thinking very seriously about the implications of what they were saying, not least for the people who actually suffered most from the division.

Christian Democrats, by contrast, accused Social Democrats of no longer even talking about reunification, or, indeed, of talking positively about alternatives to it: models for the long-term co-existence of two states, of a reformed GDR in a European peace order, and so forth. Yet in the case of the Social Democratic architects of Ostpolitik, the fact that they did not talk about unification is no sure indication of what they thought. For, in the 1960s and early 1970s at least, they certainly thought more than they publicly said. It makes more sense, they argued, to talk publicly about the issues on which we have a chance of reaching agreement with the other side than about those on which there is no such chance. 'The time seems to me to have come,' as Brandt put it in a letter to Willi Stoph in February 1970, 'to relegate that which separates and to seek that which joins.'

It was not just in 1988 but already in 1969 that Brandt said 'I must confess that I have stopped speaking about reunification.' In the short-term, this could be seen as responsible, humane pragmatism, in the interests of the individual people in Germany (*die Menschen*). In the long-run, it had more than a touch of Machiavellianism, in the national interest. German unity could only be achieved if one ceased to demand it!

Given this complex starting point, it is very difficult to make any firm judgements about public statements on long-term goals. One may suspect that the private thoughts of leading Social Democrats came somewhat closer to their increasingly reserved public statements over these twenty years, even as the private thoughts of leading Christian Democrats somewhat (or further) diverged from their public statements, so that by the mid-1980s the two sides had perhaps reached, by different routes, a quite similar point of belief, or non-belief, in the real possibility of German unification. This must, however, vary with each individual case, and in no case will one be able to prove it anyway.

One may also ask how important the theological question of whether Mr X or Ms Y truly 'believed' in German unity ultimately is, interesting though it might be, especially for the purposes of party-political polemics. It is useful, and feasible, to record what leading figures actually said on this issue, over the years. It is important, although much more difficult, to enquire what the real effects of what they said were in East and West Germany, and among Germany's neighbours. Methodologically, the rest is little better than a parlour game.

At the other end of the spectrum were the short-term, operative goals. These were well-defined and consensual. Their realisation could be quite precisely charted. Yet perhaps more interesting than either the short or the long-term goals is the question of the medium-term. How did the Bonn government propose to move from the short-term goal — the reunification of families — to the long-term goal — the reunification of Germany? Even if the long-term goal were defined slightly differently — as, say, a genuinely democratic German Democratic Republic, a third version of German-speaking statehood, next to West Germany and Austria — the question remained of how one proposed to get from here to there. We may, of course, find that there was surprisingly little — of deed, word, or even thought — in this middle ground. The most effective politicians often combine a simple, long-term strategic vision with the greatest tactical flexibility and attention to the immediately do-able, leaving the middle-term to the so-called policy intellectuals. Arguably both Brandt and Kohl were, in their very different ways, this kind of politician, while Helmut Schmidt was witheringly dismissive of the 'concepts' of policy intellectuals.

Yet it would be a remarkable feat to conduct a policy of such central importance to your country for twenty years without having at least some underlying notion, however vague and rudimentary, of where it was taking you. So one can reasonably ask: how did West German policymakers think their policies might be changing the policies, and politics, of East Germany? And then: what effects did they actually have? Of course, as we have mentioned earlier, it is extremely difficult to single out the influence of Western policy among the many factors, domestic and international, that determine the political development of a communist state, and no state was more dependent on the international constellation than the GDR. It is also very difficult to distinguish between the influence that West Germany exerted passively, by virtue of its mere existence, prosperity, freedom, openness etc, and that which it exerted actively, by virtue of conscious policy.

Thus the fact that virtually all East Germans regularly watched West German television was endlessly cited as an example of West German influence. Yet West German television beams did not reach East German television screens as a result of West German government policy. This was, as it were, an act of God. On the other hand, the fact that in the

1970s and 1980s the East Germans received from West German television vivid, first-hand, live reports by Western reporters on their own internal affairs was, without question, a fruit of West German policy, since working conditions for Western journalists were the subject of hard-fought negotiations and agreements between the two states. That the East German regime no longer attempted to prevent its citisens watching Western television, as it had done in the 1950s and 1960s; that, on the contrary, in the 1980s it actually had cable laid so that people in the Dresden area, in what was known as 'the valley of the clueless', could properly receive Western broadcasts, rather than applying to emigrate: this was a significant change in Eastern policy. Yet this change cannot simply be described as a direct 'result' of Western policy. Rather it was the result of a complex calculation of political self-interest, in which Western desires were only one element.

Yet, despite these difficulties of analysis, the German-German relationship still offers a unique opportunity to examine the impact of Western policy on Eastern politics. Nowhere else in Europe do we have a case in which essentially just one policy was applied, by one Western state, to one Eastern state, over twenty years. Of the other major Western states, only France may perhaps be said to have had a distinctive policy directed specifically at the East German state. But this consisted in going slightly further than West Germany in recognition of the GDR (to help ensure that there continued to be two Germanies for France to love). Like France, Britain and the United States had interests in East Germany, and American policy was a prime determinant of the 'overall weather conditions' for German-German relations. But neither Britain nor the United States had a distinctive policy directed specifically at the GDR. In direct relations with the GDR, their role was essentially supportive of Bonn's policy.

In what follows we shall look first at the short-term, consensual, operative goals of West German policy and the means by which they were to be realised: permanent negotiation, money and recognition. We shall then turn to the medium-term relationship between policy towards the GDR and the politics of the GDR, looking first at the intended and then at the actual impact of the former on the latter.

For people and the people

'The intra-German treaty policy,' said the common resolution of all the main parties in the Bundestag, in February 1984, 'should make the consequences of partition more bearable for the people in Germany and preserve the unity of the nation.' In Bonn usage, these central purposes were generally referred to under two rubrics, both difficult to translate: *menschliche Erleichterungen* and *der Zusammenhalt der Nation*. The former means literally 'human alleviations', and the latter 'the cohesion of the nation'. *Menschliche* implies more than simply 'humanitarian', so one might more loosely translate this phrase as 'improvements for people', that is, for individual human beings, *die Menschen*. *Nation* in the second phrase implies less than nation-state, so one might more loosely translate it as 'keeping together the people', that is, the ethnic and cultural collectivity, the *Volk* and the *Kulturnation*. In the statements of West German policymakers these two senses of 'helping (the) people' were practically elided, or at the very least a natural continuum was assumed to lead from one to the other.

No one talked more movingly about *die Menschen* than Willy Brandt. In his first state of the nation address as Chancellor, in January 1970, he concluded by answering the charge that his government was proposing to pay in advance for uncertain concessions from the East. There was a time, he said, 'when considerable German payments-in-advance to the West were considered as proof of special statesmanlike wisdom and foresight'. The reference was of course to Adenauer's Western treaties. Then he went on to spell out the potential benefits that justified the opening to the East. 'And will not Germany then herself have more security and a better peace?' he asked.

> Will not her people, every single one, profit from it? Let me put it like this: because there will be less fear; because the burdens will be lighter; because people will see each other again, who for years could not see each other; because perhaps two people from the two states in Germany will be able to marry, who today are divided by inhuman duress. These are the standards, great and small, but always related to the people (*die Menschen*), which this government sets . . .

Seventeen years later, Chancellor Kohl set the same standards and made the same elision. 'We are aware,' he said, in his 1987 state of the nation address,

> that human alleviations are not the same thing as human rights. It would nonetheless be irresponsible to underestimate the value of human alleviations. So long as the Germans are separated from each other, it is our task to ease the painful consequences of the division of our fatherland, to strengthen the consciousness of belonging together among all Germans, to preserve what unites and to create new commonalities between them. Our effort to facilitate encounters, in growing number and intensity, between the people (*die Menschen*) in both states in Germany, is central.

Most of what the Federal Republic attempted to do in its operative policy could be located somewhere on this assumed continuum between bringing individual people together and keeping the nation together. Over the years, negotiations with the East German authorities covered almost every sort of interchange within a nation: human, legal, financial, academic, social, commercial, cultural, environmental, technical, sporting, scientific; you name it, Bonn would talk about it. The West German government's interest in every case was to preserve and develop all possible kinds of exchange, link, tie or bond between the two parts of Germany, making a web to 'hold the nation together'. The idea of spinning such a web of ties and interdependencies — a process variously described as *Vernetzung*, *Verklammerung* or, most frequently, *Verflechtung* — had been central to the rethinking of Deutschlandpolitik in the 1960s, and was, as we shall see, important for the whole Ostpolitik in the 1970s and 1980s. The East German regime's interest, by contrast, was only to allow the most carefully controlled and selective development of such ties, and to exact for them the maximum price. The negotiations were therefore slow, painful and tortuous.

They were made doubly painful and tortuous by what West Germany saw as the categorical imperative of wherever possible including West Berlin in the West-East German agreements. Moreover, many of the negotiations were concerned exclusively with the special problems of Berlin. No less than fifteen of the seventeen agreements which Günter Gaus negotiated as Permanent Representative related to Berlin. Arrangements for transit travellers between West Germany and West Berlin, the physical improvement of the transit motorways and railway lines, telephone links between West and East Berlin, visits from West Berlin to East Berlin and the rest of East Germany, the anomalous exclaves of West Berlin almost entirely surrounded by the East, the local railway lines (*S-Bahn*) running through West Berlin but still administered by the *Deutsche Reichsbahn* from the East, the disposal of sewage from West Berlin: the list of Berlin issues was almost endless.

In the 1980s, the agenda of the German-German negotiations became rather more diverse and ambitious. There was some co-operation on tackling common problems like the pollution which originated in one part of Germany (mainly the East) but affected the other. A classic case was the River Elbe, which, by the time it had run diagonally across the breadth of the GDR, reached Hamburg as a poisonous sewer. There was the agreement to develop a cross-border power grid, the *Stromverbund* already mentioned. To the earlier (1974) agreement on sporting ties there were now added two on youth exchanges, although the nature of the East German signatory — the Party youth movement (FDJ) — did not bode well for the selection of young people to be sent West.

After just twelve years of negotiation, an agreement on cultural co-operation was signed in 1986. Even then it was little more than a framework agreement of principle, which some artists feared would actually increase the Eastern party-state's control over the cultural exchanges that were already happening from below. The same applied to the agreement on technical and scholarly exchanges, signed in the autumn of 1987. In 1986 there began a wave of 'twinning' between towns and cities in East and West. By the opening of the Berlin Wall, fifty-eight such agreements had been made, with another six in preparation. Although the town councils in the East were also under Party control, these town twinnings at least put the selection of contact persons lower down the hierarchy.

All these negotiations were necessarily conducted with the East German powers-that-be, under the general motto of 'co-operation'. Most West German politicians and policymakers, however, considered themselves to be negotiating on behalf of the people — *die Menschen* — meaning, first, the Germans living in the GDR, second, the Germans living in West Berlin, third, the Germans in West Germany, and fourth, the Germans altogether. The measure of 'success' for the negotiations was therefore, to quote the Bundestag resolution once again, 'directly useful results for the people'. Measured by this standard, it must be said that some of these painfully negotiated agreements produced only relatively small direct benefits, or had only just begun to do so when revolution and unification overtook them.

Yet overall there was, measured against the quite extraordinary low starting-point of post-Wall Germany, very significant progress 'for the people'. The publications of the Ministry for Intra-German relations lovingly recorded the number of letters and parcels sent from West to East and East to West, the growing number of telephone lines, telexes and telegrams, the volume of trade and the volume of people. Whereas in 1969 there had been just half a million telephone calls from West to East Germany, in 1988 (the last 'normal', that is, normalised-abnormal, year in German-German relations) there were some forty million. Whereas in 1969 there were little more than one million visits recorded from West to East Germany, in the mid-1970s the figure reached nearly eight million. In 1980 the GDR tried, as it had in 1973, to stem the presumably subverting flow of Western visitors by sharply increasing the minimum amount of hard currency that the Western visitor was compelled to exchange on each trip across the border. Yet the number of West German visits still remained above five million a year throughout the 1980s.

The improvement was most dramatic where the problem had been most acute: in Berlin. To appreciate this one has to go back for a moment to the early 1960s. With the building of the Wall, the last relatively risk-free escape route out of the GDR was closed. By September 1961 the division of Berlin and Germany was about as absolute as any territorial division in Europe could be. No ordinary German under pensionable age could now travel from East to West, except by risking their lives. Movement from West to East was also desperately restricted. West Germans could still theoretically travel in East Germany, but West Berliners could not so much as enter East Berlin. They could not even telephone to East Berlin. For ordinary people there were no telephone connections at all until 1970. Your brother three blocks up the Friedrichstrasse might just as well have been in Outer Mongolia. The permit agreements negotiated by Brandt and his team in the West Berlin city government brought some limited, temporary relief, but after 1966 the East German authorities hardened their position and demanded fuller 'recognition' as the price for further agreements. There remained only a small office giving permission for visits on 'urgent family affairs', a mere trickle of some 60,000 a year from 1967 to 1969. Even movement between West and West was severely restricted. The transit routes between West Germany and West Berlin remained theoretically open, but the ordinary citizen risked arbitrary harassment if he chose to travel by car rather than plane.

The treaty work, and subsequent German-German negotiations, transformed this situation. The transit journey between West Germany and West Berlin was still an unsettling experience when you made it for the first time, with the frontier fortifications at each end, the special mirrors to search for possible escapees clinging underneath your car, the faint scent of Le Carré in the air. After a few trips it was no more than marginally inconvenient. The transit fees for West Germans and West Berliners were paid in a lump-sum by the Bonn government, which also paid very large sums for distinctly modest improvements in the condition of the roads. Although the East German police collected fines from speeding Mercedes and BMW drivers with vengeful regularity, the risk of serious harassment was reduced to a minimum; unless, of course, one did actually try to help someone to escape. In consequence, the numbers who travelled by land to and from West Berlin increased very significantly, from just over seven million in 1970 to nearly twenty-four million in 1986, while the numbers who went by air actually declined from more than five and a half million to less than four million.

Still more marked was the improvement in access to the East, for this was an improvement virtually 'from scratch'. In March 1972, as the Bundestag began to debate the Moscow and Warsaw treaties, ordinary West Berliners were allowed to visit East Berlin for the first time in six years. Thereafter, such visits became increasingly routine. This traffic was hard hit by increases in the minimum amount of hard currency which Western visitors had to exchange on each visit — the so-called 'compulsory exchange'. But in 1988 there were still some one and a half million visits by West Berliners to East Germany, of which roughly half were day trips to the other half of the divided city. This annual flow was still probably less than the daily flow of commuters between West London and the surrounding area; but it was a great improvement on nothing. And if one did not physically go to make one's calls on relatives and friends, one could now at least call by phone. Where in 1970 there had been no normal phone calls at all between West and East Berlin, in 1988 there were more than ten million.

Behind these dry statistics were real, profound gains for hundreds of thousands of individual men and women. Yet the value to any West German or West Berliner of easier access to the East was as nothing compared to the value for an East German of travelling to the West. To use an image which in West Germany in the 1980s was widely regarded as inappropriate: the chance of visiting or being visited in prison is nothing compared with the chance of leaving prison, even for a short 'leave-out'. The crucial statistics therefore concerned the movement of Germans from East to West. The basic numbers are given in Tables VI and VIII, but so great was the importance attached to these figures by successive governments that it is worth examining them more closely.

From Germany to Germany

There were two kinds of journey 'from Germany to Germany': the temporary and the permanent. In the sixteen years between the end of the war in Europe and the building of the Berlin Wall, some three and a half million Germans moved permanently to the West from what was then still referred to as 'the Zone'. Most would then have said that they 'fled' or 'chose freedom'. The young, the better educated and the enterprising were disproportionately represented in this great movement of people. Many subsequently attained high positions in the Federal Republic, among them Hans-Dietrich Genscher, who, in 1952, at the age of twenty-five, left his native town of Halle to start a new life in the Federal Republic, first as a junior lawyer and then as a politician. Yet as Genscher himself acknowledged, his heart remained in Halle. Together with those who had earlier fled from Germany's former territories east of the Oder-Neisse line, these natives of East Germany would provide a reservoir of passionate, lasting interest in 'the East' at the very highest levels of West German public life.

After the building of the Berlin Wall had stopped the haemorrhage from what some Western observers then sarcastically referred to as 'the disappearing satellite', the flood was reduced to a trickle. In 1962, only some 21,000 Germans managed to move permanently from East to West, and a mere 4,600 did so with the permission of the East German authorities. In the same year, there were only some 27,000 visits from East to West, and even fewer visitors, since most of those who came were pensioners, invalids, businessmen, functionaries or lorry drivers, making several trips a year. For the ordinary man or woman under pensionable age there was simply no chance whatsoever of visiting or moving to West Germany.

Their freedom of movement to the West was reduced to nil, just at the time when it was gradually becoming easier for Poles, Czechs and Hungarians to travel West. The division of Germany was made deeper when the division of Europe, in this elementary sense, was already beginning to ease around it.

To restore the circulation from East to West was to be the top operative priority of the Bonn government's policy towards the GDR, arguably from 1966, and certainly from 1969. Until the mid-1980s its success was, however, very limited. In the sixteen years from 1968 to 1983 less than a quarter of a million people moved permanently from East Germany to the West: that is, just one person for every fourteen who got out between May 1945 and August 1961. One in three of these, moreover, owed their freedom less to any West German policy than to their own courage and daring. They risked life and limb to cross the German-German border, or, as that become ever more difficult and dangerous, trekked across the more loosely guarded borders from Czechoslovakia or Hungary to Austria or Yugoslavia, and thence to the safe refuge of a West German consulate. There, as we have noted already, the East German could instantaneously become a West German. In the early 1980s the West German government lent on the East German authorities to dismantle the most barbaric features on the German-German border, the automatic shooting devices and minefields, although people were still shot by frontier guards. Apart from this, Bonn's contribution was limited to offering automatic citizenship, followed by practical assistance in starting a new life in the West.

If, however, East Germans were caught and sent to prison for the offence of 'attempting to flee the republic'; if they had been sent to prison for another 'political' offence, such as conscientious objection or outright protest; if they took refuge in West Germany's Permanent Representation in East Berlin, or in a West German embassy elsewhere in Eastern Europe; if they merely applied for permission to leave legally; then the West German authorities were directly involved in attempting to win their freedom. Quantitatively, these 'humanitarian efforts' were, by the 1980s, a relatively small part of the whole network of relations with the GDR. Qualitatively, however, they remained at the very heart of the relationship, from the day the Wall was built until the day the Wall was opened. For nearly thirty years many of the details were shrouded in official secrecy, until unification allowed the main participants to start telling their remarkable stories. Only the barest outlines can be sketched here.

It began with the Protestant church. In June 1962, while attempting to secure the release of church workers imprisoned in the East, a legal representative of the (still formally united) German Protestant church made contact with an East Berlin lawyer, one Wolfgang Vogel. They arranged a deal. In return for three lorry loads of potash, prisoners from an agreed short list were released — to the West. A little later, twenty children divided from their parents by the building of the Wall were also released to the West in a similar way.

In 1963, following an intervention by the publisher Axel Springer, overall responsibility for this 'buying free' of prisoners from the GDR — *Freikauf* — was taken over by the Ministry for All-German Questions, under the then Minister, Rainer Barzel. The Ministry's then representative in Berlin, Ludwig Rehlinger, describes in his memoirs his first, agonising choices as he tried to select 1,000 especially acute or deserving cases from a list of 12,000 known political prisoners in the GDR. Then he was compelled to reduce the 1,000 to 500; the 500 to fifty; the fifty to ten. At the end of the day the GDR allowed the Bonn government to 'buy free' just eight prisoners in 1963. Bonn paid in cash. A West Berlin lawyer, Jürgen Stange, travelled across to East Berlin by *S-Bahn*, with the money in a large unmarked envelope.

When the East German authorities saw that Bonn — and the released prisoners — maintained absolute discretion about this channel, they allowed more human material to be exported through it. In August 1964, the first 'regular' transports went by bus to the frontier. A total of 880 political prisoners would be 'bought free' in 1964, and more than 1,000 in 1965. At this time, the negotiations were mainly conducted by Ludwig Rehlinger and the West Berlin lawyer, Jürgen Stange, with the East Berlin lawyer extraordinary, Wolfgang Vogel, and a certain Heinz Volpert, the senior Stasi officer directly responsible. Initially, they negotiated a price on the head of each prisoner, according to his or her prison sentence, qualifications and 'value' to the communist state. Subsequently, a standard price per head was agreed, although there were still special cases.

When the arrangement was regularised, the Bonn government paid the agreed total sums to a charitable trust of the Protestant church (in the West), the Diaconical Work, which kept a detailed record of what it called 'B-deals'. ('A-deals' were the indirect financing of the Church in East Germany through deliveries of goods, for which the East German authorities then paid the Church in the GDR, in East German Marks.) Ludwig Geissel, the man responsible in the Diaconical Work, arranged for the delivery of goods for that sum, in forms and along channels agreed with his negotiating partners in the GDR. In 1966, the GDR created a special agency called simply Commercial Co-ordination — *KoKo* — the main purpose of which was to maximise hard currency income from this and other sources. The head of *KoKo*, Alexander Schalck, and his deputy Manfred Seidel, would be Geissel's main Eastern partners.

The West German side, sensitive to the charge that this was man-trade, fondly hoped that the goods would benefit not just the state but also the people (*die Menschen*) in the East. Yet in later years the main contingents were of oil, copper, silver and industrial diamonds. And the massive investigation of Schalck's work after unification soon revealed that, from the early 1970s, *KoKo* had immediately and secretly resold many or most of these goods, often through a special firm in Liechtenstein. As an internal *KoKo* paper of 1972 noted: 'The sums are realised by deliveries of goods and turned back into hard currency by sale and manipulation.' So the diaconical supplies were laundered.

What is more, much of the hard currency thus realised was transferred to a special bank account personally controlled by Erich Honecker, and used for purposes as diverse as financing the State's thirtieth anniversary celebrations in 1979, importing Citroën cars for senior functionaries (in summer 1989!), but also importing consumer goods for wider distribution. For example, in November 1976 payment was made from this account for 800,000 pairs of shoes — or, as a retrospective report in *Die Zeit* sharply put it, shoes to the value of 1,072 prisoners.

This extraordinary set-up functioned, albeit with numerous hiccups, variations and elaborations, for more than a quarter century. Its Eastern players, Wolfgang Vogel and above all Alexander Schalck, became, in time, key intermediaries between the top political leaders in the two states. The same channels were used to discuss not just the 'buying free' of political prisoners but also the reunification of families, *Familienzusammenführung*. An especially poignant problem was that of the children cut off from their parents by the building of the Wall. Jürgen Stange estimates that in the autumn of 1961 there may have been some 4,000 of them. The release of many was quietly negotiated through the lawyers, with or without payment. But according to a confidential letter to Chancellor Brandt from the then Minister for Intra-German Relations, Egon Franke, eleven years later, in August 1972, the GDR was still holding more than a thousand such children.

After the ratification of the Basic Treaty, the Brandt government suggested to the GDR that in the twentieth century states would not normally expect to pay ransom, as in the Middle Ages. The Treaty did, after all, speak of 'normal, good neighbourly relations', and the Chancellery trio of Egon Bahr, Horst Ehmke and Günter Gaus proposed to take this seriously. Such cases should be handled directly through the Permanent Representation, and without head money. The East German authorities were deeply affronted. What matchless impudence! What Cold War confrontationism! And they broke off the talks on humanitarian cases. Many people were left literally sitting on packed suitcases. According to Wolfgang Vogel, some who had already been issued with passports actually had them withdrawn.

In this tense situation, Herbert Wehner, whose profound commitment in this field was recognised and respected by colleagues in all parties, travelled to East Berlin with the Free Democrat Wolfgang Mischnick — a fellow Dresdener — to conduct what were officially parliamentary talks with a delegation of East German 'People's Deputies'. The next day, thanks to the good offices of Wolfgang Vogel, the two of them had a long private conversation with Erich Honecker, in his house on the Wandlitzsee just outside Berlin. Although the conversation ranged across the whole palette of German-German affairs, these humanitarian issues were at the very centre of Wehner's personal concern.

Three weeks later Wehner wrote to Willy Brandt, after a talk with the man he referred to simply as 'the lawyer' (that is, Wolfgang Vogel): 'They will get serious about concrete steps in humanitarian questions. One transport can come on 11 July and one on 18 July. Children should come, 45 and again 45.' In a memorandum of a conversation on 17 September 1973, in which Wolfgang Vogel appears to have brought a long verbal message from Erich Honecker, Wehner noted:

Since [Wehner's conversation with Honecker on 31 May] he [Honecker] had ordered and received a report that ca. 300 people have emigrated . . . On 14 September he signed a further list of 178 persons, including 68 children, and ordered that this is to be handled more swiftly than before. He had heard with great concern of the difficulties which had arisen in connection with this humanitarian field, and also for me [Wehner] personally. Here it must not come to any row or break . . .

This from Erich Honecker, who twelve years before had directly overseen the building of the Wall. Oh the humanity of the gaoler!

Talking to Leonid Brezhnev in Moscow a year later, Honecker presented the matter somewhat differently. 'In the matter of family reunification,' he said, according to the East German record,

we are very restrictive. For this I am directly responsible, and permission to leave the GDR is given only with my signature. It is a closely controlled matter, which we have mainly pushed ahead to show good will. And there are many problems with it. Many children who are meant to be brought to their parents in the FRG don't want to leave the GDR, they go to school here, belong to the Pioneers and the FDJ [the Party's mass youth organisations] and are happy with us. Moreover, with this family reunification we get rid of some criminal elements to the FRG. They are treated in the FRG as political cases but in fact they are criminal elements.

Now it would clearly be wrong to conclude that what Honecker was saying to Brezhnev was the plain truth, and to Wehner, varnished duplicity. He was making a pitch to both. And there is considerable evidence that Honecker had a very emotional relationship to Wehner, in which old respect and old guilt were generously mingled. Neither Vogel nor Schalck will aver, in retrospect, that Honecker was moved by any deep humanitarian concern — except, says Vogel, when an old 'antifascist' was involved. For Honecker, both suggest, this was a chance to win credit in the West, display his personal power, earn some hard currency and get rid of some troublemakers at the same time. As Vogel pithily summarises Honecker's attitude: for him it was 'one class enemy less'.

Of course their evidence, too, must be treated with due scepticism. Whatever the mixture of motives, the fact is that from the summer of 1973 onwards, under Honecker's direct control, the procedures do seem to have run more smoothly. Indeed, over the years, to try to escape from the GDR became almost a calculable risk. Even if you were caught and sent to prison, so long as your case was known in the West you could reasonably hope that in one year, or two, or three, you would be summoned out of your cell, given your own clothes and a piece of paper certifying that you had once been a citizen of the GDR, and driven in an unmarked bus to the frontier. Bought free.

By the early 1970s, the price for a 'normal' *Freikauf* was set at DM 40,000. In 1977 the price per head was increased to DM 95,847. Wolfgang Vogel recalled, in an interview after unification, that they had arrived at a figure of DM 96,000 per head and then 'one of the participants said: we must make that figure uneven, so it doesn't look like a price per head'. The payment in cases of family reunification was generally DM 4,500 a head in the 1980s. Until 1983, the total number of men, women and children for whose freedom the West German state paid the East German state fluctuated between nine and thirteen thousand a year, of whom some one to two thousand a year were political prisoners and the rest cases of family reunification. In 1984, for reasons to be explored in more detail below, the total figure jumped dramatically to more than 37,000, and, with the exception of 1987, remained above 20,000 a year until the opening of the Wall. (See Table VIII)

In sum, over the period from 1963 until 1989 nearly 34,000 political prisoners were 'bought free' by the Bonn government, more than 2,000 children reunited with their parents, and more than 250,000 cases of family reunification 'regulated', as Ludwig Rehlinger puts it, with government help. For these humanitarian services, Bonn paid to East Berlin, in cash or kind, a round total of DM 3.5 billion.

Of course not everyone wanted to leave the GDR permanently; and the Federal Republic would have been hard-pressed to take them even if they had. So beyond the humanitarian imperative of 'buying free', the Bonn government's top priority was to persuade the GDR to permit 'ordinary', that is, temporary, travel from East to West. Whereas the channels of humanitarian relief were already working in the 1960s, improvement in this respect was directly related to the opening of German-German relations. Every year between 1965 and 1971 there had, according to the East German statistics, been more than a million visits (but not visit*ors*) from East to West Germany. Most of these travellers were, however, pensioners, plus a much smaller number of invalids, businessmen, athletes, lorry drivers, functionaries and, of course, spies. The East German authorities were not unduly worried if a pensioner or invalid decided to stay in the West. That individual had already given his useful working life to the East German state. Such a 'defection' would save it the cost of pension, housing and medical care. The real sticking point was people who still had some productive capacity for the state to extract.

Then, in May 1972, Egon Bahr finally negotiated his first full treaty with the GDR, outlining the arrangements for traffic (in a broad sense) between the two states. In an accompanying letter his East German counterpart, Michael Kohl, promised that some sorts of travel would become easier. Mostly he listed forms of travel from West to East, but in the penultimate sentence he wrote: 'The government of the German Democratic Republic will enable citizens of the German Democratic Republic to travel to the Federal Republic of Germany on urgent family matters (*dringende Familienangelegenheiten*).' The formula 'urgent family matters', like so much else, stemmed from the earlier negotiations in a divided Berlin. This central desire of the East German people and the West German government was thus first formally acknowledged in the penultimate sentence of a letter accompanying a treaty about traffic.

Five months later, the East German Interior Minister and Chief of the People's Police issued a directive according to which GDR citizens could in theory be permitted to visit 'non-socialist states' and 'Westberlin', at the invitation of relatives, on urgent family matters. 'Urgent family matters,' declared this directive, ' . . . are births, marriages, life-threatening illnesses and cases of death (*Sterbefälle*). The presence of these grounds is to be proven by legal instruments or official medical attestation.' Relatives were defined as grandparents, parents, children or siblings.

As we have noted already, a letter accompanying the Basic Treaty then had the GDR promising to take further steps to reunite divided families, and to improve the flow of visitors and 'non-commercial goods'. A set of detailed notes explained that silver and golden wedding anniversaries would also count as 'urgent family matters' and that half-sisters or half-brothers *with the same mother* would also count as relatives. (Why not, one wonders, half-sisters or half-brothers with the same father?) In a further directive of June 1973, the East German Interior Minister and Chief of the People's Police generously threw in '60th, 65th and 70th wedding anniversaries'.

According to the official West German statistics, the practical upshot of this grotesque small print was that some thirty to forty thousand East Germans under pensionable age were allowed out in 1973 for short visits to West Germany. The happy few were carefully selected. They almost invariably had to leave their spouse and children behind. The occasion for their going was as likely to be a mother's funeral as a brother's wedding. But still, they went: and often they were travelling 'from Germany to Germany' for the first time in their lives. The numbers remained relatively constant for ten years, until 1982.

In the mid-1980s, however, there was a significant increase in this 'ordinary' travel to the West, facilitated by a new travel decree of February 1982. The numbers rose to more than 60,000 a year, from 1983 to 1985, then quite dramatically to levels undreamed of since the building of the Wall. According to the (incomplete) West German statistics, there were more than a quarter of a million such visits in 1986, and over 1.2 million in 1987 and again in 1988. This meant that something like one in every six East Germans under pensionable age was able to travel to West Germany in 1988. If one included pensioners, then the total number of visits to the West in 1988 was over six million — more than in the other direction!

This 'ordinary' travel still went under the extraordinary rubric of 'urgent family matters'. In fact such high figures were only achieved by an arbitrary, politically ordered 'stretching the rules' by the responsible East German officials. In 1987–88 it was said that you could almost invent a relative in West Germany. The introduction in January 1989 of precise, legal regulations on travel thus threatened initially to be regress rather than progress, and was sharply criticised as such by the Protestant church in East Germany. In the first months of 1989 it emerged that these rules, too, could be stretched. The improvement nonetheless remained arbitrary and reversible — until the opening of the frontier between Hungary and Austria changed not the rules but the whole game.

What had been achieved in this respect by early 1989 was thus still very, very far from 'normality' in any normal usage of the word. According to a thorough survey commissioned by the Bonn government no less than eighty-four per cent of a representative sample of West Germans said they had 'no contacts' with East Germans in 1988. Even among the West Berliners there were many who lived from one year to the next without ever visiting the people next door. For an ordinary East German, travel to the West was still an almost miraculous experience, at once uplifting and deeply disturbing.

The travel possibilities for East Germans were not even 'normal' by the much more modest norms of the rest of Eastern Europe. In this respect, Poland, Hungary and Czechoslovakia had been ahead in the 1960s, and remained ahead, despite political setbacks and currency restrictions, in the 1980s. In early 1989, the possibility of travel to the West remained the exception for most East Germans, whereas it was by now the rule for most Poles and Hungarians. Poles and Hungarians could also routinely take their wives and children with them.

So by comparison with the division of the rest of Europe, the division of Germany in this elementary sense was still exceptionally acute. By comparison with the division of Germany after August 1961, however, the improvement was spectacular.

'For me,' said Chancellor Kohl in his 1987 state of the nation address, 'this development is the most important achievement of our Deutschlandpolitik so far'. When he said 'our' he surely meant in the first instance his own government. Yet most Christian Democrats would have agreed that the 'our' had also to refer to the whole consistent, patient policy of the Federal Republic, with the operative ends broadly agreed by all the main parties since 1966, while the operative means changed only slightly with the transition from Social to Christian Democrats in 1982.

Permanent negotiation

What, then, were the means by which Bonn attempted to influence Erich Honecker and the rest of his regime to concede these improvements? Indirectly, Bonn's whole Ostpolitik was designed to create an overall atmosphere of East-West détente, and relaxation in the GDR's neighbouring communist states, so that a repressive regime in East Berlin would increasingly stick out like a sore thumb — and feel itself to be so. Implicit or even explicit appeals to Moscow to lean on East Berlin were also an important part of this overall conception.

Directly, Bonn's first means of influencing the East German regime was continuous negotiation. Thus the minute of a 'meeting about GDR-issues' in the Chancellery on 21 June 1974, a month after Helmut Schmidt had become Chancellor and just as the Permanent Representations were beginning their work, is basically a list of subjects for negotiation — the special arrangements for intra-German trade, electricity supplies for Berlin, the 'compulsory exchange' of hard currency for Western visitors, transit to Berlin, humanitarian questions, projects of industrial co-operation. 'Summing up,' the minute notes, 'the Federal Chancellor said it is in our interest to put together relatively soon a palette of points on which we are ready to negotiate. In this we should use to our advantage the well-known interests of the GDR.'

Thereafter the Permanent Representative, and other West German public servants, engaged in innumerable rounds of negotiation between the two states. For hours, days, weeks, they would meet with Schalck, Vogel, or more regular functionaries such as Karl Seidel, the head of the 'FRG Department' in the East German Foreign Ministry. The day-to-day internal minutes and correspondence on Deutschlandpolitik to be found in the Schmidt papers are almost entirely concerned with the modalities and substance of these negotiations. In the 1980s, there were also a growing number of meetings between senior West German politicians and the political leaders of the GDR — above all, Honecker and Mittag.

There was a great deal to talk about. But in Bonn's view the negotiations were not just a means to specific ends. They were, taken altogether, a means to a more general end, indeed almost an end in themselves. This end was to reduce the bristling barriers of hostility, the complexes and neuroses of the powerholders in East Germany, and to replace the confrontation with a stable relationship of calm, reasonable dealing, and eventually, trust and co-operation. Initially, this somewhat resembled one of those conversations over the radio with aircraft hijackers. Whatever you do, say the hijack experts, you must keep them talking. Later, the dialogue became so broad and regular that such a comparison seemed increasingly inappropriate, although the raw resemblance would keep breaking through — when, for example, men, women and children took refuge in the Permanent Representation in East Berlin, or in West German embassies elsewhere in Eastern Europe, pleading for West Germany to set them free.

While the East German side would often capriciously refuse to talk, or suspend existing talks, the West German aim might be summarised as a Permanent Representation engaged in permanent negotiation. Over these years of dialogue and negotiation a certain style developed in the West German approach to German-German relations, a style which was also substance. In internal notes for the preparation of Schmidt's 1981 state of the nation address we read: '1. *Introduction*: 20 years after the Berlin Wall. 10 years after the Basic Treaty and Quadripartite Agreement. Necessary: prudence, persistence, predictability (*Behutsamkeit, Beharrlichkeit, Berechenbarkeit*).' These three key-words sum up the style. The representatives of West Germany would be low-key, modest, careful, cautious, calm, steady, discreet, responsible. The East Germans should know exactly where they stood with them. No surprises! This style was significantly influenced by the leaders of the Protestant church in East Germany, who had themselves 'recognised' the GDR earlier than the Federal Government by forming a separate church structure in the East, defined themselves ideologically as the 'church in socialism', and developed their own top-level dialogue with the Party leadership.

Yet, as we have seen already, this public piety sometimes went together with, and covered, secret and even conspiratorial dealings with the party-state. This was true of some (though not all) of the Bonn government's negotiators, as also of the Protestant church's chief negotiator, Manfred Stolpe. After unification, when Stolpe became the Social Democrat Prime Minister of the new-old state of Brandenburg, the nature of his contacts with the East German regime, and above all with the Stasi, would figure beside the discussion about Schalck as one of the great retrospective test cases of German-German relations — trials in the first place by the media, in the second place by parliamentary commissions, and only thirdly by the courts.

Stolpe's was a 'borderline case' in every meaning of the phrase. Yet it was also of far from marginal importance for the history of German-German relations. 'Stolpe was a détente politician,' wrote Antje Vollmer, in a perceptive comment. And defending the man in whose cabinet he had, after unification, gone to serve, West Germany's former Permanent Representative in East Berlin, Hans Otto Bräutigam, would say: 'I feel myself close to Stolpe's methods.' Whether, at the time Bräutigam made this generous defence, he knew about all of Stolpe's methods, is another question. But it is clearly true that in trying to work 'for the good of the people' key representatives of the Bonn government, as of the Church, often found themselves — *nolens volens* — alone in a misty no-man's land, with nothing but their own internal compass to rely on. Inevitably, some kept their bearings better than others.

The details of these strange encounters have more than a few overtones of black comedy. When Günter Gaus first made contact with Schalck, the East German insisted that they should meet on a parking lot up the road from the Permanent Representation. Gaus recalls telling his secretary: 'if I haven't rung in by six, alert the government!'. On a corner of the parking lot, Schalck waited in his Volvo, flashing his headlights in signal of greeting. As a scene for a spy movie this would hardly have passed muster. Some liked this conspiratorial style, others did not. Hans Otto Bräutigam recalls being heartily relieved when he could pass Schalck on to other partners in Bonn, after one or two meetings. Conspiracy was not his thing — and precisely in this, his methods differed very much from Stolpe's.

Franz Josef Strauss, by contrast, seems to have revelled in it. His secret communications with Schalck are riddled with terms such as 'the acquaintance', 'the partner', 'No.1', and even the 'third man' — a resonant phrase for British spy afficionados. Yet on inspection the German 'third man' turns out to be nothing more mysterious than the Chancellery Minister then responsible for relations with the GDR, Philipp Jenninger. Jenninger's successor, Wolfgang Schäuble, tried to regularise the encounters with Schalck a little, receiving that jovial conspirator quite normally in the Federal Chancellery. But when Schäuble visited East Berlin, he still found himself meeting Schalck semi-secretly in the office of the lawyer extraordinary, Wolfgang Vogel.

In the private as in the public talks, style and substance, medium and message, cannot be entirely separated, and the outward forms of these meetings surely are a legitimate subject of retrospective inquiry. Yet the medium could not be the only message. So what were those 'well-known interests of the GDR' to which Helmut Schmidt referred? For all the complexities of particular negotiations, in general terms one can say that throughout the history of German-German relations, starting already with the first negotiations in Berlin in the early 1960s, the GDR demanded payment in two currencies: DM and recognition. And, again with slight oversimplification, one can say that the payments made to the GDR in both currencies steadily increased from the late 1960s until the late 1980s, reaching a high-point some three years before the GDR ceased to exist.

The German Mark

The economic relations between the two states in Germany were, of course, exceedingly complex, and could not simply be described as Bonn 'paying' East Berlin. At the time, the true facts were very difficult to come by, due to official secrecy, incomplete or positively false statistics, and often inadequate analysis. Even after the end of the GDR, the web is still hard to disentangle. Our account can therefore only be sketchy and provisional, pending the necessary masterwork on this theme. Roughly speaking, one can divide the relationship into four intersecting circles: trade, hard currency transfers to private individuals in the GDR, hard currency transfers to the state, and government-guaranteed credits.

As already mentioned, for purposes of trade the two states in Germany had recognised each other from the very beginning. What is more, a protocol to the Treaty of Rome confirmed that in the new European Communities this 'intra-German trade', as Bonn called it, would continue to be treated as 'a part of German internal trade'. The Federal Republic consistently maintained that position, despite a steady drizzle of discontent from its EC partners, who spoke darkly of East Germany's 'secret membership' of the European Community and sometimes raised quite specific complaints about external goods finding their way on to West European markets through this shady back-door.

For political reasons — 'keeping together the nation' — the Federal Republic consistently encouraged this trade, offering duty-free access to East German goods, tax concessions, and an interest-free overdraft facility, the so-called 'Swing'. For economic reasons, the GDR consistently took advantage of these extraordinary privileges, despite the obvious slight to its sovereignty that they implied. One particular advantage was the ability to obtain urgently needed supplies or services at very short notice. Since, like all planned economies, the East German economy excelled in the production of bottlenecks, this was important. At the same time, for political reasons, the GDR tried hard not to become too exclusively dependent on trade with the Federal Republic.

Yet by the end of the 1980s, West Germany was far and away its largest trading partner in the West. Although its own published statistics deliberately concealed this dependence, more than half of its Western trade was with the Federal Republic. The Leipzig trade fair had become not merely an annual celebration of this trade, but a national political event, regularly attended by the East German party leader and by senior politicians from West Germany.

The Schmidt government did rather cautiously use the renegotiation of the Swing facility in 1974–5 as a card in overall negotiations, and partly for this reason secured a partial reduction of the compulsory exchange tariff for Western visitors, after a sharp increase in 1973. It even more cautiously tried to make such a linkage, with less success, when the Swing facility was renewed in 1980–81. In 1985, the Kohl government privately — that is, in talks between Schäuble and Schalck — made the extension of the Swing dependent on the GDR stopping the flow of Tamil refugees (who were flying into East Berlin airport and then taking the *S-Bahn* to West Berlin, where they asked for asylum). This the GDR did, only to let a flow of refugees from other countries use the same route a few months later. In sum this was hardly a record of very heavy or successful linkage. But for a simple reason: Bonn's own political interest in the maintenance of this trade was as strong as East Berlin's economic interest.

Much more directly connected to the development of German-German relations was the dramatic increase in public and private transfers of hard currency. Again, the picture is a complex one. Many of these transfers directly benefited ordinary people in the GDR (who were first legally permitted to possess DM in 1972). Such was the case, for example, with the 'welcome money' paid to every East German visitor by the West German government, a small enough sum in itself, but a goodly total of some DM 2 billion over the twenty years from 1970 to 1989. So also with the private presents in cash or kind that flowed across the border from West to East.

The party-state took a handsome profit on many of these transfers, when, for example, the money was spent in its hard-currency 'Intershops'. In hard currency terms, it made an even more outrageous profit by selling East German products to East German consumers for hard currency, through the so-called 'Genex' service company, a wholly-owned subsidiary of the communist party. (In particular, this was a way for East Germans to jump the sometimes ten-year-long queue for domestically produced cars.) At the same time, the Federal Republic made generous lump-sum payments to cover the real or alleged postal costs of sending presents from West to East. A leading specialist estimates that the total value of all these direct or indirect transfers to private citizens was a formidable 30 to 40 billion D-mark over the twenty years (1970–89). Yet at the end of the day, benefits clearly were enjoyed not just by the state but by private persons, *die Menschen*.

The substantial transfers from the West to the East German Protestant church — at a cost of DM 2.2 billion from 1970 to 1989, of which roughly half actually came from the Bonn government — also directly benefited the party-state. As the (West German) Protestant Church's middleman,

Ludwig Geissel, himself notes in his memoirs, he was able to arrange for the supply of goods which the GDR would otherwise have had difficulty in obtaining. Many of the goods were also laundered back into cash by *KoKo*. However, the East Marks which the party-state paid the East German Protestant church in return benefited not the Communists but believers in a God that did not fail. All this was also helping the people and holding together the nation. And to keep these large sums in perspective, it must be emphasised that other East European states (and peoples) also benefited very substantially from private or semi-private transfers in the 1980s. Thus, to give just one example, hard-currency transfers to Poland from Poles abroad were estimated to be of the order of $1–1.5 billion a year at the end of the 1980s.

In an intermediate category were the visa fees and the compulsory exchange of currency demanded of Western visitors. West German specialists estimated that the state took some DM 5 billion from this source alone over the two decades, as well as making additional hard-currency income from the 'Intertank' petrol stations which Western visitors were obliged to use, and the Intershops on transit routes. As we have seen, the West German government pressed hard, but with only marginal success, to have the compulsory exchange reduced. This hard currency went straight to the state. But at least the visitors went to the people.

The direct state-to-state transfers were the subject of more direct negotiation. They fell into three main categories. Firstly, there were the payments to buy people free: some DM 3.5 billion in all, of which about DM 3.2 billion was paid in the years 1970–89. Secondly, there were the 'transit fees' for people travelling to and from West Berlin. Following a suggestion originally made by Willy Brandt to Piotr Abrassimov, the Soviet ambassador to East Berlin, the two states agreed in the early 1970s that Bonn should make a lump-sum payment for the transit and other 'road-use' fees exacted by the GDR. In the second half of the 1970s these were DM 400 million a year, in the 1980s DM 575 million a year, and if the GDR had survived into the 1990s it would, under an agreement signed in October 1988, have got no less than DM 915 million a year from 1990 until 1999. The total actually paid over two decades was a round DM 8.3 billion. Thirdly, there were investments in road, rail and canal links between West Germany and West Berlin, as well as such minor details as taking West Berlin sewage or West German rubbish. These payments totalled more than DM 2.4 billion.

Clearly Bonn did not give everything for nothing in these transactions. It paid for the freedom of more than a quarter of a million people in the first case, and for the well-being of the hostage half-city — West Berlin — in the second and third. In the case of the large autumn 1988 agreement on lump-sum transit payments for the 1990s, the papers presented to the Politburo actually include the written draft of an 'informal verbal declaration' — presumably to be made by Schalck to Schäuble — in which the GDR promised to maintain the high level of permissions granted for East Germans to visit the West.

Moreover, the road and rail links were investments in Germany. If ever unification came, they would still be there. Yet even the most passionate advocate could not say with a straight face that Bonn got 'value for money' in any normal sense. It gave at least as much as the investments would have cost in West Germany, while the GDR paid in soft currency for what was usually a worse job. After the demise of the GDR, West German investigators found, not surprisingly, that only a small part of the hard currency payments had gone to the purposes for which they were theoretically provided. So the justification could not be in terms of any normal cost-accounting.

Last but by no means least were the so-called 'billion credits': commercial bank loans of DM 1 billion in summer 1983 and DM 950 million in summer 1984, both initially negotiated by Franz Josef Strauss with Alexander Schalck-Golodkowski, granted on unusually favourable terms by the banks and guaranteed by the Federal Government. At the time, and again after unification, these 'billion credits' provoked a heated discussion about the relationship between money and politics in German-German relations.

Now neither of the Social Democratic Permanent Representatives in East Berlin disputed that Bonn had been financially generous in the period up to 1982. Günter Gaus vigorously argued that it would pay off in other fields over the longer term. Klaus Bölling, Permanent Representative in 1981–82, concluded that 'the principle of a balance of give and take' was not worth much in practical policy. 'If we are serious about national cohesion,' he wrote in 1983, 'we shall always have to give somewhat more than the other side is prepared to. One may call this our vulnerability to blackmail. It is not dishonourable.' At the end of a long decade of Social Democratic policy towards the GDR, Christian Democrats charged them with paying 'cash against hope'. They had given too much for too little, it was said. The Christian Democrats would now look for a strict balance of give and take.

When, therefore, the Christian Democrats not only continued to make all the hard-currency transfers agreed but also negotiated generous new ones, and gave these two unprecedented 'billion credits', the Social Democrats could hardly resist retorting that 'cash against hope' was precisely what the Christian Democrats were now paying. The Christian Democrats replied that, on the contrary, they had secured valuable concessions, although to explain them in detail would be to endanger them. In time, however, they would point to a reduction of the compulsory exchange for pensioners and children, the dismantlement of the automatic shooting devices and some of the minefields along the German-German frontier, a relaxation of the border controls for West German travellers, and, as we have seen, a very significant increase in the numbers of East Germans allowed to travel West. Moreover, the billion credits were, it was argued, a clear and necessary political signal to the GDR that the Federal Republic wished to continue to improve German-German relations even as it deployed the new Nato missiles.

Documents that became available after the end of the GDR do clearly show that Strauss, for all the flattery that he was happy to give (and receive), made these linkages quite plainly in his private talks with Schalck. Thus, for example, Schalck's internal note of their talks in Leipzig in March 1984 refers to 'the complex of problems

— credit offers by West German bank consortia to the Foreign Trade Bank of the GDR.

— decisions of the GDR in the framework of its sovereign rights to determine certain alleviations in travel and visitor traffic.'

Here also are clear references to a reduction in the compulsory exchange, the dismantlement of minefields and automatic shooting devices, keeping open a particular border crossing, as well as the regulation of individual humanitarian cases 'through the well-tried channel Rehlinger/Vogel'.

On the other hand, what also emerged after the end of the GDR was the extent of the hard currency balance of payments deficit which it had run since the early 1970s, and the vital importance of the hard currency transfers and credits from West Germany. There is little doubt that these saved it from having to reschedule its soaring hard-currency debt, as first Poland and then Hungary had to do. The particular significance of the Strauss credits was, Schalck and others now testify, less the actual sums involved than the signal they sent to the international financial markets. In the early 1980s Western banks, having burnt their fingers terribly in Poland, were classifying the whole of Eastern Europe as a bad risk. However, says Schalck, after the announcement of the first Strauss credit, in 1983, the head of the Foreign Trade Bank was soon able to borrow another DM one billion, this time in dollars or yen from commercial banks.

Whether Strauss actually saved the GDR from financial disaster in 1983 is disputed, and, of course, ultimately unprovable. Günter Mittag goes so far as to suggest that without the first Strauss credit there would have been a massive crisis and civil disorders in the GDR, with incalculable consequences. Gerhard Schürer, then head of the GDR's State Plan Commission, and now a calmer and more reliable historical witness, suggests that the most acute crisis actually came earlier, in 1978–81. By 1983, he argues, the GDR had taken strenuous measures to improve its balance of trade and was not on the verge of default, although clearly the Strauss credit did very much help to restore the GDR's financial credibility. As chairman of the key operational Balance of Payments Working Group, he was in a position to know. Yet Schürer also emphatically confirms the growing preoccupation of East Germany's key economic decision-makers with the burgeoning hard-currency debt, and the unique significance of the whole economic and financial relationship with West Germany in attempting to cope with it.

The internal statistics of the GDR in this field are not yet fully available, and when they are it will need a fine combination of auditor, historian and detective to make reliable sense of them. Yet from the available documents and key witnesses we can at least make an informed guess at orders of magnitude. In 1970, the net hard currency debt of the GDR seems to have been about 2 billion Valutamarks (an East German unit of reckoning equal to one DM). By 1980 this 'plinth', as the East German experts called it, had grown to 25 billion Valutamarks.

The main reason for this spectacular growth was Honecker's strategy, drily called 'the unity of economic and social policy', of which more below. Beside other, domestic economic burdens, such as huge basic food price subsidies and a massive housing construction programme, this involved importing significant quantities of goods from the West — and more consumer than producer goods. Not for nothing was Honecker's model of socialism sometimes called 'Jeans and Golf socialism' (where the Golf referred to was not the game but the imported Volkswagen car). The hard currency expended on these imports was not recouped by exports, hence the growing debt.

It should be noted that the strategy which might loosely be described as socialist consumerism was not peculiar to Honecker alone. János Kádár used it in Hungary, although there it was accompanied by genuine (if ultimately insufficient) measures of economic reform. Edward Gierek tried it in Poland, with truly Catholic profligacy, and unaccompanied by any fundamental economic reforms. But nowhere were there more consumer imports, and less substantial reforms, than in the GDR.

The result, for East Germany as for Poland and Hungary, was what might be called a dollar gap (by loose analogy with the dollar gap faced by Western Europe in the late 1940s). Gierek's inability to bridge his dollar gap was one of the main precipitant causes of his fall, and of the birth of Solidarity. Kádár's growing dollar gap ultimately contributed to his fall, and to the more radical reforms initiated by his successors. In fact, Brezhnev was constantly warning Honecker, and other East European leaders, of the dangers of becoming too indebted to the West. The great lesson of what had happened in Poland, he told the Czechoslovak Politburo in spring 1981, was that they should all make sure that their foreign debt 'did not reach a dangerous level'.

A few of Honecker's own colleagues in the Politburo also warned, although the forcefulness and eloquence of those warnings have no doubt grown in fond recollection. Yet Honecker stubbornly refused to change the fundamentals of his political-economic strategy. Mittag, whatever his private reservations, oversaw its implementation. Instead of fundamental reform, or at least a change of strategy, they tried to plug the dollar gap with (West) German marks.

This gap-stopping function of West Germany had a long pre-history. Ludwig Geissel, the West German Protestant church's veteran middleman, recalls the Foreign Trade Minister of the GDR appealing for his help as early as 1958, because the trains were about to stop running in East Germany. Could the church middleman help out, with a rapid delivery of coal? (For which, of course, the GDR would pay in East Marks to the church in the East.) From the mid-1960s, Schalck's *KoKo* had combined the attempt to create an enclave of real-price, market-oriented economic activity with the attempt to exploit the GDR's half-nelson on the Federal Republic. Selling hostages as the first step towards a market economy!

Now Honecker's new domestic political stategy meant a sharply growing need for hard currency. But his new foreign political strategy — above all, in the relationship with West Germany — also offered increasing possibilities of obtaining it. As the need for hard currency grew, so did the responsibility of Schalck, formally in 1972 and again in 1976, *de facto* even more thereafter. Looking back, Karl Seidel, head of the department dealing with West Germany in the East German Foreign Ministry, considers that the need for DM was the single most important driving force behind the GDR's negotiations with the Federal Republic.

How much did they actually get? Here one has first to distinguish between trade conducted by the Foreign Trade Ministry inside the regular framework of the state's economic Plan, and trade, transfers, deals and everything else conducted outside the Plan, mainly in the twilight realms of Schalck. Gerhard Schürer rightly points out that the hard currency earned for the state budget by that ordinary in-Plan trade was, in a given year, between five and eight times as much as the hard currency contributed by Schalck. However, this ordinary trade did clearly benefit very largely from the extraordinary terms of 'intra-German trade'.

So far as the realms of Schalck were concerned, the king of that twilight world would himself claim, after the end of the GDR, that from 1972 to 1989 he 'secured' a remarkable DM 50 billion for the GDR, of which roughly DM 27 billion came from business and DM 23 billion from payments of various kinds from the Federal Republic. However, in conversation with the author Schalck casually mentioned that the figure of DM 23 billion included the DM 9 billion which was agreed for the transit fees for the 1990s, but not actually paid! Making this minor adjustment, we arrive at a round figure of DM 14 billion, which corresponds almost exactly with the total of the West German figures for the actual state-to-state transfers. Beyond this reasonable correlation, however, there is a very large grey area, which contains such elements as Intershop and Intertank, Schalck's subsequently notorious dealings in antiques, weapons, luxuries, the whole web of firms in the West, and a long list of more ordinary goods which were exported by hook or by crook in the increasingly desperate scramble for hard currency.

As we have seen, by no means all of the hard currency Schalck 'secured', to use his own well-chosen term, went into the state budget. The money from the 'church deals' — A, B and C — did not, but much of it went to special accounts used for the purposes of the party leadership. *KoKo* also organised supplies, personally supervised by Mrs Schalck, for the Politburo's residential compound in Wandlitz, a miniature model of socialist consumerism. Other monies clearly went into other holes and pockets. But the contribution of Schalck's whole 'out-of-Plan' area to the state budget was of the order of 2 billion Valutamarks a year in the 1980s. For comparison, this has to be set against a debt service and repayment requirement running at about 5 billion Valutamarks a year.

This was a very substantial contribution to keeping the GDR financially afloat. Taken together with Strauss's billion credits, the income from in-Plan trade with the West, and measures of retrenchment by the GDR itself, it saved the GDR from the kind of financial crunch which contributed so directly to Gierek's downfall. In a broader sense, it contributed to what in the West would be described as the GDR's relative 'stability' — a term whose full meanings, and ambiguities, will be explored more fully later on.

It did not, however, prevent the debt from growing. Exactly how big it grew is not wholly clear. The internal figures used by Schürer and others showed a net debt 'plinth' of nearly 30 billion Valutamarks in 1985 and nearly 35 billion by 1987. A memorandum prepared by Schürer, Schalck and others for the new Party leadership at the end of October 1989 suggested that the net debt could reach a staggering 49 billion Valutamarks by the end of that year. In fact these figures were probably too high. This was partly because Schalck had his own considerable reserves, held mainly in gold, and partly because, since this was a centrally planned economy, the figures were based on fixed, arbitrary exchange rates. While the Valutamark-DM rate was always 1:1, that to the dollar was periodically adjusted. Schalck himself would speak of a final net debt of 38 billion Valutamarks, or some $20 billion. In its own calculations in 1990, the Bundesbank arrived at an even lower figure, of less than 30 billion DM. But in this twilight world, even the Bundesbank could err.

So, amusingly enough, the combination of chronic secrecy and unreal statistics — two characteristic features of communist systems — may actually have made the problem seem even worse than it was. Yet, realistically, it was still bad enough. Meeting weekly, sometimes even daily, in the Balance of Payments Working Group, Schürer, Schalck, the Foreign

Trade Minister Gerhard Beil, and a handful of other key players, found themselves struggling to keep the GDR afloat. In this endeavour, they even sold off many of the GDR's strategic reserves, including arms and ammunition, for hard currency. Yet with every new billion of debt grew their sense of crippling dependency on West Germany.

By 1988, Schürer and Schalck would privately discuss the idea of some sort of 'confederation' with the Federal Republic as the only way out from under this intolerable load. At the same time, Schürer tried — very cautiously — to suggest some correction in the increasingly distorted domestic price and investment policy. Mittag and Honecker slapped down even those modest proposals for change, although Mittag would claim, retrospectively, that he too had been looking for ever closer economic co-operation with West Germany.

When these facts became known in the West, after unification, they were seized on by many as an explanation of the end of the GDR. Quite simply, it was bankrupt! To some extent that was indeed the feeling of those who had to wrestle directly with the problem. And perhaps not only of them. The figures given to the Politburo were slightly less alarming than those known to Schürer, Schalck and their colleagues. Yet Schürer recalls Alfred Neumann, one of very few Politburo members who still spoke his mind, saying to Honecker at a Politburo meeting: 'When you took over the GDR from Walter Ulbricht we had almost no debt, and now we're almost broke!' Egon Krenz knew the true facts directly from Schalck. In a memorandum written as the regime collapsed, in early 1990, the former Politburo member Werner Krolikowski colourfully remarked that the GDR had reached the financial point where an officer in Imperial Germany or Tsarist Russia would have shot himself.

It is indeed plausible to argue that this awareness of crippling debt and dependency undermined any residual faith many East German decision-makers and functionaries may have had in their own system, and hence also undermined their readiness to defend it — especially against a takeover by West Germany, without which the GDR would anyway be broke. The above-mentioned Schürer memorandum of October 1989 predicted that the net debt could soar to as much as 57 billion Valutamarks by the end of 1990.

It is also plausible to argue that among ordinary people in East Germany, the growing role of the DM both in the state's dealings with the West and in their own everyday consumer lives produced an explosive mixture of resentment and longing. Resentment at the double-standards of the rulers and at the new class divide between those who had DM and those who had not. Longing to have not just an Intershop simulacrum of West German consumer society but the real thing: the DM, the whole DM and nothing but the DM. 'Where has all the hard currency gone?' sang the demonstrators in Leipzig in the autumn of 1989, unforgettably, to the tune of 'Where have all the flowers gone?' And then East Germans voted for unification with the DM.

Yet hindsight can also mislead. While this may be the final balance of the financial relations between the two states, it was by no means necessarily the interim, subjective balance drawn up in either state at the time. In particular, we shall have to look more carefully at the attitudes of the man who was clearly the crucial decision-maker. There is much evidence that Honecker always understood little of economics and increasingly lost touch with reality altogether. As in most dictatorships, who would venture to tell him the unvarnished truth? Neumann's outburst in the Politburo was so memorable precisely because it was so exceptional. The capacity of an ageing dictator to repress unpalatable truths should never be underestimated.

Moreover, states do not simply go bankrupt like companies, let alone shoot themselves like honourable Tsarist officers. Honecker and Mittag's political economy was in many ways ruinous and irrational. But considered as a strategy for political survival it was, at some shallower (or was it deeper?) level, quite rational, so long as the Soviet Union was prepared to support the GDR politically, and the Federal Republic was prepared to save it from ruin financially. At least until 1986, those two conditions seemed to apply. And the two were intimately related. West Germany would give its kind of fraternal help to make quite sure that the Soviet Union would not be called on to give its kind of fraternal help.

There is, furthermore, a serious question as to just how realistic a picture West German policy-makers really did have of the depth of East Germany's economic and financial plight. In the early 1980s, those most directly involved clearly saw that the GDR was in a tight spot financially. For the late 1980s, Schäuble recalls Schalck telling him exactly how bad the situation was. Perhaps more important, Schalck recalls Schäuble replying that, if the worst came to the worst, West Germany would help out with another billion credit. So long as the Brezhnev Doctrine still seemed to apply, West Germany would pay to preserve what it called 'stability' in East Germany, although all the time demanding more of those 'improvements for the people' — for the negotiation of which such a stability was held to be a precondition.

Yet outside this very small inner circle, and perhaps even inside it, there were illusions about the economic and financial strength of East Germany — illusions which in turn reinforced Honecker's own. (For surely hard-nosed West German businessmen and politicians would not pay homage to a bankrupt?) In a weighty report prepared to accompany the 1987 state of the nation address, some of West Germany's economic experts did document in minute detail the extent of East Germany's relative economic backwardness. They pointed out, for example, that the average East German cow could produce only 82 per cent of the milk pumped out by the average West German cow, while an East German pig could offer only 75.8 per cent of the pork mustered by its West German counterpart. They did also suggest that the total hard currency transfers from West Germany were probably enough to cover the interest payments on the GDR's foreign debt in the years 1981 and 1982. They nonetheless failed to bring home to most policymakers in Bonn the extent to which the East German economy was already on the rocks.

Did not the official statistics show East Germany outperforming the rest of Eastern Europe? Were not the displays at the Leipzig trade fair or in East Berlin shop windows quite satisfactory, by East Bloc standards of course? Was not Mr Mittag really rather impressive and convincing? (Mittag, says Günter Schabowski, was known in the Politburo as the man who could 'choreograph the West German grande bourgeoisie'.) Did not the World Bank say that per capita income in the GDR was higher than in Britain? The East Germans might have a bad economic system, but they were, after all, still Germans.

On balance it seems fair to say that most Bonn policymakers were not fully aware of how desperate the economic and specifically the financial crisis of the GDR was, and of how crucial a difference their transfers and payments actually made. It was only very late in the day that a few of those at the heart of policy-making realised that they were dealing with a state on tick.

The result was curious. In 1986 an American political scientist, James McAdams, published an article in the journal *Foreign Affairs*. He argued that there had been a remarkable reversal in the relationship between the two German states. In German-German bargaining, East Germany now had the upper hand. With hindsight, the argument may seem slightly absurd. Even at the time it seemed overstated. Yet it was based on a careful study of the subject, and conversations with West German policymakers at that time could indeed give this impression. While the underlying reality may have been that the GDR was getting weaker and more dependent on the Federal Republic, the overlying perception in the mid-1980s was that the GDR was getting stronger, and the Federal Republic therefore needed more than ever to buy its goodwill and co-operation, for the good of the people.

Recognition

This curious reversal brings us to the other currency in which the GDR in general, and Erich Honecker in particular, demanded payment: recognition. The key-word 'recognition' had been the subject of fierce debate in West Germany in the late 1960s and early 1970s. Characteristically, much of the debate had been about fine legal distinctions: the difference, for example, between a recognition in international law and one in constitutional law. But a more important distinction was that between purely diplomatic recognition of the state and a more substantive recognition of the repressive regime.

Christian Democratic opponents of the recognition of the GDR argued passionately that the former necessarily implied, or would almost certainly lead to, the latter. It would therefore be morally unacceptable, an insult to the people suffering under this regime, and an encouragement to that regime to persist in oppressing them. 'We . . . are not prepared,' declared the terminally ill Freiherr von und zu Guttenberg, in a powerful speech to the Bundestag in 1970, 'to heed, respect, let alone recognise realities that bear the name "Injustice".' Was there anyone in the house, he asked, who would seriously maintain that injustice became justice merely because it had lasted for decades? Would anyone in the house have been prepared to make their peace with Hitler, if he had managed to hold on for thirty-seven years? 'I say no, I say three times no. For the same reason there can be no recognition for new injustice on German soil, for Herr Ulbricht.'

Social and Free Democrats replied that the purely diplomatic recognition of the state did not necessarily imply nor automatically lead to political and moral recognition of the system. On the contrary, the recognition of the state was the only practicable way to begin alleviating the hardships imposed by the system. Willy Brandt quoted a remark of the British Prime Minister Harold Wilson to illustrate the difference between the two kinds of recognition. If I go into a zoo and see an elephant, he said, I recognise him as an elephant. But this does not mean that I recognise him in the sense that, say, a scientist, writer or athlete receives 'recognition' for their achievement. The qualified diplomatic recognition of the GDR in 1972 was presented as recognition strictly in the first sense. The elephant was there. He had people under foot. To help those people (*die Menschen*) and keep the people (i.e. the nation) together, one had to do business with the elephant. But one need hang no medals round his neck. Indeed, one might still consider him a monster.

This purely diplomatic recognition was itself sorely desired and highly prized by the GDR, not least because it opened the door to membership of the United Nations and to recognition by the rest of the Western world. Well into the 1980s, East German leaders never tired of trumpeting this achievement. At the celebration of the thirty-fifth anniversary of the GDR, in 1984, Erich Honecker proudly announced that the GDR maintained diplomatic relations with 132 states 'all over the world'. The printed version of his speech actually said 131, but at the last minute the GDR had scored yet another diplomatic triumph, securing recognition from the Ivory Coast.

More seriously, the Honecker regime tried hard to get the Federal Republic to make this diplomatic recognition still more complete. The most important single expression of this was a speech Honecker delivered at Gera in October 1980. Against a background of sharply worsening East-West relations, with the Polish crisis posing a direct challenge to the domestic political stability of the GDR, the East German leader made four demands, of which the most important was that the Federal Republic should fully recognise GDR citizenship. By this, what he actually meant was *de-recognition* of the East Germans' automatic right to West German citizenship, for the Federal Republic already respected anyone's right to keep (or indeed, should they be so curiously inclined, to take) citizenship of the GDR.

The other demands were for the formal conversion of the Permanent Representations into Embassies; the closure of the West German 'Registration Unit' at Salzgitter which recorded incidents in the GDR, including shootings on the border, for which people might one day be prosecuted; and a point about the precise delineation of the border on a stretch in Lower Saxony where it ran along the River Elbe. Although there were important figures, especially among Social Democrats, who advocated conceding at least the lesser of what came to be known as the 'Gera demands', the Bonn government did not change its basic positions, above all on the key question of citizenship.

There was, however, a significant increase in what one might call *de facto* rather than *de jure* recognition. This was not exactly the substantive approval of the communist system which Christian Democrat critics of the new Ostpolitik had feared. But it was a growing substantive approbation, firstly for the humanitarian and other improvements which the Honecker regime had permitted, and secondly for that regime's commitment to preserve what had been achieved in German-German relations at a time of sharply worsening American-Soviet relations. The milestones of this growing political recognition were Helmut Schmidt's meeting with Erich Honecker in East Germany in 1981, and Erich Honecker's visit to West Germany in 1987.

Already in the late 1970s, Herbert Häber, head of the Party's so-called West Department, had extensive informal contacts with politicians of all the main West German parties. Häber's records of his conversations in West Germany, heavily annotated in Honecker's hand and kept in the Politburo's internal archive, suggest a growing ease of intercourse with leading Social Democrats, but also with Free Democrats such as Wolfgang Mischnick and Christian Democrats, such as Walther Leisler Kiep and Lothar Späth. Of course, these records must be handled with care. When Häber reports, for example, the delight expressed by a West German politician on being given a copy of Erich Honecker's autobiography (as published by Robert Maxwell), we clearly need to take this with a large pinch of salt.

Nonetheless, one recurrent and striking feature is the frequency and vehemence with which Haber's interlocutors appear to have criticised American policy, from Carter's human rights campaign to Nato's double-track resolution and from the neutron bomb to Zbigniew Brzezinski — 'a fanatical Polish nationalist', complained the German Social Democrat Hans-Jürgen Wischnewski to the German Communist Herbert Häber. Häber's report after a trip in March 1980, which Honecker circulated to the Politburo, noted that 'there was hardly an interlocutor who did not in some way express distaste for American policy and Carter', although, Häber went on, they also emphasised Bonn's need for alliance solidarity with the United States. From a trip in September 1980, Häber returned to report the characteristically salty observation of the Social Democrat Holger Börner that 'the difference between Carter and Reagan was like that between plague and cholera' — a comment marked in the margin by Honecker.

Formal top-level contacts were, however, still minimal. The first West German minister to visit East Germany officially under the Schmidt government was the Housing Minister in 1978. By the end of the 1970s, the progress made in the continuous negotiation, and the improvements achieved 'for the people', were already felt by many in Bonn to justify a summit meeting. Herbert Wehner, among others, also argued that, for all Honecker's commitment to his political system and the preservation of his own power, the East German leader personally wished to meet certain basic minimum standards of common humanity. Yet Schmidt himself clearly did not attach as high a priority to direct relations with the GDR as his predecessor had done. Despite — perhaps also because of — their conversation in Helsinki in 1975, he at this time still took a fairly contemptuous view of Erich Honecker. Previous East German suggestions of a German-German summit had been brushed aside.

It was only in the run-up to Nato's double-track resolution of December 1979 that Schmidt himself began to push for a summit. If he were to convince colleagues in his own party of the need for the military part of the double-track, he had to demonstrate his own commitment to the détente part. In January 1980, the East German Politburo member and Central Committee Secretary for international relations, Hermann Axen, hurried off to Moscow with a message to Brezhnev and the Soviet leadership. The message was that despite the double-track decision, the East German Politburo wished to go ahead with the planned 'working meeting' between Honecker and Schmidt, 'in order to put pressure on the government of the FRG'. The East German Politburo asked the Soviet Politburo 'for a swift decision on this matter'. So much for the sovereignty of the GDR! A day later, Boris Ponomaryev conveyed the Soviet Polit-buro's answer to Axen. The answer was no. But, Vadim Zagladin consoled Axen at the airport: in a few weeks things might be different.

Fortunately, the grim reaper then started to come to the aid of

East-West relations, and Tito's death in May 1980 provided for the first of what would come to be known as the 'working funerals'. The East German record of Honecker's conversation with Schmidt, on that occasion, records Schmidt observing that the medium-sized and smaller states, such as the Federal Republic, the French and the British, the GDR, Poland and Hungary, had to watch out that 'the really big brothers don't get nervous'. After discussing whether Schmidt should go to visit Brezhnev in Moscow, Schmidt raised the question of a date for his 'working visit' to the GDR. According to the East German record, Honecker said: 'you visit Brezhnev in Moscow first, then we can arrange it'. Both perfectly understood the Bonn-Moscow-Berlin geometry.

Not so long afterwards the summit was rearranged, for August 1980. But fortune would not smile on the plan. This time it was called off by the West German side, because of uncertainties created by the strikes in Poland that gave birth to Solidarity. The movement for freedom, or, as it was more often put, the 'crisis' and 'instability' in Poland, caused the East German leadership to raise its defences against possible infection from its Western as well as its Eastern neighbour. Honecker's 'Gera demands' and the simultaneous doubling of the compulsory exchange tariff for Western visitors could only be understood in this context.

By the time the summit finally happened another leitmotif had been added to the language of German-German relations. To the shared responsibility for basic, minimum human alleviations was now added a shared responsibility for the fate of humankind. Beside talking about the reunification of families, or road and rail links, or postal agreements, or trade, the two sides would now talk about arms control and disarmament. This theme had been present already in the original German-German debates and agreements a decade before. As we have seen, the formula 'war must never again go out from German soil' had been used in the Erfurt meeting and was one of Willy Brandt's twenty points at Kassel. Article 5 of the Basic Treaty committed both states to work for 'peaceful relations between European states', for 'security and co-operation in Europe', and specifically for arms control and disarmament. Yet Bahr's hope that the treaties might might lead on to major reductions of conventional forces in Central Europe had proved vain. It was only a decade later, as the number of weapons in Central Europe was about to increase rather than decrease, that the subject moved to the top of the German-German agenda.

First, Helmut Schmidt and Erich Honecker solemnly exchanged that code-phrase about war never again 'going out from German soil'. Then, at their summit meeting in December 1981, in a hunting lodge on the Werbellinsee, Schmidt urged Honecker to use his influence to modify and moderate the Soviet position on East-West relations in general, and arms control in particular. 'We have signed the nuclear non-proliferation treaty, you and us,' he said. 'The world powers have an obligation to us. We must press the great powers.' And again: 'We don't want to show off. But in truth we both, both German states, have great weight. I believe, Herr Honecker, that we have a right to throw this weight into the scales.'

Although the declaration of martial law in Poland cast a dark shadow over the last day of the summit, Schmidt felt obliged not only to complete his visit, but also to try to preserve so far as possible, atmospherically as well as substantively, what had been achieved in the German-German relationship. So as the leaders of Solidarity were thrown into camps just over the frontier, the two German leaders threw snowballs together in the small town of Güstrow, surrounded by solicitous Stasi men keeping the people at bay. At parting, Honecker handed Schmidt a boiled sweet for his train journey home.

Thereafter, the trajectories of overall East-West and specifically East-West German relations crossed, going in opposite directions. The 'overall weather conditions' deteriorated, but both German states tried to preserve, even to improve, their relations. Herbert Häber noted the Christian Democrat Walther Leisler Kiep observing in February 1982 that in West Germany there was little readiness to sacrifice the gains of détente on account of Poland. There were real concerns on the East German side following the formation of the Kohl government. But in October 1983, scarcely a month before the vote to deploy Nato missiles, Herbert Häber could record the Christian Democrat Prime Minister of Baden-Württemberg, Lothar Späth, saying cheerfully: 'these days it is almost a personal taint [i.e. for a West German politician] if one has not been to meet Erich Honecker'.

A further, crucial step in substantive recognition came after the Bundestag vote to deploy the Nato missiles. As we have seen, instead of freezing relations with West Germany, as Soviet propaganda and some of his own previous utterances suggested he should, Erich Honecker surprisingly announced that the point now was to 'limit the damage' of this deplorable decision. 'As genuine advocates of peace,' he declared, 'we are always guided by the popular wisdom that to negotiate ten times is always better than to fire a single shot.' The popular wisdom was clearly helped along by Strauss's one billion DM credit, and by other signals the Kohl government gave that it had a double-track strategy of its own: to implement the Nato decision, but also to preserve and develop what had been achieved in the intra-German détente. Yet it was by no means a foregone conclusion that Honecker would accept this de-coupling.

The Bonn government could therefore hardly believe its luck when the GDR went on to hold up such notions as a 'coalition of reason' between the two German states. West German leaders, for their part, spoke of a 'community of responsibility'. 'The two states in Germany,' Chancellor Kohl wrote to Honecker on 14 December 1983, 'stand in their relations with each other in a community of responsibility to Europe and to the

German people. Precisely in difficult times in West-East relations, both [states] can make an important contribution to stability and peace in Europe, if they come closer to each other and carry forward what is possible in co-operation.' After defending the deployment and criticising the Soviet response, Kohl went on to say that the Federal Republic would make a positive contribution to the 'constructive continuation' of West-East relations, and expected 'that the German Democratic Republic, too, will allow itself to be guided by a common interest in co-operation, security and peace'.

Two months later, Honecker replied, thanking Kohl for his letter and referring to their telephone conversation on 19 December. His reply was almost a mirror-image of Kohl's own. 'Community of responsibility,' he wrote, 'to use your expression, or better still security partnership, presently means from our point of view first and foremost what both states actively do to improve again the changed situation which has arisen out of the stationing of American medium-range nuclear missiles in Western Europe, and above all in the Federal Republic of Germany.' After further criticism of the American deployment, he observed 'the German Democratic Republic is attempting as far as possible to limit the damage done by the missile deployment'. Turning to German-German relations, he repeated his four Gera demands but nonetheless averred: 'the point is, despite the tense situation, to preserve what has been achieved and where possible to build on it, not least in economic relations'.

Remarkably, this East German line was maintained after Soviet negotiators had walked out of the Geneva arms control talks and while the Soviet press poured a torrent of execration upon Nato in general and the 'revanchist' Federal Republic in particular. Whereas a decade before it had been Honecker who devoutly reasserted, against Ulbricht, the intimate and irrevocable ties between the GDR and the Soviet Union, now it was Honecker who, like Ulbricht, asserted against the Soviet Union the special interests — and superior virtues — of the German communist state. The GDR was joined by Hungary in urging the continuation of dialogue and practical (not least, economic!) co-operation with the West.

At another 'working funeral', this time of Andropov in February 1984, Kohl and Honecker met for the first time, in a guesthouse in the Lenin Hills. Kohl renewed Schmidt's invitation to pay his first-ever visit to the Federal Republic, and thereafter detailed preparations went ahead. Only in September 1984 did the GDR announce that Honecker's visit had been 'postponed'.

The GDR blamed this postponement on offensive commentaries in West Germany, and particularly the remark of the Christian Democrats' parliamentary leader Alfred Dregger that 'the future of the Federal Republic does not depend on whether Herr Honecker pays us the honour of this visit'. (From the horrified reaction in much of the West German media and politics one might almost have gathered that the future of the Federal Republic did depend on Honecker's visit.) Documents that have become available since unification conclusively show what all realistic analysts at the time understood — that the visit was cancelled because of Moscow's objections. As late as mid-August the East German Politburo still seems to have been working on the assumption that it might be possible to go ahead with the visit, despite a sharply critical leading article in *Pravda*.

A dramatic encounter in Moscow on 17 August between a delegation led by Honecker and a full turn-out of the Soviet leadership (including Gorbachev), formally under the dying Chernenko, drew the line. Looking back in 1992, Honecker recounted proudly how he had argued over the table with Marshal Ustinov, and then in the car with Gorbachev, all the way to the airport. But it was no good. Egon Krenz vividly recalls the painful Politburo meeting in East Berlin three days later, when the Soviet 'no' had to be swallowed yet again. Dregger thus merely provided the pretext for cancellation. The Politburo minutes for 28 August record the formal decision to postpone the visit, 'on account of the policy of the government of the FRG' — a statement which everyone round the table knew to be untrue. Yet the same resolution instructed the Permanent Representative of the GDR in Bonn to continue negotiations on the basis of Foreign Ministry plans. Attached was the draft of a joint communiqué on the visit that never was. The East and West German leaders, it said, had exchanged views 'in a businesslike and open atmosphere'.

This remarkable episode, made especially complex by the confused leadership transition in Moscow, deserves to be treated at length in any history of Soviet-East European relations. Most important for our immediate purposes, however, is the impact it had in West Germany. It seems fair to say that this, combined with the demonstrative continuity of German-German relations, and the slow improvements in people-to-people contacts, produced something like a psychological breakthrough in German-German relations. Honecker was given more credit and sympathy than he had ever enjoyed before.

From this time forward there was a subtle transformation of the language in which official representatives of the two German states talked with, and about, each other: a change in the quality of their mutual recognition. This was then greatly facilitated for the GDR by the fair winds of change from Moscow after 1985, and specifically by Soviet 'new thinking' on foreign policy, with its central emphasis on the priority of 'all-human' over 'class' interests.

Now the language of the 'all-human' was, of course, particularly characteristic of Willy Brandt and the social-liberal version of détente. Indeed, as we have seen, Brandt, Bahr and Olof Palme would claim with some justification that the Soviet 'new thinkers' took much of this language directly from them. At the very heart of this vocabulary was the word 'peace'. Yet it was not Brandt but the Christian Democrat Chancellor Kohl who, at the moment of Gorbachev's succession, after meeting again with Erich Honecker on the occasion of Chernenko's funeral, agreed with the East German leader a joint statement which said: 'From German soil war may never again, from German soil *peace must go out*' (my italics).

What on earth did this mean? How could peace 'go out' from German soil? Germany was, of course, famous for its capacity to export an extraordinary range of products — including a lot of weapons — to all parts of the world. Would consignments of peace now be added to the export balance? At one level this was merely a symbolic affirmation of mutual goodwill, such as are common in international relations. A Brazilian tribe discovered by the English traveller Peter Fleming greeted him enthusiastically with the repeated word '*Ticantó! Ticantó!*'. He had no idea what '*Ticantó*' meant, but he found that it helped a great deal to repeat the word often, smiling. The Brazilian tribe said '*Ticantó!*'. The Germans said '*Frieden!*'

At another level, it reflected a genuine conviction that the Germans, through their terrible experience of both causing and suffering war, and their position at the front line of the East-West conflict, had a special responsibility to urge caution, moderation and restraint upon their respective allies. Yet there was also the special interest born of the insight that while German-German relations could, after all, be slightly better than East-West relations overall, they were still painfully dependent on this general East-West climate.

So while the two states continued to disagree fundamentally about the nation and the political system, they found common ground at the lowest level — concerning the fates of individual human beings (*die Menschen*) — and at the highest level — concerning the fate of humankind. By talking about the fate of humankind, Bonn might help a few more individual human beings in Germany. By talking about the fate of individual human beings in Germany, Bonn and East Berlin might also be helping humankind. Sublime harmony!

The symbolic high-point of this mutual recognition was the official visit that Erich Honecker finally paid to the Federal Republic in September 1987. As late as April 1986, Gorbachev was still objecting. How can I explain to the Soviet people, he asked the East German Politburo, that Erich goes to Bonn before me? In summer 1987, with the 'overall weather conditions' significantly improving, the East German leadership prepared the ground with Moscow most carefully. Shortly after President von Weizsäcker's visit to Moscow, which marked the gradual thaw in Soviet-West German relations, they despatched Hermann Axen to Moscow once again, for a 'consultation' to discuss a long document prepared by the East German leadership and entitled 'Analysis of the situation of the FRG — Conclusions for a common policy'.

Axen noted a significant difference between the positive response from Anatoly Dobrynin, the new head of the Central Committee department for international relations, and that of Vadim Medvedev, head of the department for relations with socialist countries. Medvedev counselled greater vigilance against subversive West German influence. 'That sounded exactly as in the old manuscripts', Axen sourly minuted to Honecker. In response, Axen pulled out all the stops: 'The visit would be one of the strongest blows against revanchism in history. The foundation of the GDR in 1949 was the first heavy blow, the Protective Wall in 1961 the second blow, the Basic Treaty and the GDR's accession to the UN in 1972 the third blow. In September 1987 a fourth blow would follow.'

Returning with 'the most cordial, fraternal fighting greetings (*Kampfesgrüsse*)' to Honecker from Gorbachev, Axen was able to report a mission accomplished. In the new style of Soviet-East European relations, the East German leadership did not then (as in 1980) 'ask for a decision' about the visit, but merely informed the Soviet comrades of the details.

Yet it was not only in Moscow that there were residual doubts. On the West German side, Helmut Kohl was very far from enthusiastic about the visit. By Wolfgang Schäuble's own account it was he who persuaded Kohl that, in the logic of the policy they had adopted, it was both inevitable and essential. And if it were to be done, it had better be done properly. Honecker was therefore received in Bonn with virtually all the honours usually given to the head of a completely sovereign, foreign state. Two different German flags hung before the Federal Chancellery, the West German army band played two different anthems, two German leaders stood to attention side by side.

Kohl began his keynote dinner speech — actually delivered before dinner so that viewers in both German states could watch it on prime-time television — with a powerful reaffirmation of his belief in German unity. Millions of Germans between Stralsund and Konstanz, between Flensburg and Dresden, and in Berlin — he said — were watching, often with divided feelings. 'The awareness of the unity of the nation is as alive as ever,' he went on, 'and the will to preserve it is unbroken.' Recalling the words of the preamble to the Basic Law, he declared that to complete the unity and freedom of Germany in free self-determination remained the goal, 'and we have do doubt that this reflects the wish and the will, yes, the yearning of the people in Germany'. And again: 'the people in Germany suffer from the partition. They suffer from a Wall which literally stands in their way, and repels them.'

The Stasi closely monitored popular reaction in the GDR. Its Central Evaluation and Information Group reported on 9 September that the contents of the dinner speeches had thus far been the centre of attention. 'Progressive forces' were critical of Kohl's 'presumptuous attitude', but 'hostile-negative forces' were encouraged, 'especially by his comments on the human rights problem'. Six months later, talking to the Free Democrat Otto Graf Lambsdorff, Honecker remarked, according to the East German record: 'The GDR shows great patience. He had calmly listened to the speech of Chancellor Kohl at the meal in Bonn. We had even published it.' A testimony to the impact of the speech — but also to the fact that Honecker thought the risk worth taking. For beside making these points, very forcefully indeed, to the united television nation, Chancellor Kohl also said other things.

This visit, he observed, was another step on the way to a *geregeltes Miteinander*, a 'regulated with-each-other'. (In 1969, Brandt had actually spoken of moving from a regulated next-to-each-other to a with-each-other, but perhaps the regulated with-each-other was an intermediate phase, like that of 'developed socialism' in the GDR.) Kohl gave two main reasons for thinking that the two states might now feel themselves to be 'with' rather than merely 'next to' each other. Firstly, there were the fruits of 'practical co-operation' between the two German states over the fifteen years since the Treaty on the Bases of Relations. 'With our practical co-operation despite all differences,' he said, 'we have given an example — for the well-being of people and in the interest of peace.' It behoves 'the people of Lessing, Schiller and Goethe', he explained, to display, in their dealings with each other, *Humanität* — a word beloved of Thomas Mann and only weakly translated as 'humanity' or 'humaneness'.

Secondly, the Germans in East and West had a special obligation to do 'works of peace' because

In this century terrible havoc and suffering has gone out from German soil. For that reason too it is the task of the two states in Germany to contribute to an improvement of the political climate and to confidence-building in West-East relations by the extension of their co-operation. It seems to me obvious that our governments have to press for arms control and disarmament in the framework of overall East-West negotiations.

And then he spoke of realism, recognising the limits of German possibilities, and again of the incompatibility of the political orders in the two states.

Honecker also started with the theme of realism and incompatibility. 'Socialism and capitalism,' he said, 'can no more be combined than fire and water' — a sentence that Chancellor Kohl quoted, with approval, in his state of the nation address a month later. Later in his speech, Honecker made clear his different approach to the German question, though rather by omission than by explicit statement, and to human rights. Kohl had linked the issues of peace and human rights in his almost Papal formulation that 'peace begins with respect for the absolute and unconditional dignity of the individual person in all areas of his life.' Honecker kept the two issues carefully apart, but said that human rights, 'in the complete complex of political, civil, economic and social rights, find their daily realisation in practical life in the German Democratic Republic . . .'

In between these conflicting positions, however, he restated two basic points that Kohl had made. First, that 'co-operation instead of confrontation' had 'brought good results for the states, for the people (*die Menschen*), not least for the two German states and their citizens' — although he ascribed these 'good results' somewhat pointedly to the détente of the 1970s. Secondly, that the two German states had a special responsibility to be particularly active in promoting peace, disarmament and détente.

He declared that in their joint statement of March 1985, and now again, the two leaders had agreed that everything must be done so that 'never again war, but *always only peace* will go out from German soil' (my italics) — a further rise in the rhetorical bidding. Continuing the exchanges of code-phrases, he said 'we are in favour of realising the thesis of "creating peace with ever fewer weapons" (*Frieden schaffen mit immer weniger Waffen*)'. He thus adopted Kohl's slogan for multilateral disarmament in preference to the original formula for unilateral disarmament — 'create peace without weapons' (*Frieden schaffen ohne Waffen*) — coined by the peace movement in West Germany, and then adopted by independent peace initiatives in East Germany.

Their joint communiqué summarised the two main points, saying that the two states 'in the light of a responsibility arising from the common history, must make special efforts for peaceful living-together in Europe'. Then came the familiar pathos-laden sentence: 'From German soil war may never again, from German soil only peace must go out.' The relationship between the two states, 'must remain a stabilising factor for constructive West-East relations'. It should give 'positive impulses for peaceful co-operation and dialogue in Europe and beyond'. There followed a long list of areas in both West-East German relations and the East-West security dialogue where the leaders agreed that progress had been made or could be made.

In one sense, this remarkable consensus and harmony was not surprising, since few official visits in recent history had been prepared with such exhaustive thoroughness. Moreover, most of the ideas expressed, indeed the very phrases used, had been tried out, swapped, trimmed and polished in what one might now call the national political conversation — direct and indirect, official and unofficial — between the two German states. But in the perspective of forty years, or even of fifteen, it was quite extraordinary.

After signing the Basic Treaty, Egon Bahr had remarked that after having no relations the two German states would now at least have bad ones. Fifteen years later this looked remarkably like good relations. Here they were, the man who styled himself 'Adenauer's grandson' and the man who directly supervised the building of the Berlin Wall for Walter Ulbricht, agreeing not only to disagree, and where they disagreed, and roughly why they disagreed — in itself no mean achievement — but further agreeing that the two German states had common interests and common goals. And no minor goals at that: for what could be more important than 'humanity' and 'peace'? Mutual recognition had indeed reached a new stage.

But who would recognise the recognition? Germany's European neigh-bours, and the part-European superpowers, certainly 'recognised' this remarkable rapprochement in a narrower sense of recognition. They saw it happening. They adjusted to it. The increase in the diplomatic and political attention other Western states paid to East Germany was directly related to the growth in West Germany's engagement there. Over the next year, Honecker would pay official visits to Belgium, Spain, and, most notably, to France. (Despite strenuous East German efforts, the other Western Allies, America and Britain, were less forthcoming.)

Whether they recognised the German-German achievement in the larger sense of substantive approbation, is a different question. The first German-German common goal, that of more practical co-operation 'for the people' was relatively unproblematic. This was not true of the other common theme: that of the two German states as heavenly twins, separately, yet somehow in spirit together, urging 'peace, disarmament and détente' upon their respective alliances and a recalcitrant world.

Far from endorsing this vision, the Polish People's Republic redoubled its efforts to recapture from the GDR the position it had enjoyed in the 1970s as the West's favoured partner in Eastern Europe. The French Republic redoubled its efforts to bind the Federal Republic ever more closely into the West European web, offering hitherto unexposed charms, such as a Franco-German Joint Brigade and Defence Council, with the vague distant promise of something like that (West) European Army which had been vetoed — in Paris — more than thirty years before.

As for the superpowers, they promptly held their own summit, in which there was a great deal of talk about peace, disarmament and détente, but much less about the particular initiatives or aspirations of the European powers, whether West, Central or Eastern. There was, however, one specifically German point on the agenda of the December 1987 Washing-ton summit. Under 'regional issues', point 9, 'Presidential Initiative on Berlin', this recalled President Reagan's dramatic appeal to Gorbachev in June 1987 to open the Brandenburg Gate and 'tear down' the Berlin Wall. Scant recognition there.

Publicistic reaction to the German-German summit was even more mixed. As usual, there was a large dose of exaggerated — if historically explicable — fear and doubt in many of these commentaries. It has been well said of West Germany, and to a lesser degree of the whole of Western Europe, that it was unhappy when the superpowers got too far apart, as in the so-called 'second Cold War' of the early 1980s, but also when they got too close together, as in the Nixon-Brezhnev détente of the early 1970s. Yet the same might be said, as it were in reverse, about the superpowers' attitude to the two German states: worried if they were too far apart, as in the mid-1960s, but equally worried if they got too close together. Yet both sets of fears — those of the small about the large and those of the large about the (relatively) small — had a rational kernel.

The rational kernel of Western doubts about the German-German rapprochement in the 1980s was presciently formulated by Pierre Hassner. As early as 1983 he argued that West Germany, having for a long time denied the very existence of the GDR, seeing its government as wholly unrepresentative of its people and entirely dependent on the Soviet Union, was now in danger of swinging to the opposite extreme, greatly underrating, or at least under*stating*, the differences between state and society, and the degree of the GDR's continued dependency on the Soviet Union. From the absurd extreme of complete non-recognition in the 1950s it was in danger of swinging to the opposite extreme of exaggerated recognition, in the substantive-approbatory as well as the formal-instrumental sense. To recall Willy Brandt's image of the man contemplating an elephant in the zoo: whereas in the 1950s Bonn was absurdly saying 'we see no elephant!', it now seemed almost to be saying 'what a charming eagle!'.

So far as the GDR's real ability — rather than merely wish — to influence its own 'alliance' in the direction of 'peace, disarmament and détente' was concerned, the evidence was slight. In the early 1980s it had come sharply up against the limits of Soviet tolerance, and retreated. Since 1985 it had, in foreign policy, been following Gorbachev's lead, albeit with its own particular emphases carried forward from the earlier period.

To be sure, a frank and intensive 'security dialogue' between governments in East and West had probably helped to keep the GDR, Hungary and Poland firmly behind Moscow's 'new thinking' in foreign policy. In some details of arms control and military doctrine these countries had indeed been marginally more specific, or, from the Western point of view, more 'helpful' than Moscow. Other Western governments therefore agreed on the value of maintaining this dialogue. Yet no one would have dreamed of comparing, say, Poland's role in the Warsaw Pact with Britain's role in Nato.

Now plainly, if pressed, most serious politicians in Bonn would have acknowledged the deep asymmetry between the Federal Republic's role, influence and room for manoeuvre in Nato, and that of the GDR inside the Warsaw Pact. To be sure, there were still unique restrictions on West Germany's sovereignty. But could anyone imagine an American President telling a West German Chancellor not to visit the GDR? The point is, however, that in Bonn it was no longer thought useful to dwell too much on these differences. Just as there should be said and seen to be the greatest possible harmony between German and European interests, so now there should be said and seen to be the greatest possible harmony between West and East German interests in foreign policy. Hence the rhetoric of explicit or implied symmetry. The danger here was that if the differences were not clearly recalled, they might, in time, cease to be seen at all. As the Christian Democratic specialist on foreign policy, Alois Mertes, observed in 1982: 'It's a short step from calling things the same (*Gleichbenennung*) to valuing things the same (*Gleichbewertung*).'

The other, still more serious, reason why this political recognition seemed exaggerated was the internal condition of the GDR. For the main way in which the GDR asserted its limited sovereignty and autonomy from the Soviet Union after 1985 was in resisting the application of Gorbachev's glasnost and perestroika to its own internal affairs. This it did with quite as much passion as it displayed in embracing the 'new thinking' in foreign policy; indeed with extraordinary frankness. In the spring of 1987 the West German magazine *Stern* asked the GDR's elderly chief ideologist, Kurt Hager, whether there would be perestroika in the GDR. At the end of a long answer, Hager made a remark that rapidly became famous: 'Incidentally,' he said, 'if your neighbour put up some new wallpaper, would you feel obliged to do the same in your own apartment?' So according to the chief ideologist of the GDR, Gorbachev's second Russian revolution was no more than wallpapering.

Whatever the improvement in the GDR's foreign policy, whatever the concessions it made on Western contacts, emigration and travel across its frontiers, what still mattered most to most people in East Germany was how the state treated them inside those frontiers.

Liberalisation through stabilisation?

How did West German policymakers hope or imagine their policy towards the GDR would change, or actually was changing, the domestic politics of the GDR? At the very beginning of Ostpolitik there was one rather clear hypothesis, or set of hypotheses, advanced on this crucial question. The basic lesson of the Cold War, it was argued, was that an aggressive posture by the West had led, compelled or at least encouraged the communist rulers in the East to adopt an aggressive posture, not only towards the West but also towards their own people. Such an aggressive 'Cold War' posture therefore produced the precise opposite of the intended effect. Instead of softening the regimes it hardened them. 'Increasing tension strengthens Ulbricht and deepens the division,' as Bahr plainly put it in his Tutzing speech of 1963.

The Berlin Wall was, as Bahr went on to explain, 'a sign of weakness

. . . of the communist regime's fear and urge for self-preservation. The question is whether there are not possibilities gradually to diminish the regime's quite justified fears, so that the loosening up of the frontiers and the Wall will also become practicable, because the risk will be bearable.' This was the policy which, Bahr concluded, 'one could sum up in the formula *Wandel durch Annäherung* (change through rapprochement)'. The underlying assumption was spelled out even more explicitly by Peter Bender, in his book of 1964, *Offensive Détente*. The basic feature of the GDR, he wrote, was its inner weakness. 'This weakness is the crucial reason why those relaxations (*Lockerungen*) which in other states of the Soviet bloc have already, in part, happened years ago, are still missing in the GDR. The weakness of the SED[i.e. Party]-leadership is thus the main cause of everything which urgently needs to be changed in the SED-state.' The logical conclusion was clear. The SED-state must be strengthened, so it could make those changes. 'Liberalisation of the GDR,' wrote Bender, 'requires stabilisation of the GDR.'

One of the keys to stabilisation was obviously the state of the East German economy. 'A material improvement would be bound to have a tension-relaxing effect in the Zone,' argued Bahr. To the objection that this would reduce popular discontent in the GDR he replied: 'but precisely that is desirable'. For otherwise there might be 'uncontrolled developments', like the 17 June 1953 rising or the 1960–61 emigration wave, which would lead to 'inevitable reverses', such as the crushing of the 17 June rising and the building of the Berlin Wall. No 'practical path' led via attempts to overthrow the regime. 'I see only the narrow path of relief for the people in such homeopathic doses that no danger of a revolutionary turn develops, which would necessarily lead to Soviet intervention out of Soviet interests.' So: reform instead of revolution.

Josef Joffe has forcefully argued that the concept advanced by Bahr and Bender in the early 1960s became a central underlying idea, not just of West German policy towards the GDR, but of the whole Ostpolitik in the 1970s and even into the 1980s. He calls it the notion of 'relaxation through reassurance'. Détente — that is, precisely, relaxation, *Entspannung* — between states in East and West should lead to détente between state and society in the East. An aggressive Western posture towards Eastern rulers had led, or at least contributed to, an aggressive approach by Eastern rulers not only towards the West but also towards their own people. If the West were less aggressive so, in time, should those rulers be — towards the West, but also towards their own subjects. By relaxation, and the building of trust and confidence between East and West, we could encourage the rulers to relax at home. And then they might find that this relaxation produced not explosion (as on 17 June 1953) or defection (as in the run-up to 13 August 1961) but a new trust and confidence between the rulers and the ruled.

There would then follow what Joffe nicely describes as a 'virtuous circle'. International relaxation and reassurance would encourage domestic relaxation. Domestic relaxation would produce domestic reassurance, and therefore encourage the rulers to relax still further, producing more domestic reassurance, and more international relaxation, until all sides, East and West, society and state, were so relaxed and so reassured that we could all move slowly, peacefully forward together from a mere regulated next-to-each-other to a with-each-other, and thence to the highest harmony of the European peace order.

Leaving aside the — important — historical question of how far this theory accurately reflected the real history of the Cold War, one can see that it was, in essence, a hypothesis of behavioural psychology. It was, in fact, one of two rudimentary hypotheses of behavioural psychology that underpinned Western thinking about the relationship between Western policy and Eastern politics. With deliberate oversimplification, one might call these the American and the German détente-hypotheses.

The American hypothesis was also first advanced in the early 1960s, and underlay the United States' policy of 'differentiation' to Eastern Europe. East European states were to be rewarded for good behaviour and punished for bad, and this in the short to medium term. Good behaviour was defined mainly politically, in terms of independence from Moscow in foreign policy and/or relative 'liberalism' and respect for human rights in domestic policy. Punishments and rewards were, in practice, mainly economic. The governing metaphor of 'differentiation' was that of 'carrots and sticks'. East European rulers were thus considered to be, at heart, donkeys. In the behavioural psychology of the German idea of détente, by contrast, East European rulers would appear to be, at heart, rabbits. The rabbit will freeze if you fix him in your headlights. If you frighten him too much, he may even bite. But speak to him gently, offer him carrots — above all, lots of carrots — and he will relax, loosen his grip.

These are, of course, rather childish simplifications — although it is a great mistake to believe that because our politicians and statesmen appear sophisticated the basic ideas underlying their policies are in fact sophisticated. In the case of social-liberal Ostpolitik, however, this rudimentary notion of behavioural psychology came wrapped, not merely in more sophisticated language, but in a world-historical dialectic. The central proposition of this dialectic was first publicly formulated by Egon Bahr at Tutzing in 1963, when he attributed to Kennedy the notion of 'overcoming the status quo, by first not changing the status quo'. With Willy Brandt it was extended from Berlin to Germany, and from Germany to Europe. Twenty years later this Berlin dialectic had hardened, in the hands of other leading SPD strategists, into statements such as 'Only the *unconditional* recognition of the status quo creates the precondition for a gradual changing of the status quo'.

What was this 'status quo' which one now so fully, not to say fulsomely 'recognised'? Was it merely the post-war frontiers, and the existence of new East Central European states, including the GDR, inside those frontiers? Or was it rather the 'post-war realities' as Moscow defined them, that is, including the enduring reality of communist systems in those states? In the case of Poland, Hungary or Czechoslovakia, the distinction between state and system was relatively easy to make; much less so in the case of the GDR. For what need would there be for the separate existence of an East German state if it did not have a fundamentally different system from West Germany? The GDR, said one of the Party's leading ideologists, Otto Reinhold, in a radio interview in August 1989, 'is only thinkable as an antifascist, as a socialist state, as a socialist alternative to the FRG [West Germany]. For what justification would a capitalist GDR have next to a capitalist Federal Republic? None of course.' The Bonn government might distinguish between 'recognising' the state and the system, but the GDR's leaders made no such distinction. For them, the state was the system, and the system was the state. 'Recognising' one meant 'recognising' the other.

The notion of 'relaxation through reassurance' seemed to square this circle. It suggested that by strengthening the East German state, through recognition and hard currency, in the interests of 'the people', the Federal Republic could yet also be working towards its internal liberalisation. To the general dialectical principle — accept the status quo in order to overcome it — was added the specific dialectical principle — strengthen the GDR regime in order to liberalise it. A stronger, more secure GDR could also be more acceptable to its own citisens, because, feeling stronger and more secure, it could afford to relax. This, in turn would permit a further 'coming closer' of the two German states. And this in turn . . . 'The more firmly entrenched the SED leadership,' wrote a leading Social Democratic specialist on Deutschlandpolitik in 1978, 'and the more satisfied the GDR population, the more probable is a co-operative relationship between the two German states.' 'Only a consolidation of the GDR,' wrote another sympathetic scholar in 1980, 'offers a promise of easing and overcoming the gruesome realities of barbed wire and death-strips at the intra-German frontier.' Here was the specifically German version of the 'virtuous circle'.

Now it is clearly not the case that all West German policymakers publicly endorsed or privately subscribed to this bold hypothesis. Far from it. Bahr himself modified and qualified the argument significantly over the next quarter-century. Willy Brandt cautioned against attempts at the 'dialectical resolution' of conflicts of interest, power relations and social differences. Helmut Schmidt was, as we have seen, dismissive of such 'concepts'. And many Christian Democrats had fiercely criticised it, then and subsequently. In 1983, the Christian Democrat who was perhaps most sympathetic to the social-liberal approach, Richard von Weizsäcker, described the notion of 'change through rapprochement' as a 'burden' from which Ostpolitik should be freed.

Yet it is remarkable how much of the basic thrust of this theory survived, or resurfaced in different forms and fragments, among those who were involved in policy towards the GDR over the two decades under review. One of its intellectual architects, Peter Bender, wrote in 1988 that Kohl and Strauss 'decisively reject Bahr's formula, and nonetheless pursue the policy that Bahr recommended twenty-five years ago'. This was a partisan and sweeping claim. Yet on all the evidence it is hard to dispute his next, more qualified assertion: 'Above all, they observe the basic law of social-liberal Ostpolitik and respect the status quo, in order gradually to overcome it. They know that their Deutschlandpolitik will only work if they do not attempt to destabilise the GDR, and when the GDR remains certain of that.'

Certainly this is what they said in public. While they did not adopt the explicit dialectics of social-liberal Ostpolitik, while they repeatedly insisted on the fundamental differences between East and West, the Christian Democrats nonetheless went out of their way to emphasise that they, like their predecessors, had no intention of 'destabilising' the GDR, or any other East European state. The Kohl government's Deutschland-politik was 'not aimed at a destabilisation of the GDR,' said Chancellery Minister Wolfgang Schäuble. 'We have no intention of harming or destabilising the GDR,' said the Minister for Intra-German Relations, Heinrich Windelen.

This 'stability commandment', as Eberhard Schulz well described it, for among most practitioners of Ostpolitik it had almost the sacred force of a commandment, proves on closer examination to contain two different, though closely related propositions. The first proposition is that it would be wrong for the West to attempt directly to 'destabilise' the communist state, to encourage discontent, resistance and revolt in East Germany or the rest of Eastern Europe, as had been done — or was said to have been done, and in reality had been said more than done — in the 1950s. It would be wrong politically, because it would only produce 'inevitable reverses'. It would also be wrong morally, because we might encourage people over there to resist, but when it came to the crunch it was they who would pay the price — in blood — while the West would do nothing. That was 'Yalta'.

The second proposition, closely related but not identical, was that it would be a mistake for people over there to attempt to change their government by revolution. Given the overwhelming reality of Soviet power, they would inevitably be crushed. There was thus a deep ambivalence in the West German attitude to the 17 June 1953 uprising. On the one hand it was celebrated as the first major rising for freedom in Eastern

Europe; kept as a public holiday called 'the day of German unity' in West Germany; and marked every year by a ceremonial speech in the Bundestag. On the other hand, most of those ceremonial speakers would have argued privately, and many argued publicly, that what happened after 17 June 1953 proved conclusively that an uprising was quite the wrong way to go about achieving desirable political change in Eastern Europe.

In 1978, when there were first signs of an explicitly political opposition developing in the GDR, Helmut Schmidt cautioned that

> a serious domestic crisis of the GDR, on which some people seemingly speculate, particularly in the opposition [i.e. the West German opposition], could not bring the state unity of our nation one centimetre closer.... Expectations of a crisis-like internal development in the GDR, with a consequent political change, derive from a fatal misjudgement of the existing realities and power relations there. No-one should forget the sacrifice of human life which such a misjudgement has already cost.

So rebelling or protesting was not what the East Germans were to be encouraged to do. And not just the East Germans. When, in the summer of 1980, the Poles started protesting once again — continuing the chain begun by Germans on 17 June 1953 — the reaction of the Schmidt government was extremely defensive, and subsequently critical. This was, in the first place, because the Polish protests had a direct negative impact on German-German relations. But it was also because German policymakers simply did not believe Solidarity's attempt could succeed. A contrast was drawn between the 'unrealism' of the Poles around Lech Wałęsa and the 'realistic' German-German policy — where the essential, constitutive part of 'reality' was the Red Army. The declaration of martial law in Poland seemed only to bear out this sober contention. Here was yet another of those 'inevitable reverses'.

So what was needed was not revolution from below but reform from above. West German policy might be made for — that is, on behalf of — the people in the GDR, but they could not be expected to change their own state. Policy for the people therefore had to be made not with the people but with the rulers. There, with the rulers, lay the key not just to short-term alleviations but also to medium-term reforms. Although the assertion cannot be proved, since policymakers can always claim that they thought more than they said, the evidence points to this having been a basic working assumption of the Bonn government's policy towards the GDR, in the 1980s as well as in the 1970s.

Now the political value of this constant reassurance, particularly in Moscow, should not be lightly underrated. Nor should the genuine moral concerns which informed the commandment of 'no destabilisation'. Yet the moral balance of the commandment was not entirely clear. It is one thing to say 'we should not risk other people's lives', but quite another to say 'you, other people, should not risk your lives'. Responding to Bahr's original Tutzing speech, Harold Hurwitz, an American with a deep and somewhat romantic interest in the history of the German left, wrote (in English) to his friend Willy Brandt: 'It is in the liberal and socialist traditions a somewhat disgusting example of "Hochmut" [arrogance, German in the original] to imagine that, knowing best, one has the right to usurp from an enslaved people its right to insurrection.' From a quite different tradition, conservative and Catholic, Alois Mertes would later make a very similar point about what he called 'the important, the many-layered word "destabilisation"'. 'We do not have the right,' he said, 'to stabilise a system that abuses human rights . . .' This was a difficult line to draw for every Western country, for the Americans in relation to Russia or the French in relation to Poland, but it was doubly difficult in the case of Germans dealing with Germany.

The classic image, almost the mandala, of this dilemma is the photograph of Willy Brandt at the window of the hotel in Erfurt on that first, moving official visit to the GDR in 1970. Here was the crowd of ordinary East Germans, full of emotion and hope, chanting 'Willy, Willy!' There he stood, just for a brief moment, with a tense look on his face, making a desperately strained, almost apologetic gesture of pacification, pushing downwards with the hands splayed out and both wrists pressed against the window frame. 'I was moved,' he wrote in his memoirs, 'but I had to consider the fate of these people: I would be back in Bonn next day, they would not . . . I made a gesture urging restraint, and my point was taken. The crowd fell silent. Turning away with a heavy heart, I noticed that many of my aides had tears in their eyes. I was afraid of kindling hopes that could not be fulfilled, so I adopted a suitably low-key manner.' In a sense, the leaders of the Federal Republic were to go on making this gesture to the people of the GDR for the next twenty years: in some cases still with that deep, inner moral and emotional tension, yet in others with what was almost a routine complacency.

If the moral balance of the stability commandment was not quite so clear as was generally claimed, nor was the political balance. This was, in fact, to enter one of the great political arguments of modern Central European history. On the one hand there were those — Poles, Czechs, Hungarians, Germans — who argued that the interests of people and the people, *die Menschen* and the nation, could best be served by accommodating, with many moral compromises, to the 'realities' imposed by outside powers. One should first adapt to the 'realities' in the hope of then gradually, quietly modifying them. On the other hand there were those who argued that it was more important to uphold certain absolute moral principles and national aspirations, to defy 'reality', even if the attempt was doomed in the short term:

For freedom's battle once begun,
Bequeathed by bleeding sire to son,
Though baffled oft is ever won.

In nineteenth-century Poland the latter were described as romantics, the former as 'positivists' (in this special Polish sense). In the twentieth century the conflict has been described as that between 'realism' and 'idealism' (although not in the special German sense).

Now in the latest round of this great Central European argument, the leaders of Solidarność in Poland stood in the latter, romantic or idealist tradition, albeit in a modern, cautious, carefully moderated form, resolutely abjuring violence. Albeit in a modern, cautious, moderated form, carefully restating positions of principle so far as one's own state was concerned, the makers of Ostpolitik stood in the former tradition. They stood, explicitly, for 'realism' — 'German realism' as Brandt put it in a powerful speech on the ratification of the Basic Treaty. But who, in the long run, was more realistic? The romantic idealists or the self-styled realists? The answer to this question certainly looks different after the revolution of 1989 than it did before them, but it is not simple, and can only be given, insofar as it can be given at all, in that full context. What is important for our purpose here is to establish that up until 1989 the 'realist' premiss was dominant in policy towards the GDR.

The 'realities' of communist rule and Soviet domination were held to preclude a success for revolution from below. The key to political change was therefore held to lie in reform from above. 'Stability' was the key-word in this connection. Like other key-words of Ostpolitik, like 'recognition' or 'normalisation', its meanings were many, and not clearly distinguished from each other. In the original détente hypothesis, 'stability' referred to the strength of the communist state, and 'stabilisation' was seen as a means to liberalisation. Over the years, however, the means began to be taken for an end. This was particularly tempting since the term 'stability' — with its connotations of peace, calm, predictability, order — was considered a positive value in West German domestic and foreign policy more generally.

In the early 1980s, as the subject of 'peace' moved to the fore of German politics in general, and German-German relations in particular, the term 'stability' was linked more closely to the concept of peace. Thus, to take an extreme example, Günter Gaus averred in 1983: 'Polish conditions such as [prevailed] in the last three years, such *polnische Wirtschaft* in Central Germany, understood in the sense of the old, evil, arrogant German metaphor — this would be the eve of a war in Europe.' (Incidentally, if the metaphor was old, evil and arrogant, why use it?)

In more sober government usage, the term stability came to be applied increasingly not to the state or regime, but to German-German relations altogether. The Minister for Intra-German Relations talked of the 'stability' of intra-German travel. Hans Otto Bräutigam, Permanent Representative in East Berlin for most of the 1980s, spoke of the 'stability' of the whole relationship. All the leading practitioners of policy towards the GDR agreed on the need for 'stability' in this modest sense. The internal political 'stability' of the GDR was, however, thought to be necessary for the 'stability' of relations, since it was argued that only a strong, secure, self-confident GDR leadership would be a reliable and forthcoming partner in the Permanent Negotiation. If they protested too much, the people in the GDR would therefore get in the way of negotiations on behalf of the people in the GDR. On the hypothesis of 'relaxation through reassurance', neither they nor the West German government should put too much pressure on the communist rulers of East Germany.

For all his impatience with the 'concepts' of policy intellectuals, Helmut Schmidt makes clear in his memoirs that he, too, adhered to the original nostrum of behavioural psychology. Describing his approach to his summit meeting with Erich Honecker he writes: 'I wanted to help to increase the self-respect of Erich Honecker in the international context and reduce the inferiority complexes of the GDR leadership. In this way I hoped to contribute to a growing sovereignty and generosity of the GDR government in its treatment of its citizens. This had been the dominant motive for me since the beginning of the Ostpolitik of the social-liberal coalition.'

Whether or not they analysed it in precisely this way, Chancellor Kohl and his team in practice largely continued this approach, with growing outward 'recognition' of the Honecker regime, up to the remarkable crescendo of the Honecker visit in 1987. After the visit, leading politicians of all the main parties still regularly went to visit Erich Honecker in East Berlin, and to be photographed smilingly shaking his hand. To judge by the available East German records of these meetings — which of course have to be treated with caution — only a few of these prominent West German visitors directly raised issues of human rights, although many discreetly handed over lists of 'humanitarian cases'. All were respectful and polite. For were they not by their very politeness, yes, even by their flattery, 'helping the people'? (What was certain, however, was they were helping their own political 'profile' in the television democracy of the West.) Hermann Axen, summarising the main points of his own conversation in April 1988 with perhaps the most outspoken of all these visitors, Volker Rühe, was still able to write, in an internal memorandum to Honecker: 'CDU not interested in destabilisation GDR'. That was Bonn's message, sent and received.

To be sure, there was also some criticism of this whole approach, notably from those who had some direct, personal experience of the inner workings of the East German system. Wolfgang Leonhard made a powerful critique of the theory of liberalisation through stabilisation, arguing that a degree of pressure on the rulers, both from below and from outside, was not the obstacle to, but rather the essential prerequisite for, change in communist systems. The Federal Republic, he said, should distinguish more clearly between regime and people, and be more explicit in its demands for more respect for human rights, liberalisation and democratisation.

In 1988, the twin brothers Bernd and Peter Eisenfeld, the latter only recently deported from the GDR, made an even more swingeing critique. They argued, like James McAdams, that the GDR had got the upper hand in the German-German relationship. The Federal Republic should, they said, be much tougher in its negotiations with the regime, and more prepared to support independent and oppositional groups. Similar criticisms were made by other disillusioned intellectuals from East Germany, such as Hermann von Berg, Franz Loeser and Wolfgang Seiffert.

Yet these remained isolated voices. At least until 1988, virtually all those who actually made the policy, in government, opposition or civil service, subscribed to the commandment of 'no destabilisation', in both senses analysed above. Not all went to the opposite extreme, arguing that stabilisation was the only path to liberalisation. Yet this remained a powerful underlying notion, if only because no one seemed to have a better hypothesis about the way desirable change might come about in the GDR. Hans Otto Bräutigam, who was in many ways the walking personification of Bonn's GDR-policy, says — looking back — that he never believed that a stabilisation could lead to a liberalisation of the GDR, but he did believe that one might move through stabilisation to a modest humanisation of the GDR.

In any case, stability (inside the GDR) was thought to be a precondition for stability (in the German-German relationship) which was itself felt to be a contribution to stability (in East-West relations) — also known as 'peace'.

Stabilisation without liberalisation

What were the actual effects of policy towards the GDR on the politics of the GDR? The question is not easily answered. As we have noticed already, it is difficult to distinguish between the effects of the active policy and those of the mere, so to speak, passive reality of the Federal Republic, especially since one of the aims of the former was to expose ordinary East Germans to the charms of the latter. How can one summarise the myriad interactions of two societies, let alone of two societies in one nation? How do these relate to the domestic interactions of state and society in the GDR? And those to the influence of developments in the Soviet Union and elsewhere in Eastern Europe? Moreover, all criticism of a given policy is based on assumptions about possible alternatives. But we cannot, by definition, know 'what would have happened if . . .' All we can know is what actually happened, and even that we know only partially.

What is clearly wrong, however, is to judge the policy only by its final ending — revolution and unification. This may be good enough for politicians, but it is not good enough for historians. That outcome was very far from inevitable, and we must look at an interim as well as at the final balance-sheet. Perhaps the best interim vantage-point is the spring of 1986, when the ruling Socialist Unity Party held its eleventh party congress.

The choice of date is not arbitrary. Boring though they might be, Party congresses were very important moments in the life of communist states. They were important even if their message was, as in this case, 'no change'. This was especially important when the simultaneous message from Moscow was 'change!' The year 1986 also marked fifteen years of Honecker's leadership, while the two states in Germany had had 'relations' for nearly as long. Moreover, as we have seen, this year was felt in Bonn to mark something of a breakthrough in the crucial area of travel 'from Germany to Germany', a pleasure Honecker was himself to taste in 1987.

So, taking stock in spring 1986, what do we find? We find, first, a political system which in its fundamentals was quite unchanged. More than in any other East European state, more even than in the Soviet Union, the GDR had preserved and, so far as possible, made more efficient the basic structures of a Leninist-Stalinist one-party state. The pyramid command system of so-called 'democratic centralism', the external mobilisation of a mass membership, the 'language drill' of ideological conformity — all were maintained in the GDR to a degree long since abandoned even in Gustáv Husák's 'normalised' Czechoslovakia, let alone in Hungary or Poland.

The state bureaucracy, the mass organisations and the media all remained correctly subordinated to the leading role of the Party. Last but by no means least, the formidable domestic state security apparatus — the 'Stasi' — was more numerous and more formidable than ever. Although it certainly had very significant elements of operational autonomy, it remained, to use its own self-description, the 'shield and sword of the Party'. The head of its espionage operations, Markus Wolf, well described the Stasi as a 'hypertrophied function of the system'. At the top of this pyramidical party-state was an autocratic form of rule, with the Party leader increasingly making key decisions on his own, or in direct consultation with the Politburo's key functional bosses: Günter Mittag for the economy, Erich Mielke for security, Joachim Herrmann for the media.

The Party leadership had, however, significantly developed and modified the strategies by which it endeavoured to win from its own citizens some active, voluntary support or 'legitimacy'; if not 'legitimacy', then at least loyalty; if not loyalty, then at least acceptance; if not acceptance, then at least the absence of explicit protest — or what in Bonn was called 'instability'.

The central appeal for popular acceptance made by the Party under Honecker was staked out already at the 8th Party congress in 1971, and only re-stated and embellished at this 11th congress, fifteen years later. The appeal came under the awkward ideological formula of 'the unity of economic and social policy', but in plain words what it said to people in the GDR was roughly this: We do not ask you, as we did in the 1950s, to support us just because of our rejection of a terrible past ('anti-fascism') and our promise of a golden future (the communist utopia). Nor do we claim, as Khrushchev and Ulbricht did in the 1960s, that we will 'bury' the West with our superior economic performance. But we do claim that in our 'really existing socialism' we can sustain economic growth while at the same time providing you with an improved standard of living and a social security which you would never get in the West, ridden as it is with unemployment, crime, drugs etc. You will have cheap food, free medical care and education, safe streets, cheap holidays organised by the party-state's mass organisations, and there will be apartments — Honecker's particular concern — for everyone.

Whereas under Ulbricht the motto had been 'as we work today we will live tomorrow', people were now to enjoy more of the benefits today. Socialism was to be made more attractive — or, as the ideologists carefully reformulated the proposition, as attractive as by its nature it was. In 1986 all this was summed up in the key-word *Geborgenheit*, meaning sheltered, cosy safety. This was an understanding of socialism from a man, indeed from a generation of German communists, who knew from personal experience what it meant not to have enough to eat, warm clothes or a dry roof over your head. At the same time, it was, at least in the short-to medium-term, a fairly shrewd strategy for political survival.

It is important to note that the economic growth to underpin this welfare and consumer provision was not to be achieved by further market-oriented economic reforms, such as had been timorously attempted in the 1960s. On the contrary, the 1970s saw a consolidation of traditional, Soviet-type central planning, with some modifications to make it less inefficient, but with nothing that could seriously be spoken of as reform in the sense that Kádár's Hungary had embarked on economic reform. Instead, the underlying economic growth was supposedly to be achieved, first, by making the existing system (and people) work as hard and efficiently as possible; second, by technological innovation — Honecker himself was particularly keen on micro-electronics; and, last but not least, by opening to the West.

Economists talk of a strategy of 'import substitution', when economies in difficulty substitute alternative, domestic products for costly imports.

One might describe this political strategy as one of reform substitution. Social benefits and consumer goods were offered to the people not as complements to a reform of the system but as substitutes for a reform of the system which the Party leadership considered would be too dangerous (for the Party leadership). And one of the main substitutes for reform was — imports. Imports of Western technology, whether obtained legally, or illegally through the efficient espionage of Markus Wolf's intelligence department of the State Security Service. Imports of Western goods. Imports of DM.

As we have noticed already, this political strategy was not peculiar to East Germany. Edward Gierek did the same thing in Poland, albeit with catholic profligacy rather than puritan self-restraint. In Czechoslovakia, Gustáv Husák also offered material and social goods as substitutes for the crushed reforms and stolen freedoms of the Prague Spring, although he was able to do so without incurring large hard-currency debts. Even János Kádár's 'goulash communism' in Hungary tried initially to make economic without political reforms. When the difficulties of combining plan and market became acute, the Hungarian leadership, too, partially substituted foreign credits and imports for further steps of radical economic reform.

Peculiar to the GDR were, however, two features. On the one hand, Honecker was able to sustain this strategy virtually unchanged into the second half of the 1980s, thanks partly to (East) German good housekeeping, efficiency, hard work and so forth, but also crucially, and increasingly, to the financial and economic advantages of the relationship with West Germany. In Poland and Hungary, the hard currency loans which in the 1970s had been to some extent a substitute for reforms became in the 1980s a vital goad to reform. The West made rescheduling and new loans contingent on measures of economic reform, and on respect for human rights and political liberalisation. In the GDR this medium-term effect was lacking, because the very substantial monies from West Germany came with other, less immediately pressing linkages.

On the other hand, the risks of opening to the West were obviously greater for the GDR than for the other East European states, for while they risked subversion of their communist regimes, the GDR risked undermining the very basis of its existence as a state. In response to Bahr's Tutzing speech, the GDR's then Foreign Minister, Otto Winzer, spoke darkly of 'aggression in felt slippers'. The Minister for State Security, Erich Mielke, was constantly warning about the danger of an undermining of socialism in the GDR through contact with the West.

From the outset, therefore, much more than anywhere else in Eastern Europe, the opening to the West was accompanied by redoubled efforts to maintain the Party's political control and ideological rigour. The phase of 'peaceful co-existence' was openly declared to be one of heightened ideological struggle, directed primarily, of course, against the Federal

Republic. In a series of top-level internal briefings in the early 1970s, Mielke would instruct his subordinates in the Ministry for State Security that for them peaceful co-existence meant 'above all struggle'. Every possible operative step should be taken so that what happened at Erfurt should never be repeated. Following the signature of the Basic Treaty he warned that the process of 'normalisation' of relations with the Federal Republic would be a 'hard and complicated' area of class struggle. Visiting West Germans would have to be kept under close observation. The transit routes would have to be 'secured in depth'. Officers would need to investigate the 'whole personality' of East Germans who applied to travel West. And so on and so forth.

Beside this political-police response there was also an ideological escalation of what was officially called *Abgrenzung* (with connotations of 'drawing the line' and 'fencing off'). The escalation of *Abgrenzung* was the ugly twin sister of the opening to West Germany. In ideology and propaganda, this was particularly apparent in the GDR's new line on the national question. The 1968 constitution had declared that 'the GDR and its citizens . . . strive for the overcoming of the division of Germany forced upon the German nation by imperialism, the step-by-step rapprochement (*Annäherung*) of both German states until their unification on the basis of democracy and socialism'. In October 1974 this passage was deleted from the constitution, which now affirmed that the GDR was 'for ever and irrevocably allied with the Union of Soviet Socialist Republics'.

In the same period it was decided that the words of the GDR's 'national anthem' should no longer be sung, since it declared 'let us serve you for the good/Germany, united fatherland'. Indeed the GDR's ideologists now discovered that there were not just two states but actually two nations in Germany. The GDR was a separate 'socialist nation'. As late as 1987 the Party's veteran ideologist, Kurt Hager, could declare — in the interview already quoted — that the GDR was a 'socialist German nation'.

Looking back from 1992, Erich Honecker insisted that this so to speak anti-national *Abgrenzung* had been done largely at Moscow's behest. The assertion will clearly need to be tested against the evidence in the archives in Moscow and East Berlin. Yet what is demonstrably true is that Honecker always left himself an ideological loophole. Although the nation was now socialist, and its people's citizenship that of the GDR, their *nationality* was, he declared, still 'German'. And through this ideological loophole the GDR began, very tentatively at first, then with growing range and confidence in the 1980s, to acknowledge its own indubitable Germanness. When an East German astronaut was taken up in a Soviet spaceship, the East Germans were informed in a banner headline that he was the first *German* in space. Later, more seriously, there were quite spectacular celebrations to mark the 500th anniversary of Martin Luther's birth, and a cautious rehabilitation of Frederick the Great, even of Bismarck. All were now added, albeit with careful reservations, to the previously thin red line of 'progressive' elements in German history.

Again, the basic direction was not peculiar to East Germany. In their quest for new sources of popular support, the regimes in Poland and Hungary, not to mention those in Romania and Bulgaria, engaged in much more vehement appeals to patriotism — and nationalism — in the same period. There, too, the exercise was fraught with ambivalence. In every case, the appeal to patriotism — or nationalism — was used, at least in part, as an alternative to reform, liberalisation, or democratisation. In every case, there were non- or even anti-democratic national traditions to which the regimes could turn, and which found some echoes in the surviving political culture of at least some parts of the population. Thus, for example, it has been argued that parts of the surviving bourgeoisie in Hungary went quite smoothly from Horthyism to Kádárism. In the Balkans, the echoes were even more crass. Yet in every case there was ultimately an ineradicable tension between the regime's reading of national history — its lesson being: support us! — and the readings of national history that independent citizens made for themselves, which rendered lessons such as: give us back our pre-war freedom and independence!

Nowhere was this tension more acute than in East Germany. On the one hand there was much in traditional German political culture that was serviceable for a dictatorship. In the cliché of 'Red Prussia', as in most clichés, there was a grain of truth. The tradition of blind obedience to the state (the *Untertan* mentality), and the inner emigration of the unpolitical German (*machtgeschützte Innerlichkeit*), both survived and could be built on in the East more than in the West. In this sense, too, East Germany was, to repeat another cliché, 'more German' than West Germany. On the other hand, to emphasise national traditions was inevitably to concentrate people's minds on the enduring fact of division. And could even Erich Honecker be certain, in his heart of hearts, that they would then conclude the GDR was the better Germany?

Two other, related modifications of the ideological and political rigour of *Abgrenzung* should be mentioned here. In the 1970s, the opening to the West had been accompanied by redoubled efforts to ensure that young East Germans' readiness to defend the 'socialist fatherland' against the evil, capitalist, militarist, imperialist Federal Republic should not be diminished by actual contact with the beast. 'Defence education' was stepped up, with verses exalting a soldier's readiness to shoot his West German counterpart — 'perhaps my brother but . . . my enemy'. Yet in the 1980s, as we have seen, the official line became, increasingly, that the two German states had a joint responsibility for 'peace', that, indeed, in their 'coalition of reason', they were together helping to keep the peace, despite the less responsible behaviour of outside powers — meaning, above all, the United States.

Now this, too, was double-edged. It could bring the regime some popular appreciation, even active support. Yet it also had worrying implications. As the architects of West German policy towards the GDR had always hoped and intended, it made it increasingly difficult for the regime to present West Germany to its own people with any plausibility as a dangerous enemy or threat. Precisely this concern is reflected in a summary report of the Stasi's central evaluation group on popular reactions to Honecker's visit to Bonn. University and school teachers, said this report, found themselves confronted with such questions as: 'Do we still need an enemy-image (*Feindbild*)? . . . Is the Wall still necessary? Has the imperialism of the FRG changed its character? Western politicians also want peace.' The 'coalition of reason' also brought the risk that some citizens of the GDR, inspired by the images of the West German peace movement brought them every day by television, would start wanting to 'do something for peace' themselves, independently. What is more, they might, like peace activists elsewhere in Eastern Europe, link the theme of peace to that of human rights.

The second important modification concerned relations with the Protestant Church. Here the themes of German history and tradition, peace and human rights all came together, but in ways that were not merely double-but multiple-edged. Indeed, the history of church-state relations inside the GDR is scarcely less complex than that of German-German relations. Crudely stated, the basic political facts are that under Erich Honecker there was a cautious rapprochement between the party-state and the Church. This rapprochement was symbolised by a summit meeting between the head of the Federation of Protestant Churches in the GDR, Bishop Albrecht Schönherr, and Erich Honecker, on 6 March 1978. In the 1980s, there was a more or less permanent dialogue or negotiation between the party-state authorities and the Church, at lower as well as higher levels. There were, however, numerous ups and downs in the relationship, and wide variations between regions, dioceses, and individual parishes.

Whereas the minority Catholic Church was highly centralised and authoritarian, the majority Protestant Church was highly decentralised, with important historical differences between individual regional churches (*Landeskirchen*) and a quite democratic internal structure, with much lay participation in Church councils, synods and the like. In the GDR — unlike in Poland — the Catholic Church mainly concentrated on purely religious themes and ecclesiastical interests, keeping its distance from the regime. The Protestant Church, by contrast, addressed a whole palette of social and political issues. Diversity was therefore its hallmark. With considerable over-simplification one might, however, identify three main strands.

Firstly, there was a small but active minority of priests and lay Christians who saw themselves, in the tradition of Dietrich Bonhoeffer and the *Bekennende Kirche* as working in outright opposition to an evil, dictatorial state — although few would have accepted a direct comparison of the GDR with the Third Reich. Secondly, there was a somewhat larger minority of clergy and laity who, while they would surely have condemned the collaboration of the so-called German Christians with the authorities of the Third Reich, now more or less actively collaborated with the authorities of the GDR.

Thirdly, there were the many who attempted to navigate a path between those two extremes. Sometimes they believed in the genuine possibilities of Christian-Marxist dialogue, leading to a partial agreement on such issues as welfare provision, social justice and, indeed, peace. The formula of 'the Church in socialism' seemed to imply that possibility, while at the same time implicitly denying that this was a regime which intrinsically and necessarily demanded a Christian's outright resistance. (Compare the barely imaginable formula: 'the Church in national socialism'.) Instead, they saw their political function as that of mediators between state and people. In playing that part they developed a style and language which, as we have already suggested, also influenced the style of West German policymakers — prudent, persistent, predictable. As the extent of Stasi penetration of the Church became apparent after unification, so the political and ethical borderline between these last two categories would become the subject of a fierce debate, personified in the case, at once extreme and exemplary, of Manfred Stolpe.

The putative advantages to the regime of this still barbed and cautious rapprochement with the Church were considerable. It widened its potential basis of support. It gained the possibility of more fully engaging the talents of Christians, and the resources of the Church (including its monies for the West), especially in such areas of common interest as social welfare provision. Co-operation with the Churches on such issues as 'peace' gave it badly needed credibility. Through some churchmen, at least, it could also hope to moderate, even to pacify discontented citizens. All this was, to use the West German key-word, 'stabilising'. The political culture of Lutheranism was itself ambivalent, containing the potential for both collaboration and resistance. There was obviously a profound connection between German Protestantism and the substance of the *Kulturnation*, of German cultural unity in music, thought, literature. Yet so long as the political division seemed set in concrete this, too, could work for as well as against the interests of the regime.

Unambiguously negative from the regime's point of view were four things. First, the Church represented a fundamentally different view of the human person, a view which went back slightly further than the Marxist one and might be found to make more sense of the life even of a completely secularised young person in the GDR. Second, the Protestant Church in the GDR was both *de jure* and *de facto* autonomous to a degree unique in Eastern Europe, while the structure of its internal self-government was partly democratic. Third, it formed enclaves of free speech and free association, which the church-state rapprochement made it more difficult to encroach upon.

Finally, the Church could, if it wanted, offer the security of these enclaves to critics and even outright opponents of the regime, some of whom would certainly not otherwise have been regular churchgoers. Here, in churches, church halls and vicarages, they could talk about environmental and social problems, about peace, and about human rights. This they did, in growing numbers, at the beginning of the 1980s. They would, they said, taking their motto from the Bible, beat 'swords into ploughshares'.

Yet as soon as they stepped outside the church doors they were liable to be picked up by the police, harassed or arrested. The Stasi would make difficulties for them at work, or, if they were young, prevent them from going to university — as the children of clergy were still, anyway, regularly prevented from doing. Even the transport police on the trains would stop you just for wearing a 'swords into ploughshares' badge on your denim jacket. So with a touch of that glorious semiotic ingenuity which was to be seen all over East Central Europe in 1989, some young people displayed simply the bare round patch where a badge might have been. Yet the swords remained: in the National People's Army, in which all but a few still had to do armed service, despite the peace movement's demand for civil alternatives, and in the self-styled 'shield and sword of the Party', the Stasi.

The Church-protected groups survived as a small counter-culture, an important fragment of what all over East Central Europe would come to be called 'civil society'. They were dissidents in the original, Latin sense of the word: they 'sat apart' (*dissidere*). But the state successfully prevented them from becoming a lasting democratic opposition. In fact, the authorities dealt decisively with the leading lay activists of the Church-based peace movement; as they had with the leaders of a would-be democratic socialist opposition, the Robert Havemanns and Rudolf Bahros, and with the balladeer Wolf Biermann and other critical writers who had taken seriously Erich Honecker's initial announcement that there would be 'no taboos' in East Germany's cultural life. The methods of dealing with this opposition were, to be sure, less crudely brutal than in the 1950s. People were no longer shot — except at the frontier. But this improvement, this 'humanisation', to recall Hans Otto Bräutigam's term, was common to the whole Soviet bloc, with East Germany still close to the rear of the pack.

When the lesser repertory of intimidation and harassment failed, the dissident activist was faced, sometimes quite explicitly and cynically, with a stark choice. Here, in this room, said the police or state prosecutor, we are preparing the case against you, 'you'll get three years'. (No need to worry about independent judges, the sentence could be predicted in advance.) But there, in the next room, we have a completed application to emigrate, 'just sign and you'll be in the West next week'. It was, as one young Christian put it, like the choice between Heaven and Hell. In the circumstances it is not surprising that, often under acute psychological pressure, most of these courageous men and women chose emigration. And so the opposition was bled, and bled.

In sum, one has to conclude that after some fifteen years of Honecker's rule and West German 'GDR-policy', there had been a significant, although still fragile, stabilisation of the party-state, but no significant liberalisation. If the West German hope had been liberalisation through stabilisation, the interim balance was stabilisation without liberalisation. And our standard of comparison is not, let it be carefully noted, the freedoms of the West, but the much more limited freedoms of the East. In his original Tutzing speech, Bahr had himself observed that the 'Zone' was behind Poland and Hungary in political development, because of the special difficulties posed by the presence of West Germany. Yet on any meaningful measure of 'liberalisation', the GDR was now further behind Poland and Hungary, despite more than fifteen years of a West German policy designed to close that gap.

While people were more able to withdraw into an unpolitical private life — Günter Gaus coined the vivid term 'niche society' — the tribute of external conformity, that is, of public lying, expected even of the ordinary citizen was still much greater in the GDR than in that neighbouring 'niche society', Czechoslovakia. While there were fragments of civil society, above all in the churches, this was nothing to compare with the spectrum of independent activity in culture, the universities, the media, and the explicitly democratic opposition in Poland and Hungary. While there had been important changes in the tactics and even the strategy of the Party leadership, there was nothing that seriously deserved the name of reform in the political, economic or legal system. The Stasi was more numerous and ubiquitous than ever.

This stabilisation without liberalisation was, of course, primarily the achievement of the GDR itself. West German historians agreed with their East German colleagues that the consolidation of the party-state really dated from the building of the Berlin Wall in 1961. Yet both the main instruments of West German policy had contributed to this stabilisation. In the medium term, Bonn's growing transfers of DM and recognition had greatly helped the party-state. The importance of the DM has already been discussed. The importance of the recognition is well illustrated by the notes of one participant in the regular top-level meetings of senior editors with the head of the Agitation department of the Central Committee. 'Important, important strong GDR,' went the propaganda argument at the time of Honecker's visit to West Germany. 'If the GDR were on crutches, the leading representatives of business and politics would not have met with E.H., his delegation and our "captains of industry". We are a stable soc. [ialist] country in the heart of Europe: a political and economic factor.' And even more cheerfully: 'If Bavaria and Baden-Württemberg help us to build socialism — that's just great!'

We have been at pains not to over-simplify this story. The gains were double-edged. The GDR paid both an economic and a political price. The short- to medium-term financial relief to the state brought medium- to long-term financial dependency. The currency and goods that went to the people diminished immediate material dissatisfaction. Yet they also diminished the economic credibility of a state which treated its own currency with such contempt. The main political price the GDR paid was to permit the growth of ties between West Germany and West Berlin, contacts between the Germans in West and East, and slightly more travel (temporarily or permanently) for East Germans to the West. The reports of the Stasi's Central Evaluation and Information Group clearly indicate that ordinary East Germans responded to every major step of German-German summit diplomacy, whether Brandt in Erfurt, the Basic Treaty, Schmidt on the Werbellinsee, Brandt's meeting with Honecker in 1985, or Honecker in Bonn, with hopes of easier travel.

Yet even the balance of these concessions was not simply destabilising. Of course the presence of a prosperous, vital West Berlin in the very heart of the GDR, and visits from thousands of prosperous, vital West Germans, was not liable to increase satisfaction with one's own grey reality — although the vulgar arrogance of some West German visitors could actually prompt a curious defensive loyalty. As for travel to the West: since the lack of that freedom was one of the main grievances of the East Germans — the 'Wall sickness' was universal — the gradual, controlled granting of that freedom could perhaps reduce rather than increase the discontent. And since this freedom was granted not as a right but as a privilege, it was also a means of control. With this instrument, too, the regime could 'divide and rule'.

Even the most sensitive aspect of West Germany's efforts 'for the people' — family reunification and the 'buying free' of political prisoners — was double-edged. To be sure, when too many people applied to leave, as they did, for example, after the text of the Helsinki Final Act was published in *Neues Deutschland* in 1975, then the authorities made strenuous efforts to reduce the pressure. All sorts of intimidation were regularly used for this purpose. Moreover, three former East German intellectuals suggested that the GDR had in the 'emigration movement' something analogous to Solidarity in Poland. Those whose applications were refused swelled the ranks of the discontented at home; those who succeeded made new connections across the frontier and encouraged others to follow; while those short-term visitors to the West who went back to the GDR would spread the word about the attractions of life in West Germany. Ludwig Rehlinger has also argued that the business of 'buying free' must have demoralised the police and judicial authorities who thus routinely subverted the rules by which they supposedly lived.

Yet the effect of emigration and the 'buying free' was also, and more immediately, to demoralise those who probably had rather more morale (and morality) to lose in the first place: the would-be opposition. Asked, in July 1989, what they considered to be the main reason for the relative weakness of the opposition in the GDR, as compared with Poland, Hungary and Czechoslovakia, a circle of dissident activists in East Berlin unanimously gave as their first answer: emigration. Of course many other factors contributed: the efficacy of the Stasi; the relative constancy and cheapness of basic consumer supplies; the continuity of an undemocratic political culture; the lack of support from prominent writers and artists; the attitude of parts of the Church leadership; last but not least, the lack of any direct or explicit support from the Federal Government or any of the main parties in Bonn, with the partial exception of the Greens and a few individual Social Democrats. But the main reason remained: emigration.

After unification, Bärbel Bohley, one of the few who both opposed and stayed (indeed, returned), charged the Federal Republic with the 'slice-by-slice' buying of the opposition. Now it may be objected that the numbers of those actually 'bought free' were relatively small. But if one considers what a difference the one to two thousand members of the democratic oppositions in Hungary and Czechoslovakia were to make to the political life of their countries, then it seems reasonable to suggest that the departure of between one and three thousand of East Germany's brightest and best citizens *each year* must have had some debilitating effect. In fact, General Jaruzelski and Gustáv Husák could have dreamed of nothing better than to export their dissidents for hard currency.

This is not to make a final judgement. It is to explain why, in 1986, Erich Honecker could conclude that the balance of German-German relations was favourable to the stabilisation of his unreformed regime. Taking out that protocol of his memorable conversation with Leonid Brezhnev back in July 1970 (see p. 77f), the 74-year old Party leader might nod and say: 'Yes, indeed, how right you were, dear Comrade Leonid Ilyich, to suggest that Brandt's Ostpolitik would increase our "international authority" and "consolidate the position inside the GDR". And so it has! You rightly warned against Brandt's hopes of "penetrating" us, but on balance I think we have that under control.' Unfortunately the man in Moscow was now called Mikhail Gorbachev, and he was embarking on a course of reform which would have Brezhnev turning in his grave.

Liberation by destabilisation

How should the GDR respond to the challenge from the East? The constitution of 1974 said that the GDR was 'for ever and irrevocably allied to the Soviet Union'. Honecker's wife Margot, the Minister of Education, had the GDR's children taught that 'to learn from the Soviet Union is to learn how to win'. On the other hand, by late 1986 Gorbachev was indicating to East European rulers that they were now much more at liberty than under Brezhnev to pursue their own individual domestic strategies. This could be taken, as it was in Poland and Hungary, as an invitation to try further reforms. But it could also be taken as (albeit grudging) licence to continue as before. Honecker, like Husák, took this latter option. But he did not merely batten down the hatches in hope of calmer seas. Instead, he took what looks in retrospect like a remarkable gamble.

Honecker's last gamble was reform substitution on a grand scale. As in the 1970s, but much more boldly, he would use the burgeoning relationship with West Germany as a substitute for political and economic reform at home. Since, however, the example of reform was now coming from Moscow, and being enthusiastically embraced in Budapest and Warsaw, the further opening to the West was accompanied, not, as in the early 1970s, by a redoubling of fraternal ties with the East, but rather by a limitation of those ties. In the 1970s the opening to the West had been accompanied by *Abgrenzung* against the West. Now the further opening to the West was accompanied by *Abgrenzung* against the East.

In relation to Poland the fences had been up since the birth of Solidarity in 1980. But after 1986 the 'fencing-off' was turned against the Soviet Union itself. A Church weekly was forbidden to reprint an article from *Moscow News* on the grounds that this would be 'interference in the affairs of another state'. The Soviet journal *Sputnik* was banned from circulation in the GDR. Honecker lauded the superior economic and social performance of 'socialism in the colours of the GDR'. Yet along with the rejection of the Soviet reforms went a further intensification of German-German contacts, not only between the political élites — referred to in Politburo minutes as the GDR's *'Dialogpolitik'* — but also between ordinary people. As we have seen, from 1986 onwards the number of ordinary East Germans under pensionable age allowed to travel West increased dramatically.

To describe this as a conscious gamble or strategy is of course a speculative interpretation. Rich as they are in many ways, the archives of the former party-state are poorest precisely in documenting the background to decision-making at the very top. Honecker's sometime crown prince and eventual successor, Egon Krenz, suggests that the whole process was more confused, reactive and improvised. Certainly Honecker did not look like a gambler. Yet others who had been close to him argue that he did have a real political intelligence, and even a penchant for taking risks. What is more, in conversation with the author in late 1992, Erich Honecker himself quite emphatically confirmed that the decision to let more people travel was part of a conscious strategy. It was his own response to the challenge from the East, and a further step to 'normalize' relations between the two German states. He believed that his people would become more not less satisfied if they were allowed to travel.

That this is not merely retrospective rationalisation is suggested by perhaps the most striking of all Honecker's comments during his visit to West Germany. Speaking in the town of Neunkirchen in his native Saarland, he said:

> The German Democratic Republic is an active member of . . . the Warsaw Treaty, and the Federal Republic of Germany is firmly anchored in the Western Alliance. It is only too understandable that under these conditions the frontiers are not as they should be. But I believe that if we act in accordance with the communiqué that we agreed in Bonn, and thereby achieve a peaceful co-opera- tion, then the day will also come on which frontiers no longer divide us, but unite us, as the frontier between the German Democratic Republic and the People's Republic of Poland unites . . .

Since the frontier between the GDR and Poland had been virtually closed since the emergence of Solidarity, this could almost be taken for a bad joke. Yet the message that the frontiers were not 'as they should be', and the clear implication that it was the alliances that prevented them from being so, was still remarkable. If there was to be a new era of East-West détente, then this time East Germany would make sure it was in the vanguard.

What Honecker would still vigorously deny in 1992 was the motive of financial need or dependency on the Federal Republic. For those who actually had to keep the state solvent from day to day, this was clearly a dominant concern. But Gerhard Schürer recalls Honecker treating the issue in Politburo as almost an administrative, departmental problem — as if the 'plinth' of net debt could be halved by decree. Talking to the author in 1992, the deposed leader would refer to the Bonn government's recently announced conclusion that the final net hard-currency debt of the GDR was 'only' about DM 30 billion. This, said Honecker blithely, was a level 'usual in trading relations'. And in a striking display of economic naïvety, he suggested that the GDR's debit balance in hard currency should be set against its credit balance in transferable roubles. So even if the GDR's hard currency debt and financial dependency was an objective reason for the further opening to West Germany, and a conscious ground for some of Honecker's close associates, the balance of the evidence suggests that it was probably not a major motive for him.

Beside the political gamble there were no doubt also more personal and emotional elements in the behaviour of the key decision-maker. In 1985 Willy Brandt called him 'the last all-German' in the East German leadership. Helmut Schmidt observed that over the years Honecker became 'more German'. Perhaps this was partly a result of the increasingly intense German-German conversation. Partly it may have been simply old age. Old men remember, and, in his seventies now, Honecker would often hark back to his early days in the Saarland and the tragic division of the German labour movement between Social Democrats and Communists, which had allowed Hitler to come to power.

This was a leitmotif which can be found as early as his intensely emotional meeting in 1973 with Herbert Wehner, with whom he had worked as a young Communist in the Saarland, and of whom he would often speak with deep respect. In the Brandt papers there is a remarkable text — typewritten by Herbert Wehner himself — of what appears to be a letter which Honecker sent him in February 1974. Thanking Wehner for his summary of and commentary on their previous exchanges, Honecker wrote 'I hope that a man like Herbert Wehner can long go on working for views "which another not yet or no longer has". This will make it possible to discuss questions of mutual interest and bring them to a solution.' After emphasising the closeness of the GDR to the Soviet Union, Honecker wrote that he, like the Brandt government, also wished to fill the German-German treaties with life, 'although I assume that even with the best relations, polemics will not be wholly avoidable on account of the different social orders' — a quite extraordinarily mild formulation at a time of fierce public *Abgrenzung*. Honecker and Wehner subsequently met a number of times, in or near East Berlin.

Looking back after his fall from power, Honecker again warmly recalled Wehner's role, saying that although Wehner had rejected the Communist Party 'his goal was still the unity of the labour movement and the building of a socialist German republic'. In 1992 he affirmed that this had also been his own goal. Of course one must allow for the colouring of retrospect. But this all-German leftist perspective was certainly there, and grew stronger rather than weaker with advancing age and the development of German-German relations. 'We are going the German way,' he told Willy Brandt in 1985.

At the same time, he visibly enjoyed the 'recognition' that was increasingly accorded his regime and him personally. Trivial though it may sound, the element of simple vanity should never be underrated in explaining the conduct of men and women in power. Honecker's own visit to West Germany would be the crowning glory — especially if it could include a sentimental return to his native Saarland. And if West Germany wanted more ordinary East Germans to travel too: well, the experience of the last fifteen years suggested that the political risk could be worth taking.

As we have seen, one of the underlying ideas of the West German approach was to produce 'relaxation through reassurance'. Arguably, the reassurance did indeed produce relaxation — but not in the intended form of domestic liberalisation. Instead, it came in the classical form of *hubris*. So reassured was Honecker that he miscalculated the strength, popularity and stability of his own regime. As numerous witnesses testify, he was already suffering from that growing distance from everyday reality which affects all long-term rulers in dictatorships. Asked about public attitudes, he would refer to the happy expression on people's faces at the May Day parade.

In an almost touching conversation with the Czechoslovak Communist Party ideologist Jan Fojtík, in January 1989, Honecker observed (according to the East German record) that it was plain 'that the majority of the population prefers the kind of socialism which respects Engels' view that people need food, clothing etc before they talk about politics. Socialism in some other countries was no example for that. Since in the GDR socialism had something to offer people, it was unshakeable.' One could hardly ask for a more pregnant summary of Honecker's basic political philosophy, strategy, and illusions. But West Germany, with its increasingly fulsome 'recognition', reinforced those illusions.

Plainly, any such interpretation of a leader's motives and calculations can never finally be proven. Yet whatever the precise mixture of causes, the results were visible for all. More East Germans than ever since the building of the Wall travelled, like Honecker himself, to West Germany in 1987. More East Germans than ever returned through the Wall to find an unchanged, indeed a worsening state of affairs at home. The young East German writer Gabriele Eckart concluded a moving account of her first trip to West Germany, in 1987, with the words: 'I would wish everyone who rules over us to peer into the heart of a GDR citizen in the hour after their return from West Germany'.

Their reactions to some aspects of West German life might be ambivalent, but they certainly did not conclude on their return that, as the Central Committee of the Socialist Unity Party had only recently informed them, the GDR was 'one of the freest countries in the world'. In fact, as we now know, secret police control was further stepped up in 1986, with the recruitment or infiltration of Stasi 'officers on special duty' in all key areas of East German life, while a further clampdown on dissent followed soon after Honecker's own return from Bonn.

The people of East Germany now lived with a double contrast: that between their own grey, stagnant reality and the West, which more of them had now seen at first hand; and that between their own unreformed, repressive regime and the increasingly daring reforms in the Soviet Union, Hungary and Poland. It is impossible to say which contrast was more important. They came together. In June 1987, young East Berliners gathered at the western end of Unter den Linden to hear the British rock band Pink Floyd playing just across the Wall, in West Berlin. When the police tried to disperse them, they chanted 'Gorbachev! Gorbachev!' The influences of West and East conspired against Honecker.

Talking to Western visitors, Honecker would often insist that youth was behind the party-state. But polls conducted by its own Institute for Youth Research in Leipzig gave a dramatically different result. Whereas in 1985 some 51 per cent of apprentices, 57 per cent of young workers, and no less than 70 per cent of students said that they felt themselves 'strongly or very strongly' tied to (*verbunden mit*) the GDR, by October 1988 the figures had sunk to 18, 19 and 34 per cent respectively. 28 per cent of the apprentices, 23 per cent of young workers and even 15 per cent of students now replied: 'not all all'. In part, these results may reflect less a change in underlying attitudes than a reduction in fears about the consequences of an honest answer. But whether loss of loyalty or simply loss of fear, the results were devastating.

There were two main outward expressions of growing popular discontent. Firstly, the number of applications to emigrate increased. Figures given to the Politburo by Egon Krenz in April 1988 put the number of applications to emigrate at 112,000, compared with 78,000 in 1987, and 87 per cent of the applicants were under the age of forty. Western estimates of the numbers wishing to leave in 1988–9 varied widely, from a quarter of a million to more than a million. Whatever the true figures, the trend was clearly upward. Honecker hoped that freer travel to the West would make people more satisfied, as arguably it had done in the previous fifteen years. But now it made them more dissatisfied. The combination of direct experience of the West, change to the East, and no change at home, turned the safety-valve into a steam-hammer.

Secondly, despite the sharper repression that followed soon after Honecker's return from West Germany, the dissident groups grew in strength and boldness. When an official mass rally in East Berlin to commemorate the murder of Karl Liebknecht and Rosa Luxemburg was joined by independent demonstrators carrying banners with Rosa Luxemburg's words 'freedom is always freedom for those who think differently', they were rounded up by the police. Several leaders of those who thought differently were now more or less compelled to leave the country, albeit in a few cases with the promise that they could subsequently return. Church synods pointedly sang the praises of perestroika. In a striking echo of Martin Luther, a priest from Wittenberg read '20 Theses' for a reformation of the GDR. Then, in May 1989, the dissidence acquired — for the first time — the breadth and quality of a democratic opposition, with a quite widespread action to monitor local elections. While the regime instantly claimed a 98.85 per cent 'yes' vote, the independent monitors could virtually prove that the results were falsified.

It is important to note that these two tendencies, the growing pressure to emigrate and the growing opposition, were not merely complementary. While they were both expressions of the same discontent, they were in a sense opposite answers to the same challenge. The one said: 'I will stay and fight for improvements here.' The other said: 'that is hopeless, I will leave'. Although would-be emigrants often became oppositionists while they remained, and would-be oppositionists very often ended up as emigrants, it was only in the autumn of 1989 that the two movements really came together as one.

What both indicated was the disappearance of that middle option of steady, controlled reform from above which West German policy had hoped to promote. First the medium-term stabilisation without liberalisation, facilitated by the relationship with West Germany, then the further opening to the West, as a substitute for reform at home, at a time of galloping reform to the East: this sequence had produced a situation which from the viewpoint of the active citizen seemed to offer only two alternatives — resignation (of which emigration could also be an expression) or revolution (to which the wave of emigration finally contributed). From the viewpoint of the state this meant that the domestic political situation was at once very stable — with the combination of state repression and popular resignation — and very unstable.

In June 1989 the Ministry for State Security sent a report to Honecker which estimated the total number of 'hostile, oppositional or other negative forces' in the GDR at about 2,500, with some 600 leaders and a hard core of just sixty 'fanatical . . . unteachable enemies of socialism'. There is no reason to doubt the thoroughness of the Stasi's researches. Two months later Mielke asked a crisis meeting of his regional commanders: 'is it that tomorrow the 17 June will break out?' No, said the commander from Gera. And his colleague from Leipzig averred: 'so far as the power question is concerned, Comrade Minister, we have the thing firmly in hand, *it's stable*' (emphasis added).

Shortly thereafter a '17 June' did begin — in Leipzig — and transformed the GDR out of all recognition. But this was a new 17 June: a peaceful, sustained, candle-bearing 17 June, one which bore the marks not just of the internal learning process of the Church-based opposition in the GDR, but of the much larger East Central European learning curve that began with the German rising of 17 June 1953 and continued through the Hungarian Revolution and the Polish October of 1956, through the Prague Spring of 1968, through the Polish December of 1970, the Polish protests of 1976, the Polish Solidarity born in 1980, the Polish and Hungarian 'refolutions' (reform-revolutions) of the first half of 1989, before returning at last to East Berlin.

Who could but be touched when Willy Brandt declared, in Berlin on the day after the opening of the Wall, 'now what belongs together is growing together'? Who could begrudge Helmut Kohl his moment of glory at the opening of the Brandenburg Gate, or Hans-Dietrich Genscher his triumphant returns to his native Halle? And perhaps most moving of all, to those who knew, was the sight of Willy Brandt once again at the window in Erfurt, twenty years on, this time not pressing his palms downward in that gesture of painful restraint, but raising his arm in a cheerful wave, with the strain only of memories touching the lined familiar face.

Looking at such scenes it seems almost churlish to ask the historian's dry questions about causes and intentions. All's well that ends well. 'The final measure of any policy is its success,' as Adenauer once remarked. And this was an extraordinary success. What need to say more? Yet the question of the real contribution made by Bonn's policy towards the GDR to the end of the GDR is still an interesting one. It might even, perhaps, carry a few indirect lessons for the future. Of course the reasons for the success of the peaceful rebellion and its transformation into unification cannot be understood without looking at the change in Soviet policy, the 'refolutions' and revolutions elsewhere in Eastern Europe, overall developments in East-West relations, and, not least, at the Federal Republic's own relations with the rest of the East. Yet there are some tentative conclusions that may be drawn, and questions still to be asked, about the specific story of policy towards the GDR.

Success and failure

The success was rich in ironies. For a start, the opening of the Berlin Wall was already the fulfilment of the operative goals of the Ostpolitik which began after the building of the Berlin Wall. What followed in 1990 went beyond what the architects of Ostpolitik had thought to be possible. Originally, in the early 1960s, they still hoped for unification in their lifetime. Over the years they gradually, painfully, buried the hope. Now, just as they had thoroughly buried the hope, just as not only they but the Christian Democrats who took over their GDR-policy had become soberly convinced that it would not happen in their lifetime — it happened.

Insofar as they had a concept of promoting desirable political change in the GDR, West German policymakers had aimed at reform from above. Instead, the change came through rebellion from below. As Robert Leicht observed in *Die Zeit*, this was not *Wandel durch Annäherung* (change through rapprochement) but *Wandel durch Auflehnung* (change through rebellion). If the original, and remarkably long-lived, idea had been liberalisation through stabilisation, what actually happened was liberation through destabilisation.

Yet the irony goes deeper still. For we have argued that both the Federal Republic's objective contribution to Honecker's fifteen-year long stabilisation

204 · *In Europe's Name*

without liberalisation, and the subjective contribution of Bonn's increasing, flattering 'recognition' of Honecker and his fundamentally unchanged party-state, including all those assurances about 'no destabilisation', helped to lull Erich Honecker and his colleagues into taking that final political gamble of opening to the West, instead of reform, while fencing-off to the East.

Now one could, of course, suggest, with hindsight, that this was a magnificent piece of long-term strategic deception by West Germany: a triumph of Machiavellism on a grand scale. Destabilisation through stabilisation! Precisely by allowing the Honecker leadership to continue without reforms, Bonn had actually helped the GDR down the road to ruin. So perhaps Franz Josef Strauss had 'saved' the GDR in 1983 only the better to strangle it in 1989? Yet unless hard evidence is produced to the contrary we must be permitted to doubt that the great Bavarian foresaw what no one else did.

So also with the inventor of *Wandel durch Annäherung*. In a conversation in June 1991, Egon Bahr told the author that when Otto Winzer had warned in response to his 1963 Tutzing speech of 'aggression in felt slippers' that was good enough for him. He, Egon Bahr, could not say anything like this, or it would have the reverse effect. Once, in 1968, he had incautiously told an interviewer that the real hope was that a Prague Spring would break out in Moscow. But fortunately the GDR hadn't noticed.

Yet as late as September 1989, Egon Bahr could say, in a discussion in which there were only Western participants: 'If our demands add up to taking away their state from the people (*die Menschen*) over there, then they will certainly not allow it. In this sense reforms in the GDR are only conceivable if the SED [Party] leadership can be certain that one doesn't want to take away their state.' Here the elision was not of people (*die Menschen*) and nation, but of people and Party leadership. Now the stenographic record of these proceedings was subsequently printed and circulated to a small audience. One could therefore theoretically argue that tactical caution explained even these remarks. After all, perhaps a copy might fall into the hands of the East German leadership, and then, instead of relaxing (because reassured) they would sit up and say 'my goodness, they really want to subvert us!' — and therefore clamp down. But it is more plausible to suggest that these remarks indicated not just tactical caution but also some genuine, substantive misassessment of the nature of the East German state and the intentions of its subjects.

Yet were not precisely these Western misapprehensions in a paradoxical way a contribution to the originally desired, but now largely abandoned, end? Was not the reassurance which contributed to Honecker's hubristic misjudgement the more effective precisely because the West German politicians and policymakers at least partly believed what they were saying?

It was, as we have been at pains to stress, by no means only leading Social Democrats who displayed symptoms of cognitive dissonance in relation to the GDR in the mid-1980s, overrating, or at least overstating, its economic strength and its contribution to 'peace' and *Humanität*. In this sense Honecker was not merely the victim of his own illusions. He was also a victim of the Bonn politicians' illusions.

Paradox was the characteristic intellectual figure of German-German relations (itself a paradoxical phrase): the two-in-one of the 'community of responsibility'; accepting the status quo in order to overcome it; strengthening the regime in order to loosen its grip; not demanding German unity being the only means to achieve it. So perhaps the architects of policy towards the GDR might enjoy this final paradox: they got it right because they got it wrong!

It does not, of course, follow that getting it wrong is an advisable course in future dealings with other dictatorships. The *salto mortale* from stabilisation without liberalisation to liberation by destabilisation only succeeded due to overriding external factors, above all the changes in Soviet policy and East European politics, plus a generous slice of luck. Nor does it follow that everything that was actually done in policy towards the GDR was right only because it was wrong.

At least until 1987, and even up until the summer of 1989, the working hypothesis that protest in the GDR would meet with domestic repression, and outright revolution would be crushed by the Red Army, was justified on the information available to policymakers in the West. That was 'Yalta'. It is entirely reasonable to ask: what would have happened if there had been widespread popular discontent, rebellion even, in the GDR in 1983? But we have tried to suggest that the answer is not quite as simple as is often assumed. Almost certainly the protest would have been violently suppressed, with or without the help of Soviet troops, which did not even need to threaten to invade since they were there *en masse* already. So any such protest would have been defeated. But one should note the curious fact that in East Central Europe people celebrate their greatest defeats — from the battles of Mohács and the White Mountain to the Hungarian Revolution, the Prague Spring and Solidarity.

The great Central European argument between idealism and realism is an argument precisely about the meanings of victory and defeat. Even defeated protests leave their mark, and can sometimes, in the end, become victories. This can never be said of non-existent protests. No one has the right from a position of comfort and safety to encourage others to risk their lives; but equally, no one has the right to deny others that possibility. Treading along the narrow line between not encouraging an oppressed people to revolt, and actively discouraging them from exercising what Harold Hurwitz called their 'right to insurrection', the Federal Republic erred on the side of discouragement. 'German realism' underrated the possible contribution even of apparently failed revolts — like the 17 June 1953 — to a final victory. Until very late in the day, West German policymakers failed to distinguish clearly between the two meanings of 'destabilisation': between West Germany trying to liberate the East Germans and the East Germans trying (albeit step-by-step) to liberate themselves.

If for most of this period the East Germans did not seem to be making many efforts to liberate themselves, the relative passivity of the majority was to some extent an effect of West German policy, while the minority received little or no encouragement from Bonn. The ultimate, external justification — the Red Army — did, however, seem persuasive so long as Moscow's attitude did not change. And in the rest of Ostpolitik Bonn was attempting to change Moscow's attitude, partly by the repeated reassurance of 'no destabilisation'.

One cannot, moreover, simply dismiss the claim that, whatever the stabilising effects on the internal political life of the GDR, this policy was justified by the help it gave individual people, *die Menschen*. How can we possibly put a value on the freedom which the Bonn government bought for nearly 300,000 people? And the temporary freedom for the millions who could travel to the West? Yet one may at least ask if the overall price paid for these gains was not a worse existence at home for the majority.

Here we again enter the treacherous realms of the counter-factual, of 'what would have happened if . . .' If the Bonn government had pursued a somewhat tougher policy in the 1980s, being less generous in its financial dealings, making explicit linkages to respect for human rights inside the GDR, pressing more loudly for reform, 'recognising' the independent groups as fully as it did the regime, could this have resulted in, or at least facilitated, that combination of reforms and the growth of civil society which one saw elsewhere in East Central Europe?

Some have gone a step further and argued that such a combination, if introduced early enough, might even have saved the GDR. In 1990 this argument was made, with different emphases, by leading figures from the younger generation in the Party, by some members of the opposition groups which led the peaceful protests in autumn 1989, and by some sympathetic politicians, scholars and intellectuals in the West. In whatever precise form the argument is made, it assumes that there was a possible 'third way': a system attractive enough to compete with the liberal capitalist democracies of the West, yet different enough from them to justify a separate state. Since it was precisely this hope of a 'third way' which 1989 marked the end of all over Eastern Europe, and 1991 in the Soviet Union, it is difficult to see how it could have survived just in the GDR — for all the considerable resources of ideological ingenuity present in that small space.

Even if there were such a 'third way', which might conceivably have justified a continued division of Germany, it is almost impossible to see how this could have justified the continued division of Berlin. Democratic socialism at one end of the Friedrichstrasse and social democracy at the other? And a state frontier in between? Yet without East Berlin there would hardly be a GDR, and West Berlin could not seriously be expected to risk joining the great new adventure.

Earlier reforms and a stronger civil society might, however, have meant a different end to the GDR: one in which a reformist Party leadership made a more constructive retreat, while the population had its own experienced and sophisticated political counter-élite, its shadow government in waiting. Both were notable features of the 'refolutions' in Poland and Hungary. As a result, the East Germans as a whole might have gone in to the process of unification with somewhat more self-respect and higher morale. In other words, there is a question whether West German policy did not, in some small degree, also contribute to that demoralisation of the people in East Germany which was so apparent during and after unification. Did not the patronising approach (*Bevormundung*) by the government in the West aggravate, at least to some degree, the systematic denial of adult responsibility (*Entmündigung*) by the regime in the East? Yet this is, we must stress again, a suggestion made on a highly speculative basis of 'what if . . ?'

Another, related, speculation concerns the rapid turn in East Germany after the opening of the Wall from the cry of 'we are the people' (*Wir sind das Volk*) to that of 'we are one people' (*Wir sind ein Volk*). Here two claims for West German policy are made. The first is that the defensive Deutschlandpolitik of the Christian Democrats, rhetorically holding high the constitutional claim to unity and jealously guarding the fine legal distinctions that underpinned it, contributed to keeping alive the hope of unification in the hearts of ordinary East Germans. The second claim is that the offensive GDR-policy of promoting contacts of all kinds between the people in the two states, pioneered by Social and Free Democrats, did indeed keep alive among people in the GDR the consciousness of belonging to one nation. Neither claim can be lightly discounted, nor does one contradict the other.

Yet given the context in which revolution turned to unification, some scepticism is in order. The fact is that all over Eastern Europe in 1989, as in 1848, the ideas of liberty and nation went together. Everywhere, but everywhere, the hope of one was seen in the other. Moreover, the common sense case for joining the Federal Republic, as the fastest route to secure prosperity, liberty, democracy, the rule of law — and protection from possible reversals in the East — was so overwhelming, that one may doubt if the earlier nuances of consciousness made a decisive difference. One is tempted to suggest that even if the Federal Republic had totally ignored the German Democratic Republic for the previous twenty years, the East Germans would still have come knocking on West Germany's door.

The degree to which the German nation actually had been 'held together' can also be overstated. We recall the startling figure that eighty-four per cent of a representative sample of West Germans had 'no contacts' with East Germans in 1988. And if one was impressed by the cry of 'we are one people' in East Germany, then one could also be struck by the degree to which profound differences between 'Easterners' and 'Westerners' persisted — and even grew — after unification.

With all these 'if' arguments, however, we still have to bear in mind one rudimentary constraint on West German policy: the position of the hostage city West Berlin. Even if all the criticisms made above were allowed, one could still argue that West Germany had to deal with the GDR in more or less this way because of West Berlin. As we have seen, the largest part of the direct financial transfers to East Berlin was related directly to improving the position of West Berlin.

This position was sometimes compared to that of Hong Kong. Now, in 1991 the British Prime Minister became the first Western leader to pay an official visit to Peking since the massacre of students on Tiananmen Square in June 1989. The Prime Minister had to do this, British officials said, because of the position of Hong Kong. Loud moralising and megaphone diplomacy would not help the people on the spot. Quiet diplomacy was best. The resemblance to the argument made by Brandt and his team from Berlin was very striking. Yet when the Prime Minister actually got to Peking, he spoke out strongly and publicly on human rights — not least because of pressures from public and political opinion at home.

So even in such a tightly constrained policy there is a range of possibilities in what one says and how one says it. When the Mayor of Bonn went to the new partner town of Potsdam in 1988 he pleaded publicly for the release of those arrested after the Luxemburg/Liebknecht demonstration, and declared that he would speak out for human rights 'whether in Potsdam or in South Africa'. Far from Mayor Daniels earning all-round applause from political and public opinion in the Bonn republic, however, he was widely criticised. The Social Democratic Bundestag member for Bonn, Horst Ehmke, suggested that he should apologise to his East German hosts.

The most serious questions about West German policy are perhaps ultimately less about what was done than about what was said — or not said — to the leadership of the GDR and the people of the GDR; and what was said — or not said — about the GDR. For in the condition of permanent communication between the two halves of Germany created above all by television, there was no clear dividing line between speaking to and speaking about.

This is a complex subject, but let us start with a simple assertion: the public picture of the GDR presented by most West German policy makers and opinion-formers in 1987 was hard to reconcile with the public picture of the GDR presented by most West German policy makers and opinion-formers in 1991. The former was remarkably positive and friendly. The negative features of the GDR, and especially of its frontiers, were of course mentioned, but the general syntax of commentary was: *on the one hand* there is the Wall, the Stasi, shortages, greyness etc, but *on the other hand* there are small improvements for *die Menschen*, social security, the rediscovery of Germanness, the commitment to humanity and peace. And 'the other hand', that important but easily abused intellectual instrument, worked overtime.

The commentary in 1991, by contrast, was almost uniformly negative. A whole vocabulary for the description of a dictatorship — starting with the word 'dictatorship' — which had largely disappeared from the polite society of German politics, was rediscovered overnight with the end of the dictatorship. To substantiate this generalisation would of course require extensive documentation, for how otherwise can one show what is 'typical' and what not? Here the reader will simply have to take the generalisation on trust.

Now as we have seen, it is possible, and even, up to a point, plausible to argue that this flattering treatment of the GDR was part of a long-term strategy designed to change the way in which the rulers of the GDR ruled. Here was recognition and reassurance designed to produce relaxation and reform. We have tried to show how oblique and paradoxical were the real effects of this long-term strategy on the GDR. But there remains the question whether West German policymakers did not actually come to believe some of what they said. And even if — as experienced politicians — they did not believe what they said, whether other people in the Federal Republic, especially younger people, did believe it.

An ambassador, according to a famous English definition, is a good man sent to lie abroad for the good of his country. The Federal Republic carefully emphasised that its Permanent Representative in East Berlin was not an ambassador. And his task differed from that of an Ambassador also in this: that he was a good man sent to lie in his own country for the good of his country. And this did not just apply to the Permanent Representative. Because of the condition of permanent communication between the two halves of the divided country, politicians, officials, journalists, academics, priests, writers — all were players in the great game of intra-German relations. All could feel themselves to be, in some small degree, permanent representatives. Their words had political weight. The temptations into which this could lead were strikingly anticipated in a letter which one of West Germany's most famous writers, Günter Grass, wrote to Willy Brandt in February 1970.

'As a result of the new Ost- and Deutschlandpolitik of the social-liberal coalition,' wrote Grass, 'the Stalinism inside the GDR is no longer critically treated and Stalinist attacks from the Honecker camp rightly [*sic*] go unanswered. This behaviour, relaxed and right in itself, can nonetheless lead inside the SPD to the false conclusion that there might soon be a reconciliation with the SED . . . Already the understandable desire for détente is producing curious side-effects.' And then he came to the point, which was that West German television (ARD) was declining to broadcast his play about the 17 June 1953 rising, *The Plebeians Rehearse the Uprising*, on the grounds that this could disturb relations with Moscow and, above all, negotiations with the GDR.

'In other words,' wrote Grass:

> the change of climate in the Federal Republic brought about by the change of government has, beside a whole series of favourable and liberating democratic developments, encouraged increasing uncertainty in the judgement of the social systems in the two German states. Extreme swings in Germany, familiar of old, suggests that the cold warriors of yesterday can in no time transform themselves into effusive peace-apostles . . .

(The letter is marvellously characteristic of the writer's — all writers' — train of thought: there must be something wrong if they won't broadcast my play!)

The development that Grass anticipated, and then at times himself seemed to exemplify, went through self-censorship to relativism. It is important to understand the shape this relativism took in the 1980s. It was not a simple restatement of the 'convergence' theories of the 1960s, according to which communist 'industrial society' and capitalist 'industrial society' would necessarily converge; although if one listened carefully echoes of that theory could still be found. But explicitly and repeatedly the leaders of West German political opinion said that the two systems could not be reconciled, an interpretation heartily endorsed by the East German leadership.

Socialism and capitalism were like fire and water. However, both fire and water have their uses as well as their dangers. This new relativism consisted, firstly, in a concentration on the overarching common problems — the threat of nuclear war, environmental destruction, hunger and overpopulation in the Third World — beside which mere system differences in Central Europe could appear insignificant. Secondly, it was founded on a consistent effort to look at the 'brighter side', the positive qualities, of the East German state and/or society — with the distinction between state and society often being blurred. Out of the attempt at 'normalisation' came, gradually, the conclusion that a certain normality had been achieved, that, for all its faults, the GDR was another possible version of Germany, or at least, that life in the GDR offered another possible way of living as a German.

In place of the clear, and to be sure simplistic, contrast between freedom in the West and dictatorship in the East, there was now talk of the two states' different 'terms of business' (Klaus Bölling), of a 'Peace of Augsburg' between the two systems (Günter Gaus), implying that the difference between communism and liberal democracy was comparable to that between Protestantism and Catholicism. After all, did not both worship the same God, the God of peace? Klaus Bölling wrote in his 1983 memoirs that Erich Honecker's self-confidence had grown because he knew 'that time has passed by all the reunification ideas of the Adenauer era, because it is the general consensus in East and West that peace is after all a higher good than those articles dedicated to the thought of freedom which can also be found in the constitution of the GDR'. So much for freedom.

Of course there were countless variants and gradations of this relativism. And of course it cannot solely be ascribed to the effects of a détente policy towards the GDR. It was certainly more widespread on the left than on the right. The years that saw the birth of the social-liberal Ostpolitik also saw fierce criticism of the real, existing Federal Republic, against which was counterposed the vision of 'another republic'. Not only in the generation of Herbert Wehner but also in the class of '68 were attitudes to *the* other German republic related, albeit in very complex and often contradictory ways, to hopes of *an* other republic at home. Somewhere in both was still the hope of a 'third way'. The specific story of the West German Social Democrats is examined in more detail in Chapter Six.

Almost as important, and overlapping this particular history of the left, was the peculiar history of German Protestantism, in West as well as East. From this quarter, for example, came the notion that the division of Germany was in some way God's punishment for the sins of the fathers. There is a very important book still to be written on the political history of German Protestantism over the whole period from 1933 to 1989.

There is also a distinctive history of journalism, and of scholarship. In journalism, political, ideological and cultural motives mixed with simpler common factors, such as competition for a good story and self-censorship out of the fear of expulsion or visa-refusal — that 'visa syndrome' familiar from writing about the rest of the Soviet bloc. In scholarship, there were also the familiar conflicts of generations and disciplines. A younger generation of scholars embraced a social scientific approach to analysis of the GDR, ostensibly value-free, 'taking the system on its own terms', against an older generation of political scientists and lawyers, with their value-loaded theory of 'totalitarianism'. After anti-communism came anti-anti-communism.

In 1990, once the East had voted for the West, the West generously supplied it with West German schoolbooks, so that young East Germans could learn the true facts about German history and politics. Opening these schoolbooks, the young East Germans — some of whom had just been on the streets demonstrating to get rid of the dictatorship — could read that 'both states [the Federal Republic and the GDR] understand themselves as democracies'. Elsewhere they would learn that the 17 June 1953 was 'the rising of a minority in the GDR, concerned mainly or even exclusively with social questions'. 'Read No. 10.24,' they would be instructed by another textbook, 'and try to explain why many citizens of the GDR are self-confident and proud of their state'.

None of this should be made simpler than it was. In a liberal democracy it should, however, be possible to distinguish clearly between the politicians and the intellectuals: the latter jealously guarding their independence, and attempting, as Havel put it, to 'live in truth', the former necessarily working in half-truth. Yet one of the features of the intra-German détente was that this distinction was very substantially blurred. The intellectuals — writers, journalists, scholars — became participants in the policy. Their analyses were coloured by the hopes or expectations of the policymakers, which their analyses in turn reinforced, which in turn . . .

So far as the politicians and policymakers were concerned, we may point to another palette of special causes. After unification not a few remarked, notably in relation to the economic weakness of the GDR, 'we didn't know . . .'. Although, as we have indicated, their own Western analysts did partly fail them, the strict answer to this must be that they could have known. There were, beyond this, a number of reasons specific to their *métier*. Politicians have to claim success, and that in the fairly short term. Since all parties now practised the policy of small steps, they all had to claim success for it. Small successes, to be sure, but if one goes on claiming small successes for a long time, then a lot of small successes must begin to add up to a larger one.

Secondly, there is the problem of repetition. An associate of Adenauer's has suggested that one of the reasons Adenauer came genuinely to believe in the goal of reunification near the end of his life, having perhaps originally embraced it more tactically, is that it is very difficult to go on repeating something publicly for twenty years without beginning to believe it yourself. Perhaps what happened to Adenauer with the aspiration to reunification happened, in reverse, with some West German politicians in the 1970s and 1980s. Constantly repeating that the GDR was a strong, stable, improving state, worthy of growing recognition, did they not come — just a little — to believe it?

For those most directly involved there was also sometimes an emotional element of discovering that older Germany which lay just under the surface of the Soviet-type state, following the familiar East European paradox of revolutionary conservation. In the case of Günter Gaus —

revealing precisely because it was extreme — it would not be too much to say that he fell in love with the GDR. Indeed, in a curious novella he wrote at the time of unification he portrayed her — if she it was — as a lost woman. While West Germany's leaders constantly insisted that the Federal Republic was not and would never be a 'wanderer between the worlds' (that is, East and West), a veteran practitioner of policy towards the GDR described himself precisely as a 'wanderer between the worlds'. And strange bonds developed between some of these intra-German nego-tiators, advocates, as they saw it, of elementary humanity, and defenders of the people.

If this sounds fanciful, there is another speculation which may seem even more so. There is a well-known psychological phenomenon — sometimes called the Stockholm Syndrome — in which hostages come to identify with their captors, or at least to show extraordinary appreciation of their 'humanity'. Now West German policymakers, while not them-selves hostages, were nonetheless, as we have seen, acutely conscious of negotiating on behalf of hostages — the hostage city West Berlin, and *die Menschen* in the GDR. In a sense, from 1961 to 1989 Germany lived through a twenty-eight year long hostage crisis. It is quite difficult to work with people over many years, smiling for the photographers, doing the honours, sitting at the same table talking about peace and humanity, and still regard them as criminals. For if they are criminals, what am I doing shaking their hand and paying them compliments and hard currency?

In a remarkable article to mark Honecker's visit to Bonn, Helmut Schmidt concluded that the West Germans, having spoken for years of the oppressed East Germans as 'our brothers and sisters', should now welcome Erich Honecker as 'one of our brothers'. But then, in his memoirs, he observed: 'the charge that the Federal Government allowed itself to be blackmailed in the "buying free" of prisoners always angered me, although *or rather because* it was factually correct' (author's italics). Those three little words — 'or rather because' — surely capture an important psycho-logical truth. Trying to make a virtue out of necessity, one ended up ascribing some of the virtue to the necessity. My blackmailer, my brother.

In his valedictory speech to the Bundestag in 1986, Schmidt himself identified the emotional tension that he also exemplified. 'The suffering caused by the partition,' he said, 'brings the recurrent danger that the chronic German inclination to emotional overreaction breaks dangerously through.' Indeed, in looking at the ups and downs of the West German perceptions of East Germany, one thinks of nothing so much as of 'The Marquise von O.' Readers may recall that in Kleist's story the Marquise believes herself to have been saved from a fate worse than death by a noble Russian officer, only to discover that he himself had raped her while she swooned — yet finally marries him. At the end of the story her new husband asks her why, after the discovery, she shrank away from him as if he were a devil. She would not have taken him for a devil, sighs the Marquise, if she had not first taken him for an angel.

In the history of West Germany's relationship to the GDR we see a double reverse Marquise von O. effect. First, in the 1950s, the GDR was demonised. Then, in the 1970s and 1980s, it was increasingly idealised. And then, in the early 1990s, it was demonised once again. Yet through all this the most salient feature of the GDR was just how little it changed: arguably less than any other state in Eastern Europe. Certainly the way the GDR treated its own citizens changed much less than the way the Federal Republic treated the GDR.

Now some might feel that such an impressionistic account of states of mind — and heart — has no place in a serious analysis. How much safer to stick to sober facts about trade and traffic and rail links! And really such statements should only be made biographically, for each individual is a special case. Yet the real dereliction of intellectual duty would be not to mention the emotional depths at all, for, difficult as they are to describe, they were nonetheless very, very important.

After the end of the dictatorship comes the process known in West Germany after 1945 as *Vergangenheitsbewältigung*, that is, overcoming or coming to terms with the past. In the case of the Third Reich, beside self-examination by the Germans there was a less acute self-examination by peoples to the west. How much had Britain, for example, contributed to the horrors, by the policy which gave the previously positive term 'appeasement' a lasting bad name? Should Britain not have done more to encourage, or at least to recognise the efforts of the German resistance to Hitler?

Now the GDR was not the Third Reich. It did not practise genocide and it was in no position to start wars. Its army and security forces took part in one invasion in Europe — that of Czechoslovakia in 1968 — and a few lesser 'advisory' actions in the Third World. Otherwise, its evils were confined to home, and even its domestic evils were, on the whole, lesser evils than those of the Third Reich — although their effects could be more insidious because they lasted so much longer. The self-examination of those who served, or merely accepted, this regime was made in some ways easier, but in many ways more difficult, by the fact that they were doing it no longer 'among themselves', like the Czechs or Hungarians, but in the same house as the West Germans.

Yet there was also a lesser self-examination to be made on the West German side. For the Federal Republic's responsibility for what happened in the GDR was greater than that of any other Western state in relation to any other Eastern state. Did West Germany really do all that was in its power to combat, limit, or at least moderate the everyday evils of the GDR? Was the right balance struck between the interests of West Germany itself, of West Berlin, and of the people in the GDR? Did policymakers distinguish clearly enough between party-state and society? Was 'buying free' the best and only possible way to help those who dared to protest? Did all that negotiation, hard currency, recognition and self-censorship really achieve the desired effects? Even if it did, what was the price, in demoralisation in the East and relativism in the West? Did not some West Germans come, after all, to accept the GDR as another sort of German normality? And if so, what did that say about their own norms?

V

Beyond the Oder

History and frontiers

In a seminal essay on West German foreign policy, the historian Richard Löwenthal once described the Federal Republic as the product of a 'double conflict' with the Soviet Union. There was, he wrote, a common conflict of the West, including the West Germans, based on the shared desire to preserve freedom this side of the 'Yalta' dividing line. But there was also a special conflict of the West Germans, based on the desire for reunification and a refusal to accept the loss of German territories east of the Oder-Neisse line. In this latter conflict, the Federal Republic could count only on limited, and dwindling, support from the West. Writing in 1974, Löwenthal described the Eastern treaties as the Federal Republic's 'liberation' from this special conflict, a liberation that was 'on the whole successful'.

Yet looking at the Federal Republic's relations with Eastern Europe in the 1970s and 1980s, his optimistic verdict seems more than a little premature. For what is most striking about these relations is the extent to which they continued to be shaped both by the legacy of the past and by the Federal Republic's own continued pursuit of a set of special, national goals. West Germany's relations with the states and societies of Eastern Europe since the Eastern treaties cannot possibly be understood without reference to the results of pre-1945 German Ostpolitik, on the one hand, and to the intentions of post-1961 Deutschlandpolitik on the other.

The past did not weigh equally on all the Federal Republic's Eastern ties. West Germany's relations with Hungary, Bulgaria and Romania were markedly easier than her relations with Poland, Czechoslovakia or the Soviet Union. It has been suggested that this is partly because the first-mentioned countries have never had a common frontier with Germany. There is some truth in this. It is a general rule of modern European history – at least until 1945 – that neighbouring states are more likely to be enemies, while the neighbour's neighour is more likely to be a friend.

Thus Germany goes with Russia against Poland, France with Poland against Germany, and so on. The great Polish-Jewish-British historian Lewis Namier memorably called this 'the rule of odd and even numbers'.

Yet Germany's post-1945 relationship with the neighbour's neighbour Soviet Union and with unadjacent Yugoslavia was heavily burdened, while that with adjacent Switzerland was clearly less so. For beyond, and cutting across, this general factor, the specific causes lie in the period 1938-47, and the question of who did what to whom in that terrible decade. If we look more closely, the crucial difference seems to be that between wartime allies and wartime enemies. Hungary, Bulgaria and Romania were – less or more willingly – allied to, or satellites of, Hitler's Reich for most of the Second World War. They neither suffered so heavily from German occupation, nor inflicted such heavy suffering on Germans in return.

It is no accident that the diplomatic 'normalisation' of relations with just these three countries was accomplished without major, fraught negotiations, and, indeed, without formal treaties. Other factors subsequently made a particular relationship more difficult (e.g. Ceauşescu's dictatorship, and ill-treatment of the German minority), or easier (Hungary's reforms, and good treatment of its German minority). But the history of these countries' relations with Germany and the Germans before the founding of the Federal Republic was not in itself a major, ongoing burden.

It was such a burden with Poland, Czechoslovakia and the Soviet Union. The complex, rich and troubled history of their relations with Germany is reflected in a complex, rich, but also very troubled historiography. Partisan interpretations, polemics, apologies, double standards and special pleading have abounded, even in supposedly scholarly work written decades after the disputed events. There were always notable and honourable exceptions, both in Germany and in Eastern Europe. There has more recently been a general although uneven improvement in standards both of national scholarship and international scholarly exchange. (Each requires the other. Good scholars talk and listen to their foreign peers, but it is no good talking to scholars who are no good.) To attempt to make any concise generalisations or overall judgements nonetheless remains an extremely difficult and risky undertaking.

Insofar as it directly affected Ostpolitik, this history may very crudely be divided into five main chapters: the whole, long period up to the moment of first territorial encroachment by *Wehrmacht* and *SS*; the period of war with Germany and German occupation; the post-war reprisals against, and mass expulsions of, the Germans; the major conflict that still persisted after the founding of the Federal Republic on the issue of the new frontiers drawn in what we call in shorthand 'Yalta' Europe; and, last but not least, the position of the remaining German minorities in what was now called Eastern Europe.

Only in the Polish case was the balance plainly negative even in that first, long chapter. Men and women of goodwill on both sides of the Oder-Neisse line have tried to evoke the happier moments of German-Polish relations. They recall the rich cultural and technological interchange in the late middle ages or the period of German liberal enthusiasm for the cause of Polish independence in the 1830s, when every romantic poet worth his salt (and many not worth it) penned a song for Poland. Yet the sad truth is that long before 1939 the German-Polish relationship was one of the most tense and difficult in Europe.

Both German views of Poles and Polish views of Germans were poisoned by the fact that, from the partitions of the late eighteenth century until 1918, Germans had ruled over Poles, often bringing good administration and economic progress, to be sure, but also crushing the Poles' insurrections and, in the late nineteenth century, attempting to 'Germanise' their children. In this period, too, the whole previous history was rewritten by both sides, in textbook, ballad and historical novel, through a nationalist prism.

The re-creation of an independent Polish state in the bitterly contested Versailles settlement of 1918/19 meant the transfer to Poland of territory in which Germans had not only lived but ruled for more than a century. Co-existence was tense wherever Poles ruled Germans or Germans ruled Poles, not to mention in the Free City of Danzig (Gdańsk). Poles and Germans engaged in armed struggle for control of Upper Silesia, a conflict that was hardly resolved by arbitrary partition. The German minority in Poland was discriminated against by the Polish authorities, who viewed it as a 'fifth column' for the 'revisionist' or 'revanchist' aspirations which German governments, including that of the harmonising Europeanist Gustav Stresemann, did indeed harbour. And then Hitler's Germany and Stalin's Soviet Union joined forces to erase the Polish state from the map of Europe, in what has been called the fourth partition.

'*Placet*', wrote the Habsburg empress Maria Theresa in the margin of the first partition decree of 1772, 'because so many great and learned men wish it so. When I am long dead, people will find out what will come of this violation of everything that up to now was sacred and just.' Writing in 1990, Bishop Josef Homeyer, a dedicated advocate of Polish-German reconciliation, commented wryly: 'We have found out.'

In the Czechoslovak – or rather Czech and Slovak – and Soviet – or rather Soviet-Russian – cases it is possible to derive a less wholly negative balance from at least part of the pre-war chapter. The shared history of Czechs and Germans, in some respects even until 1938, was one of compromise as well as conflict, of mutual enrichment as well as bitter rivalry. The formal renunciation of the Munich Agreement in the 1973 treaty with Czechoslovakia did begin to make it possible for Czechs as well as Germans to start looking back 'before Munich', although the legally qualified nature of that renunciation, combined with the strength and radicalism of the Sudeten German lobby, would combine to reopen the wound after 1989. The Slovaks' historic oppressor was Hungary rather than Germany, and the wartime Slovak republic was another ally of Hitler's Reich, until honour was saved at the eleventh hour by a brief uprising.

The German-Russian relationship is one of the most contorted, and psychologically complex, in all European history. It contains, as Sebastian Haffner has written, almost every conceivable variant of relations between two nations. But throughout, on both sides, there was admiration as well as distrust, fascination as well as repulsion. Germans might be more ready than Russians to recall the part played by Germans, since the eighteenth century, in the attempted modernisation (and westernisation) of Tsarist Russia. Russians might be more ready than Germans to recall the spirit of Rapallo. Neither might like to recall the Hitler-Stalin pact. But none of this shared history, good and bad, could be completely forgotten.

Of course, these pre-war histories were buried under the memory of war, occupation and post-war reprisals. Here, too, the balance was somewhat different in each case. Poland was again the extreme. With the single, unique exception of the Jews, no people suffered more terribly under German occupation than the Poles. Beside three million Polish Jews, some three million ethnic Poles were killed, more than a million were forced to go to work in Germany, hundreds of thousands were driven out of their homes to make way for ethnic Germans from further east, all were deprived and oppressed. But it was then to Poland that nearly a quarter of post-1918 Germany was assigned, at Stalin's behest, with the assent of the United States and Britain. It was then from these territories that the largest number of Germans was expelled, at Stalin's behest, with Roosevelt and Churchill's assent, but also with the direct brutality of Poles taking revenge. The British historian of Eastern Europe, Norman Davies, writes: 'For the first time in their lives, a great mass of ordinary and decent Germans were reduced to the sort of predicament which most ordinary and decent citizens of Central and Eastern Europe had come to regard as normal.' Horror followed horror.

'One ought,' observes the German historian Golo Mann, 'to look upon events and decisions between 1939 and 1947 as a chain of evil actions and evil reactions.' Yet the image of the chain invites the question: where does the chain begin? With Hitler? With Stalin before Hitler? With the First World War before Stalin? And so one enters that historiographical danger zone where the necessary, balanced account of a full historical context can slide into moral relativism and national apologies – a minefield now staked out with signs marked *Historikerstreit*.

Plainly the tangled web of causality and responsibility – more skein than chain – cannot even be properly laid out, let alone disentangled, here. Perhaps the only just comment on this whole terrible last act of Europe's second Thirty Years' War is the verse written in 1939 by the poet W H Auden:

> I and the public know
> What all schoolchildren learn
> Those to whom evil is done
> Do evil in return.

Such light sovereign compassion may be possible for an Englishman, particularly an Englishman watching from New York. It was not possible for those directly involved.

The post-1945 Polish and German historiographies of this period were therefore like distorted mirror images of each other. German historians at once documented, with minute acerbity, the horrors of the Polish expulsions. Only later, in the 1960s, did they move on to document the prior horrors of German occupation. Polish historians at once documented, with minute acerbity, the horrors of German occupation. Only much later did a few independent scholars and intellectuals try to open up the question of the Polish deportations. (The asymmetry was compounded by the asymmetrical position of the two historical professions. From the 1950s, West German scholars were free agents in a way that Polish contemporary historians only began to be in the 1980s).

The Czech case was comparable, if not quite so extreme. The wartime occupation was terrible, but not as comprehensively murderous as in Poland. The post-war reprisals and expulsions were often brutal, and they were carried out not, as in Poland, on the orders of a puppet communist government directly under Stalin's thumb, but on the instructions of a legitimate and still semi-autonomous Czechoslovak government. Here too, the distorted mirror image was broken by free West German scholars in the 1960s, and by independent, isolated – indeed banned – Czech scholars a decade later. The shadow remained, but it was not as long or dark as in the Polish case. Nor did it find quite such persistent expression in official relations, whereas Polish government claims to compensation payments for victims of German occupation, and German government demands on behalf of the remaining German minority, continued to figure high on the Polish-German agenda throughout the 1970s and 1980s.

The Soviet case was different again. Soviet citizens of all nationalities suffered terribly in the war and under German occupation. The totemic phrase 'twenty million Russian war dead' may be allowed to stand for this suffering, even if, as Norman Davies has observed, it was probably not twenty million, many of them were not Russian, and quite a lot were victims of Stalin's dictatorship rather than Hitler's war. Yet the fact that Soviet citizens also suffered terribly under their 'own' dictatorship, both before and after the war, gave the memory at least a different context from the Czech and Polish ones. So did the Hitler-Stalin Pact, and Soviet-German co-operation in the fourth partition of Poland.

Moreover, the Soviet Union won the war – more, it won an empire.

Germany lost a Reich stretching into the east of Europe. The Soviet Union gained an empire stretching into the centre of Germany. The overall German-Soviet balance sheet for the years 1939 to 1949 thus showed huge profits as well as losses on the Soviet side: at least, so long as one considered gaining an empire to be a profit. As we have seen, some West German policymakers, particularly those of the 'front generation', felt a deep psychological need to make moral 'compensation' to the Soviet Union for its wartime losses – a feeling sometimes curiously mixed with the awe of the vanquished for the superior strength of the victor. But Stalin took his 'compensation' at once, in lands and men. What is more, he took it more from Poland than from Germany. This is perhaps the deepest irony of the historical legacy.

The history of wartime diplomacy is exceedingly complex, and in part still unclear due to the shortage of Soviet sources. Yet there is little doubt that the incorporation of eastern Germany into Poland was fundamentally dictated by the incorporation of eastern Poland into the Soviet Union. It is of course true that the Western allies wished to punish, and themselves contemplated dismembering, Germany – and above all Prussia, the imagined heart of darkness. It is true that some Polish leaders saw the more developed territories in the west as, in the circumstances, a good swap for the lost eastern territories, as well as providing a militarily more defensible frontier. But it is also true that in the last years of the war the legitimate Polish Government-in-exile bitterly opposed this westward shift. And Churchill, who in 1943 had encouraged Stalin's scheme, argued at the Potsdam conference that the southern part of Poland's new western frontier should follow the line of the eastern rather than the western River Neisse. (In 1939 some 2.7 million Germans had lived in the large part of Silesia between the two Neisse rivers.) It was Stalin's unbending insistence on keeping almost all the territory that he had first acquired by the Hitler-Stalin pact which led directly to the 'compensation' of Poland in the west, and it was Stalin – speaking both in his own name and through his Polish puppets – who insisted on the western Neisse.

For the Soviet Union, this was a double gain. Not only did it acquire vast new territories, under its direct or indirect control. It also ensured that the new Poland and Germany would be in bitter conflict over the lost German territories, and therefore that the new Poland – whatever the precise complexion of its regime – would be beholden to the Soviet Union for the security of its western frontier, so long as Germany would not accept the permanence of that frontier. For who else would actually defend the Oder-Neisse line? In one move, Stalin destroyed the German Reich, tied Poland to Russia, and added yet one more cause for hatred between Germans and Poles.

Having achieved the new frontiers *de facto*, the Soviet Union then devoted its formidably consistent diplomatic attention to securing full, formal, binding, ceremonial recognition of these frontiers *de jure*. The concluding protocol of the Potsdam conference said that 'the final delimitation of the western frontier of Poland should await the peace settlement'. However, the final peace conference, with a formal settlement and treaties, such as had taken place after the First World War, did not happen. It was pre-empted by the Cold War. Beside the legal recognition of frontiers, the Soviet Union wished so far as possible also to secure recognition of the political status quo that it had established behind those frontiers, of all that it comprehensively styled 'the post-war realities'.

In the circumstances of the time, the new East European states had little choice but to recognise both the Soviet Union's new western frontiers, which deprived Hungary, Czechoslovakia and Romania as well as Poland of some of their pre-war territory, and each other's new frontiers. The new German leaders in the Soviet Zone of Occupation were initially loath to recognise the Polish western frontier. (It is sometimes forgotten that they had proportionately almost as many refugees and expellees from the east.) As late as 1947 Otto Grotewohl declared: 'The Socialist Unity Party regrets any change of frontiers. It rejects the Oder-Neisse line as much as frontier changes in the west.' But they were soon drummed into line. In the 1950 Görlitz Agreement between the GDR and the Polish People's Republic, East Germany ceremonially recognised the Oder-Neisse line not just as the frontier between the two socialist states, but as 'the state frontier between Germany and Poland'.

The challenge was, therefore, to secure recognition from the major Western powers and from the new Western Germany, which claimed to be the legal heir of the German Reich and to speak for all Germans. To recall Löwenthal's distinction, this was an issue both in the general East-West conflict and in the special conflict of the Federal Republic with the East.

In the struggle for recognition of the frontiers, the Soviet Union was joined formally by all its East European allies, but with particular emphasis by Czechoslovakia, Poland, and of course the GDR. As we have seen, 'recognition' was, for the East German state, an issue of life or death. The same might almost be said for the new Polish state, and this in a double sense. Given the Soviet incorporation of eastern Poland, the Polish incorporation of eastern Germany was a *sine qua non* for the continued existence of any but a rump Polish state. The Poles deported from eastern Poland physically took the place of the Germans deported from eastern Germany. Polish Lwów moved to German Breslau, and made it Wrocław. At the same time, the Soviet-imposed regime in Poland had a special interest in the Oder-Neisse line, since this was the only issue on which it could firmly reckon with the support both of the mighty Catholic Church and of the majority of the population. Similarly, although with less intensity, all Czechs were interested in a final, definitive recognition of what they saw as the pre-Munich rather than the post-Yalta frontiers of Czechoslovakia.

The story of this 'frontiers issue', the *Grenzfrage*, is one of the most intricate in contemporary European history: a pleasure-ground for connoisseurs of legal and diplomatic detail, and an impenetrable thicket for the layman. For our purpose, the essentials are these. In 1975, Leonid Brezhnev seems to have believed that he had finally achieved definitive Western recognition of the post-war status quo in Eastern Europe, and therewith of the Soviet position in the heart of Europe. The Helsinki Final Act was this recognition from the West as a whole: the sealing of Yalta. The Federal Republic's Eastern treaties were the recognition from West Germany. Both the general and the special conflicts were thus apparently resolved. The fruits of his generation's sacrifice in the Great Patriotic War were now secured 'for ever', as he had candidly expressed the thought to Alexander Dubček when justifying the invasion of Czechoslovakia in August 1968.

The West saw it rather differently. It is true that the Helsinki Final Act contained the most solemn undertakings to 'regard as inviolable ... the frontiers of all States in Europe', to 'refrain now and in the future from assaulting these frontiers', and to 'respect the territorial integrity of each of the participating states'. But before that it declared, in a formula negotiated by Henry Kissinger on behalf of the Federal Republic, that the signatory states 'consider that their frontiers can be changed, in accordance with international law, by peaceful means and by agreement'.

It is true that the Moscow Treaty emphatically and exhaustively declared that both signatory states 'regard as inviolable now and in the future the frontiers of all states in Europe, as they run on the day of signature of this treaty, including the Oder-Neisse-line, which is the Western frontier of the People's Republic of Poland, and the frontier between the Federal Republic of Germany and the German Democratic Republic'. It is true that the Moscow, Warsaw and Prague treaties all declared that the contracting parties 'have no territorial claims ... and will not raise any such in future'. But, as we have seen, these commitments were qualified in a number of important ways.

The 'Letter on German Unity', handed over by the Bonn government on signature of each of the main Eastern treaties, asserted that these treaties did not contradict the 'political goal' of the Federal Republic to 'work towards a state of peace in Europe in which the German people regains its unity in free self-determination'. The Bonn government simultaneously assured the Western allies that their 'rights and responsibilities relating to Germany as a whole and Berlin' were not affected by the Moscow Treaty – a contention crucially underlined by the subsequent conclusion of the Quadripartite Agreement on Berlin. The Common Resolution of the Bundestag emphasised that the Eastern treaties were no substitute for that final, binding, legal peace settlement which had obviously been envisaged at Potsdam more than a quarter-century before. The Federal Constitutional Court, in a judgement calculated to confound all but the most hardened jurist, averred that the German Reich continued to exist in the frontiers of December 1937 – the original Allied definition of 'Germany as a whole'. The Federal Republic, said its highest court, was as a state identical with that German Reich but 'so far as its territorial extent is concerned "part-identical", so that to this extent the identity does not aspire to exclusivity'. (Is that clear?)

These reservations were thus at once legal, with reference to past arrangements, and political, with reference to possible future arrangements, where, however, both kinds of reservation were more emphatically expressed by West Germany than by the other major Western powers, while the legal and the political, the past and the future, were all ambiguously intertwined. The diplomatic-political language had to bridge not only differences between East and West, but also differences between West Germany and the rest of the West, and, what is more, significant differences within the West German body politic.

The West German argument of the early 1970s, which continued to rumble on right through the 1980s, might at first sight be described, with obvious and deliberate oversimplification, as one between politician-journalists of the left and politician-jurists of the right. The politician-journalists, typified by Brandt and Bahr, and supported by much of published opinion, argued on grounds of morality and realism. While they acknowledged the formal constitutional and legal position, and had of necessity spent a great deal of time negotiating fine legal and diplomatic details, they were impatient of what Brandt called the *Formelkram* (formula stuff). For them, the Warsaw Treaty was a frontier treaty. That was the reality. Germany had given up the territories east of the Oder-Neisse line. Here was the price, a heavy and bitter price, to be paid for the crimes of Nazi Germany. Morality demanded that this should now be stated clearly.

Yet more even than morality, it was political realism that demanded this. For only by making a clear and explicit statement could one begin bringing the Germans in East and West Germany closer together, with Soviet acceptance, if not approval. Trust – Soviet and East European trust – was a vital part of the political capital that West German Ostpolitik had to build up. The firmer the acceptance of the German-Polish frontier, the greater the chances of opening the German-German frontier.

The position of the politician-jurists of the right was more complex. As late as 1989, a suggestion by a leading German specialist on international relations (and Social Democrat) that Konrad Adenauer had already privately given up the territories east of the Oder-Neisse line for lost in the early 1950s would provoke a storm of controversy. Adenauer's most authoritative biographer, Hans-Peter Schwarz, considers that at the beginning of the 1950s Adenauer was still genuinely a territorial revisionist. Yet as early as 1955, Adenauer reportedly told the leader of the Social Democratic opposition 'Oder-Neisse, Eastern provinces – they're gone! They don't exist any more!' Schwarz also shows that by the late 1950s Adenauer had come privately to accept that, realistically, recognition of the Oder-Neisse line would now be a *quid pro quo* for the Western allies' support for any reunification of the Germans between Rhine and Oder. This had by no means always been the American or British position. Indeed, following Byrnes' Stuttgart speech in 1946 the United States had rather encouraged questioning of the Oder-Neisse line. But at the very beginning of détente, Kennedy and Macmillan as well as de Gaulle made it clear that this now was their common position.

Why, then, attempt to qualify, obscure or even deny this political reality with legalistic paper castles? Three reasons can be adduced. First, the surrender of any claim to the territories east of the Oder-Neisse line was still a diplomatic card for Germany to play. An increasingly faded and dog-eared card, to be sure, but you do not simply throw away a card still notionally representing a quarter of the German Reich without getting something more than promises in return.

Second, the complex legal positions continued to have real political substance inasmuch as they were the only basis in international law for the claim to reunification even of West and East Germany, however remote that prospect might seem. If it ever became possible, the starting point for the international negotiation of unification would still have to be the unfinished post-war settlement, and the fragile origami of international and constitutional law which held that unfinished settlement in permanent suspension over Germany and Europe. Even if one wished to settle the specific Oder-Neisse question finally, one could not excise the part without jeopardising the whole.

Where the politician-journalists of the left said that opening (even a little) the German-German frontier required a final sealing of the Polish-German frontier, the politician-jurists of the Right argued that a final sealing of the Polish-German frontier might actually preclude, or at least make much more difficult, a final opening of the German-German frontier. Where the former spoke in the name of moralism and realism, the latter urged legalism and idealism. The conversion to painstaking legalism came very soon after 1945. (The historian Elizabeth Wiskemann, who had witnessed Nazi Germany trampling all principles of law all across Central Europe, wrote that 'it is difficult for Germany's neighbours not to smile sourly over this post-1945 legalism'.) This legalism was not just the *déformation professionelle* of lawyers or legally trained diplomats and politicians. It was also, as Egon Bahr's closest legal adviser on the Eastern treaties observes, the classic resource of the weak and the defeated.

At the same time, however, there was in the best version of liberal-conservative legalism an element of genuine idealism. Alois Mertes, an outstanding and influential representative of this liberal-conservative tradition, argued that to maintain these legal positions was also to hold up for people in East Germany the prospect – however remote – of free self-determination. The realists, in this view, were thinking too much in the short-term, and not paying sufficient regard to the great imponderables of history. In this sense the position of Germany's liberal-conservative legalists might be compared to that of the Poles who maintained a government-in-exile in London in the 1980s. Unrealistic, anachronistic, absurd – but it was from the President-in-exile and not from President Jaruzelski that President Wałęsa chose to receive the insignia of his new office in 1990, thus asserting the ideal continuity of a legitimate Polish government. Similarly, the balance-sheet of this German upholding of legal principles, in defiance of political realities, might look rather different after 1990 than it did in the late 1980s.

As Alois Mertes expressed it, the liberal-conservative position was that the constitutional claim for the continued existence of the German Reich in the frontiers of December 1937 was the necessary starting-point for any negotiation about German unification, but by no means the target of any such negotiation. On the contrary, he repeatedly emphasised that the quality of the German-German frontier, which divided one people, was now fundamentally different from that of the Polish-German frontier, which now divided two peoples. As Adenauer's close associate Wilhelm Grewe also insisted, reunification therefore meant reunification of East and West Germany. An interesting exchange of letters between Mertes and Egon Bahr in 1984 makes clear that on this basic point those bitter opponents of the early 1970s were actually in agreement, though the journalist Bahr cattily remarked that the jurist Mertes put in 'too much effort' to work out the legal niceties. (The devil, replied Mertes, is in the detail, as Soviet diplomats well knew.) And it was on precisely this point that the liberal conservatives crossed swords with ageing leaders of the expellees like Herbert Hupka and Herbert Czaja, who still somehow wished to regard the frontiers of 1937 as a target, not merely a starting-point.

In the essential substance, then, one might argue that the crucial divide was actually not – as it seemed – between politician-journalists of the left and politician-jurists of the right, but rather between the liberal conservative legalists, on the one hand, and the genuinely revisionist, nationalist right, with its hard core among the expellees, on the other. Yet it required a sharp, informed and dispassionate eye to notice this, especially since neither left nor right was interested in emphasising in public the common ground across party lines, while the more Social Democrats (or Free Democrats) pointed up divisions in the Christian Democrat ranks the more Christian Democrats would be at pains to deny them. Here we come to the third main reason for maintaining these legal-symbolic paper castles: the relationship of the Christian Democratic leadership to its own nationalist right wing, especially in the Bavarian Christian Social Union, to the leaders of the expellee organisations, and to the expellee vote.

West German leaders almost ritually invoked the 'Stuttgart charter' of the German expellees from the East, in which, as early as 1950, the expellees renounced any thought of 'revenge or retaliation'. This is true, and admirable. But it is also true that many of the German refugees and expellees from the East would not, or simply could not, accept the loss of their ancestral homelands as history's last word. (If Poland had been a free country in the 1950s there would surely have been a mighty organisation of Polish expellees.) In the 1950s this was still a burning issue in West German politics. No major German party would dare publicly to declare the territory to the east of the Oder-Neisse for lost, whatever the private conviction of this or that politician might be. (The West German Communists' public support for the Soviet and East German position on this issue was a major step in their self-marginalisation.)

Looking back from the 1970s, Willy Brandt himself observed that the peaceful integration of these millions of refugees and expellees was one of Konrad Adenauer's greatest services to his country. This was a double integration. It was, first, a social and economic integration. With a large initial investment by the state, partly financed by a special tax, the Silesians and Pomeranians and East Prussians and Sudeten Germans were successfully integrated into what then became (partly through this process) West German society. Indeed they contributed much to the so-called 'economic miracle', with the energies of the uprooted. But it was also a party-political integration. In the course of the 1950s, the Christian Democratic Union and the Bavarian Christian Social Union managed to mop up the right-wing expellee vote, squeezing the expellees' and right-wing nationalist parties down below the five per cent hurdle, and thus into parliamentary oblivion. This was a major contribution to the stability of West German democracy. But it also carried a price in the (growing) disparity between the private conviction and the public rhetoric of Christian Democratic leaders on the issue of frontiers, and the dismay this public rhetoric could cause abroad. At the same time, the fear of nationalist splinter parties remained in the bones of the Christian Democrats, revived as it was by electoral challenges from the National Democratic Party in the 1960s, and from the *Republikaner* in the 1980s.

It is only against this background that one can understand the public posture of Chancellor Kohl and his government on this issue. An author who knew Helmut Kohl well recalls that already in 1970, over a glass of good Palatine wine in the cellar of the state chancellery in Mainz, the then Prime Minister of the Rhineland-Palatinate thought of making a public declaration that the Federal Republic should accept the Oder-Neisse line.

This would be the beginning of a German reconciliation with Poland, such as Adenauer had achieved with France, and would enable Warsaw to view the prospect of German unity with greater equanimity. The next morning, however, after telephone conversations with a few prominent colleagues in his own party, including Richard von Weizsäcker, he rapidly concluded that the time was not ripe.

Of Helmut Kohl's private recognition of this frontier there could really be little doubt. Yet again and again, throughout his Chancellorship, right up until the early summer of 1990, he allowed uncertainty and doubt and misunderstanding to arise around the issue. Near the beginning of his Chancellorship, it was Friedrich Zimmermann, the Interior Minister from the Christian Social Union (with particularly strong expellee representation within its ranks), who put the cat among the pigeons by averring, as a political rather than merely a juridical claim, that Germany continued to exist in the frontiers of 1937. In 1985 the Chancellor himself was at the eye of the storm, when he seemed to be about to address a meeting of refugees and expellees from Silesia, on what was billed as the 'fortieth anniversary' of the expulsion, under the remarkable motto 'Silesia remains ours'. Eventually he did address the meeting, under the revised motto 'Silesia remains our future in a Europe of free peoples'.

In his speech, Kohl said that the Federal Government's position was predictable and *unmissverständlich*, that is, literally, unmisunderstandable. He then simply listed, as he had done so often before, the legal bases of his government's position, from the Basic Law to the judgement of the Federal Constitutional Court. These, he blithely repeated, made the German legal position unmisunderstandable. His government could not and would not change this legal position, he said, but it 'constituted no threat to our neighbours'. The expulsion of the Germans was a wrong, but so would another expulsion be – and he was able to quote a resolution of the Silesian association to this effect. Two wrongs would not make a right. 'Today,' he said, 'Silesia is inhabited almost entirely by Polish families, for whom this country has in the meantime become home (*Heimat*). We will respect this and not put it in question.' He went on to say that the real issue was not sovereignty rights but that of freedom for all those who lived beyond the East-West divide in Europe.

Now to deliver this message to an audience which raised banners saying defiantly 'Silesia remains ours', and in which a banner declaring 'Silesia remains Polish' was immediately torn down, was not merely appeasement. But nor was it, to use the Chancellor's own word, unmisunderstandable. Earlier in the year, the foreign affairs spokesman of his own party, Volker Rühe, had made the important statement that the Federal Republic's commitments in the Eastern treaties would also have a 'political binding effect' on a united Germany. Kohl did not venture even that far. And this was a summer in which the whole of Europe reflected on the fortieth anniversary, not just of the expulsion of the Germans but of the end of the Second World War, an occasion memorably and self-critically marked – just six weeks before – in a famous speech by the new Federal President, Richard von Weizsäcker.

What is more, Kohl's appearance before the Silesians came at a time when the Soviet media and Jaruzelski's Polish regime were engaged in a virulent propaganda campaign against West German revanchism. To be sure, the specialists in Moscow and Warsaw could perfectly well tell the difference between the liberal-conservative and the truly revisionist positions: between Helmut Kohl and his host at the meeting of Silesians, Herbert Hupka. But in the political context of the moment their political masters did not want to see that difference. The last revanchists in the West furnished ammunition for the last revanchists in the East. The actual effect on public opinion was probably not very great: even in Poland, where an independent opinion survey showed that only 4.7 per cent of those asked in 1984 saw a threat to Polish independence from the Federal Republic. But the effect on inter-governmental relations was serious. In distancing himself from Kohl's position, Hans-Dietrich Genscher was certainly in part 'winning profile' in the eternal Bonn game of coalition politics. Yet he was also representing real, immediate interests of German foreign policy.

In the second half of the 1980s, the issue faded somewhat from the public (if not from the Polish) eye, especially with the dramatic improvement in German-Soviet relations. It was revived in 1989, once again by a minister from the Christian Social Union talking about Germany in the frontiers of 1937, and not accidentally at a time when the right-wing *Republikaner* were seen to be gaining electoral ground, especially in Bavaria. In an attempt to clear the path for his great symbolic reconciliation with Poland, dreamed of already two decades before in that wine cellar in Mainz, Kohl supported a Bundestag resolution which contained the important new formulation – originally coined by Genscher – that 'the Polish people should know that its right to live in secure frontiers will not be put in question by us Germans now or in the future through territorial claims'.

Yet when the opening of the Berlin Wall, during Kohl's visit to Poland, opened the door also to German unification, the question of the frontier was still there. That it was still there as a point for international legal settlement was clear to all. Although Brezhnev had celebrated the Eastern treaties and Helsinki as the final peace settlement left unfinished in Potsdam, neither West Germany nor the West as a whole had ever accepted that spurious claim of finality. That it was still an issue of actual political controversy was, however, also the result of the specific developments inside West Germany that we have described above, and notably of the neo-Adenauerian domestic political strategy used by Helmut Kohl.

Bronisław Geremek, the outstanding Polish historian, Solidarity adviser and politician, whose own Jewish family was murdered by Germans in the war, records his conversation on this issue with Chancellor Kohl, in the autumn of 1989. 'The Chancellor tried to calm my fears concerning, among other things, the German position on the frontiers issue. I have the impression that he spoke sincerely. But when I asked him if I could make public the substance of our conversation he replied that if I did that he would immediately deny it. The justification given for this position was the realities of German politics.'

In his 'ten-point programme' of November 1989, which laid out steps leading to unification, Kohl did not mention the frontiers issue at all. The absence of this 'eleventh point' was much criticised, and not just in Poland. In March 1990, the Chancellor then surprised and appalled most of the partners with whom he was negotiating the unification of Germany by suggesting that a final treaty on the frontier was conditional on satisfactory binding commitments from the Polish side on the rights of the remaining German minority in Poland, and the renunciation of any further Polish claims to reparations for war damages. While the Chancellor soon retreated from this position, in the '2+4' negotiations for German unity, it was the other five (including Markus Meckel, the Social Democratic Foreign Minister of the now democratised German Democratic Republic), who pressed most forcefully for the unconditional recognition of the frontier precisely as it now ran between Poland and East Germany. For the Federal Republic, the final ratification of the final frontier treaty with Poland in the autumn of 1991 was still linked by the Bonn government to a further bilateral Polish-German treaty in which, among other things, the issue of German minority rights was addressed.

In a retrospective conversation with the author, in the autumn of 1991, the Chancellor left no doubt that this domestic political factor had been very important in his thinking. The strategic purpose had been to show the nationalist right and the last unteachables among the expellees that this was the price which Germany simply had to pay for the unification of the Germans between Oder and Rhine. (By his seemingly insensitive suggestions, provoking a storm of international criticism, he had indeed demonstrated this brilliantly.) He could then say, in effect, to the real nationalist-revisionists: do you wish to be responsible for sabotaging the unification of Germany?

If the liberal-left, as represented supremely by Willy Brandt, worked from the bases of moralism and a realism which included more than a touch of Machiavellism in foreign policy, the liberal-right, as represented by Chancellor Kohl, proceeded not only from legalism and idealism but also from a sort of Machiavellism in domestic politics – a Machiavellism which was in the real tradition of Konrad Adenauer quite as much as the desire for reconciliation with historic enemies. Some would say that without first securing their domestic power base the leaders of democracies will never have the power do the right thing in foreign policy, and the reckoning paid off magnificently in the end. Others would say that this approach helped to keep fading illusions alive, to rub salt in wounds that could have been more quickly healed, and that, in any case, there are issues in international affairs where such domestic political tactics, or even strategies, must yield to higher imperatives. What actually happened is now clear. The judgement must be the reader's.

Compatriots

The past therefore would not pass away, or at least, passed away much more slowly than many had anticipated in the early 1970s. There was another, more direct way in which the Federal Republic's 'special conflict' with the East continued to shape its relations with the Soviet Union and Eastern European. This was what may be called the permissive function of those relations for the Federal Republic's efforts on behalf of the Germans in the East. As we have seen, one of the two most important purposes of developing relations with Moscow was to permit Bonn to deal with the powers-that-were in East Berlin, in the interests of the people. Following the imperative of synchronisation, relations with East European states played an important supporting role in this overall scheme of Ostpolitik.

Yet beside this general, indirect permissive function there was also a specific, direct permissive function. This concerned the treatment by these states of their remaining German minorities. Like the frontiers issue, this is a subject of extraordinary historical complexity and emotional, legal and political sensitivity. Like the frontiers issue, it continued to haunt the Federal Republic's relations with the Soviet Union and Eastern Europe – and above all with Poland – even at the end of the 1980s. Unlike the frontiers issue, it remained a major point on the operative agenda of German Ostpolitik.

The basic outlines of the problem are as follows. After the vast movement of peoples, the modern *Völkerwanderung* across Central and Eastern Europe in the terrible decade from 1939 to 1949; after the expulsion of Slavs from their homes and their replacement by settlers from other parts of Germany or by ethnic Germans (*Volksdeutsche*) summoned by Hitler 'back into the empire' (*Heim ins Reich*); after the flight of millions of Germans before the advancing Red Armies; after the so-called 'wild expulsions' of Germans in the immediate aftermath of war, with Russians, Poles, Czechs, the peoples of Yugoslavia, and, in lesser measure, all the other peoples of Eastern Europe, taking bitter and often brutal revenge, sometimes on guilty but also on quite innocent Germans; after the more systematic 'transfers' of Germans, with the Western allies attempting – often vainly – to ensure that the pious wish expressed in the

Potsdam Agreement that these transfers should be 'orderly and humane' was not entirely ignored; after all this, some four million Germans nonetheless remained in the newly constituted communist states east of the Oder-Neisse line and south-east of the Erz mountains at the beginning of the 1950s.

The background and position of these Germans varied widely. There were German soldiers still held as prisoners of war in Stalin's camps. There were ethnic Germans invited to settle on the Volga and the Black Sea by Catherine the Great and Alexander I, but then deported to Central Asia and Siberia by Stalin during the war, as collective punishment for being German. Of the ancient German settlements in Bohemia, Moravia and Slovakia very little was left after the expulsions. Still intact, though beleaguered in the new Romania, was one of the most ancient of all the German communities in the East: the Germans of Transylvania, the Siebenbürgen Saxons, settled there since the early Middle Ages and described already by the eighteenth-century German historian August Ludwig Schlözer as *Germanissimi Germanorum*, the most German of Germans. Also relatively intact, though also beleaguered, were the more recent settlements at the invitation of the Habsburgs: the Germans in Hungary and the so-called Swabians of the Banat, now in Romania. From what was now Yugoslavia the Germans were almost entirely expunged.

Most complicated of all was the background and position of the remaining Germans within the frontiers of the new Poland. At one extreme there were those who were both indubitably German in culture, language and tradition, and had held German citizenship in the Reich in its frontiers of 1937. At the other extreme there were vaguely Aryan-looking Poles who had taken up the Nazi occupiers' offer to become Germans through the third and fourth categories of the so-called *Volksliste*, but had then smartly become Poles again after 1945. In between there were a great many people, above all in Upper Silesia, who for generations had lived amidst and between Polishness and Germanity, now turning one way, now the other, mixing blood, language, tradition, culture into an identity which was, simply – or rather, not at all simply – Silesian. Most of them were allowed to stay by the Polish communist authorities, being officially classed as 'autochthones'.

Such, then, were the sad puddles of Germanity which were all that was left, at the founding of the Federal Republic, of more than a thousand years of German settlement in the East. Given the real confusion of the time, and the deliberate confusion sown by the communist states' nationality statistics, all figures must be approximate, but of the total, the largest number – perhaps some two million – were in the Soviet Union, another one to two million – depending greatly on definitions – were in Poland, up to half a million in Romania, less than a quarter of a million in Hungary, still fewer in Czechoslovakia.

All Bonn governments, from Adenauer to Kohl, made it their business to help these Germans in the East. Socialists, liberals and conservatives agreed that this was a national duty: to help the Germans who were still suffering most from the consequences of the war and the 'Yalta' division of Europe. This concern, indeed this priority, was understandable. But it also saddled the Federal Republic with difficulties faced by no other Western state. Moreover, contrary to the expectations of 'normalisation' in the 1970s, the problems posed were in some respects actually more acute at the end of the 1980s than they had been at the end of the 1960s.

From the outset, Bonn governments were faced with a choice between two lines of action: to help the Germans in the East to stay there, by working to support their material, cultural, educational and legal position as a group in the given state, or to help them to leave, as individuals. Of course, one could in theory attempt to do both, as Bonn did in relations with East Germany. But there was at the very least a strong tension between the two approaches. Moreover, because of earlier German policies, each course laid Bonn open to suspicions and charges from the East.

Efforts to help the Germans to stay, by improving their lot as a minority, all too swiftly recalled the support given first by the Weimar Republic and even more by the Third Reich to what were then called the *Auslandsdeutsche* in the Versailles successor-states. In that period, German Foreign Ministry support, carefully laundered through foreign bank accounts, to organisations with such innocuous names as the *Konkordia Literarische Gesellschaft*, had paved the way for territorial revisionism. On the other hand, efforts to bring the Germans individually 'home' could be tarred with the brush of Hitler's '*Heim ins Reich*', while at the same time the new East European states feared to lose people who made an important contribution to their economies.

Bonn was thus likely to be damned one way or the other. Yet given the hatred, both popular and manipulated, of Germany and the Germans in the new Eastern Europe, given the obvious determination of the Stalinist leaderships to Polonise, Magyarise or Czechify their remaining Germans, the first option seemed nearly hopeless. In the early years of the Federal Republic, government policy therefore concentrated on helping individual Germans to get out. If in 1945 Germans were expelled against their will, in 1950 Germans were seen to be detained against their will.

This first priority was reflected in the terms applied to the Germans who came to the Federal Republic from the East. The prisoners of war in the East were described as *Spätheimkehrer*, late homecomers, the others as *Spätaussiedler*, literally late out-settlers. So far as prisoners of war were concerned, the term expressed an obvious and terrible truth. They were late homecomers indeed. As we have seen, the main immediate objective of Konrad Adenauer's trip to Moscow in September 1955 – the 'beginning of Bonn's Ostpolitik' – was to free those prisoners. Adenauer remarked that he was ready to talk to the devil's grandmother to get 10,000 people home, ten years after the end of the war. However, this trip also brought significant improvements for the ethnic Germans banished by Stalin to Siberia and Kazakhstan, in many cases releasing them from more than a decade of forced labour. In a second, extremely difficult round of negotiations with the Soviet Union, in 1957–58, the issue of 'repatriation' was a major bone of contention. Yet here it was already questionable whether Germans whose families had been settled in the Baltic states or Russia itself for generations should be described as late leavers. And had the Germans in Transylvania really been sitting on packed bags for eight hundred years?

In the 1960s, West German usage settled down with the simpler, although still curious term out-settlers, *Aussiedler*, not to be confused with the over-settlers, *Übersiedler*, from East Germany. The 1961 Bundestag initiative for a more active Ostpolitik was explicitly linked to the position and concerns of the Germans who remained in the East. The Brandt and Schmidt governments, like their predecessors, continued to press for emigration possibilities for the Germans in the East, and to point to the statistics of out-settlers as a measure of their 'success'. Moreover, they continued to do this using the remarkably generous definition of 'a German' established at the founding of the Federal Republic.

In the official translation, Article 116 of the Basic Law read as follows:

Article 116 (Definition of 'German', Regranting of citizenship)

(1) Unless otherwise provided by law, a German within the meaning of this Basic Law is a person who possesses German citizenship or who has been admitted to the territory of the German Reich within the frontiers of 31 December 1937 as a refugee or expellee of German stock (*Volkszugehörigkeit*) or as the spouse or descendant of such a person.

(2) Former German citizens who, between 30 January 1933 and 8 May 1945, were deprived of their citizenship on political, racial or religious grounds, and their descendants, shall be regranted German citizenship on application. They shall be considered as not having been deprived of their German citizenship if they have established their domicile (*Wohnsitz*) in Germany after 8 May 1945 and have not expressed a contrary intention.

There were thus two key categories, German citizenship (*Staatsangehörigkeit*) and German stock (*Volkszugehörigkeit*). German citizenship was defined according to a modifed version of the 1913 citizenship law of the (second) Reich, which gave central importance to the so-called *ius sanguinis*, that is, citizenship by descent. Whereas in America or Britain the *ius sanguinis* had long been complemented by the *ius soli* – that is, a person was American if born on American soil –, in Germany the emphasis remained on descent. A young Turk born and brought up in Germany had no automatic right to German citizenship, and, indeed, would find that citizenship quite difficult to acquire. On the other hand, a glance at the guidelines drawn up for officials at the Friedland reception camp for out-settlers shows that the descendants of people who had at any time between 1913 and 1945 been declared by the German Reich to be German citizens, whether in the former German eastern territories, the Memel, Danzig, the Sudetenland or even the Reich Commissariat of the Ukraine, would automatically qualify for citizenship of the Federal Republic.

But this was only half the story. The other, even more difficult half concerned the category of German stock. What was this? The Federal Law on Expellees and Refugees said: 'A member of the German *Volk* is . . . one who in his *Heimat* declared himself for Germanity (*deutsches Volkstum*), insofar as this declaration is confirmed by certain attributes such as extraction (*Abstammung*), language, upbringing, culture.' Beside the former German eastern territories (in the frontiers of December 1937), the possible *Heimat* in this definition was held to include Danzig, Estonia, Latvia, Lithuania, the Soviet Union, Poland, Czechoslovakia, Hungary, Romania, Bulgaria, Yugoslavia, Albania and China!

As the 1980 official guidelines for the application of this law indicate, there were thus two essential ingredients: the subjective declaration for Germanity (*deutsches Volkstum*) in your *Heimat*, and objective attributes to confirm this declaration. The guidelines went on to indicate that applicants must have shown 'by their behaviour the consciousness and will to belong to German *Volkstum* and to no other *Volkstum* . . .'

For people who lived in former German areas east of the Oder-Neisse line it would suffice that 'their overall behaviour show[ed] no demonstrative inclination towards another *Volkstum*'. In the case of mixed marriages one had to determine which parent had a dominant influence: 'If the dominant influence of one or the other parent cannot be established, the formative influence of the German parent is to be assumed.' The relevant moment for establishing whether there was a declaration for Germanity was 'immediately before the beginning of the persecution- and deportation-measures directed against the German population' – that is, in late 1944 or early 1945. For *Jewish* applicants, however, the relevant moment was before 30 January 1933, since after that date 'they could not be expected to declare themselves for Germanity'.

At this point the 1980 official guidelines defensively remarked: 'the concept of German stock (*Volkszugehörigkeit*) in the sense of article 6 . . . is fundamentally different from the national-socialist theory of *Volkstum*'. Yet the profoundly embarrassing fact was that, as a result of the definition in the Basic Law, and the way in which it was subsequently interpreted, West German officials at the Friedland reception camp were obliged to accept or reject candidates for German citizenship on the basis not merely of criteria that eerily recalled Nazi criteria (declaration for Germanity *and for no other Volkstum*), but actually on the basis of Nazi selection.

For example, as part of the attempt to Germanise occupied Poland, the Nazis in some places simply, arbitrarily, and often grotesquely declared Poles to be Germans, entering them in groups three or four of the so-called *Volksliste*. Group three membership, accorded to some 1.7 million people between 1941 and 1944, brought the right to citizenship after a period of ten years. So: produce your father's *Volkslistenausweis* in 1989, and you automatically became a West German citizen. Enrolment in the *Wehrmacht*, or other mass organisations of the Third Reich, had generally depended on a certification of Germanity, and was therefore accepted by the Federal Republic as evidence of it. Question 15 of the questionnaire for applicants asked whether you, your spouse, father, or another close relation belonged to the German *Wehrmacht*, *Waffen-SS*, Police, RAD (*Reichsarbeitsdienst*) or the *Organisation Todt*. They did? Welcome to West Germany. One way or another, roughly half of those accepted as out-settlers from Poland in the 1980s came through what one might call the Third Reich route. The others were descended, one way or another, from citizens of the Second Reich.

The general principle remained wholly understandable: the Germans enjoying freedom (and prosperity) should help the Germans who did not. So far as the Germans coming out of Romania were concerned, there was also relatively little difficulty in the concrete application of that general principle, for these people were self-evidently as German in descent, culture, language, upbringing, as any German in the Federal Republic – indeed, in some ways they were more German, *Germanissimi Germanorum*. The same applied to some, though by no means all, of the Germans in the Soviet Union. But for those areas of 'floating nationality' where for centuries people had been sometimes Czech or Polish, sometimes German, always Masurian or Silesian; for those areas, moreover, where, after 1939, the German authorities had tried to turn Poles into Germans, and then, after 1945, the Polish authorities had tried (perhaps less brutally, but more systematically and tenaciously) to turn Germans into Poles: for these areas the specific application of the general principle became simply grotesque.

Young Poles seeking – also quite understandably – a better life for themselves and their families in the West, would scrabble for proof of a Nazi skeleton in the family cupboard. Your father fought for freedom during the war? Conceal it as best you may. Not a family past in the Polish resistance but a past in the *Waffen-SS* would bring you freedom today. That a complete 'German past' could reportedly be bought on the black market in Poland for about $8,000 (1988 prices) seems, in the circumstances, less a criminal subversion of German nationality law than an ironic commentary upon it.

It was the Federal Republic's relationship with Poland, above all, that was bedevilled by this problem throughout the 1970s and 1980s. In the early 1950s the Polish communist authorities had tried to Polonise the remaining Germans within the frontiers of the new state. Following the Polish October of 1956, the Gomułka regime did permit very limited cultural freedoms to German communities in Lower Silesia, although not in Upper Silesia or the former East Prussia. At the same time, it permitted a wave of German emigration: just under a quarter of a million people came out in the years 1956 to 1959, more than one hundred thousand in the course of the 1960s.

When the negotiations for the Warsaw Treaty began in 1970, the Polish authorities at first maintained that there were no longer any Germans living in Poland. The German Red Cross said there were some 400,000 who wanted to leave, and estimates based on the legal definition outlined above brought a figure of more than one million potential German out-settlers. The social-liberal coalition reckoned that it could not get the treaty through parliament without some provision for these Germans to leave. The eventual compromise was a so-called '*Information*' of the Polish government which said that 'some tens of thousands' of Germans might still be found to be living in Poland. Unpublished 'Confidential Notes' confirmed that these persons should be allowed to leave in 'one to two years'. In the event, some 38,500 were allowed out in the next two years, but the flow then dwindled.

After coming into office in 1974, the new Chancellor, Helmut Schmidt, and the new Foreign Minister, Hans-Dietrich Genscher, made a determined effort to resolve the whole complex of problems related to the German minority. Following a long and emotional late-evening talk between Schmidt and Edward Gierek in the margins of the Helsinki Conference in August 1975, their negotiators produced a package of agreements. This included a pension agreement covering the German minority, for which the Bonn government agreed to pay DM 1.3 billion over three years, and an extraordinary miniature treaty for a DM 1 billion loan at an annual interest rate of 2.5 per cent. In an accompanying 'Protocol' the Polish side stated that 'on the basis of investigations by the responsible Polish authorities . . . some 120,000 to 125,000 persons would receive assent to their applications [to leave] in the course of the next four years'.

Like the first Warsaw Treaty, however, this supplementary package was the subject of heated political debate in the Federal Republic, with the right shaping up for the 1976 federal election campaign by accusing the Schmidt government of giving in to communist blackmail and trading money for people. The attack on the billion DM loan was led by Franz Josef Strauss. (The billion DM credit he himself orchestrated for the GDR just seven years later was, of course, something completely different.)

Since the social-liberal coalition did not have a majority in the *Bundesrat* (the second chamber of parliament with representatives of the federal states), it was compelled to lean on the Polish government to make further, quite humiliating public assurances on the issue of German emigration, in order to give more liberal conservatives in Bonn (including Helmut Kohl) sufficient grounds to allow the package through. This done, and the money paid, the Polish authorities did in fact allow roughly the agreed number of people to leave.

Now an economic 'linkage' on the emigration issue was not wholly unknown in the Ostpolitik of other Western countries. The Jackson-Vanik amendment in the United States Congress made the development of US economic relations with any 'nonmarket economy country', and specifically the grant of Most Favored Nation status, dependent on that country allowing its citizens 'the right or opportunity to emigrate'. What had originally raised Senator Jackson's ire was the imposition of a per capita 'exit tax' on Jews wishing to emigrate from the Soviet Union. If the Soviet Union ended the tax, and generally made Jewish emigration easier, then it might get the Most Favored Nation status. In the case of Romania, Most Favored Nation status was awarded by Washington partly as recognition of concessions on Jewish emigration, though also of Romania's maverick stance in foreign policy. Yet this case also showed how difficult this sort of linkage was to make, for in the American political and policy-making process, the MFN status, once granted, proved extraordinarily difficult to withdraw, even when Romania had ceased to offer most of the original favours.

West Germany, by contrast, was effectively paying the 'exit tax' itself – but for those it considered to be its own citizens. As we have seen, this it did, both directly and indirectly, in relation to the GDR. So also with Romania. Here the business of 'buying free' began after a visit to Romania by President Heinemann in 1971. As with the buying free of Germans from the GDR, it began tentatively and conspiratorially, with cash being carried to the border in unmarked envelopes, but then gradually became regularised. Under an agreement reached between Chancellor Schmidt and President Ceauşescu in 1978, the Romanian dictator agreed to allow out at least 12,000 Germans per year for the next five years. The Bonn government agreed to pay a well-rounded per capita sum for these emigrants, a sum increased, when the agreement was renewed for another five years in 1983, to nearly DM 8,000 per head.

The 1975 deal with Poland was, however, uniquely ambiguous. What was this DM 1 billion 'jumbo credit' at knock-down terms being granted for? Was it an act of historic reconciliation or even delayed reparation? Or was it just a thinly disguised exit tax: cash for Germans? Was it a personal declaration of friendship from Schmidt to Gierek? Or was it, as the preamble to the agreement declared, 'to advance the conditions for the development of economic and industrial co-operation'? The problem with the 'jumbo credit' was precisely the cloudy mixture of motives and goals: moral and national, personal, political and economic. The one thing it certainly was not was good business – for either side. Between 1976 and 1980 the West German taxpayer paid DM 290.5 million in interest subsidies for this credit alone. Meanwhile, Gierek and his colleagues so misspent this and other Western credits that they not only ruined the Polish economy but also diminished rather than increased the country's chances of 'economic and industrial co-operation' with the West.

The only people who benefited (presumably) in the longer term were the more than 120,000 Polish Germans or German Poles thus 'bought free'. Yet the problem still would not go away. The more that left, the more there were who wanted to leave. The Germans in Poland multiplied like relics of the true cross: a development not unconnected with Poland's deepening economic crisis. At the end of 1983 the then Minister of State in the Foreign Ministry, Alois Mertes, observed that 'at least 120,000 Germans in the Oder-Neisse area and neighbouring areas of the People's Republic of Poland demonstrably desire to move permanently to the Federal Republic of Germany'. As we have seen this was not merely a practical problem. It was also a symbolic-political one.

In the same document which brought this answer – in the form of a long letter to a parliamentary colleague – Mertes estimated, on the basis of scrupulous calculations, that there were probably some 1.1 million people still living in Poland who were 'Germans' according to German law. He went on, however, to emphasise that 'over ninety per cent of the population' were Poles who 'now regard the Oder-Neisse area as their final *Heimat*'. And he concluded by recalling that liberal-conservative interpretation of Germany's position in international law which clearly indicated that a putative 'reunification' would include only the territory west of the Oder-Neisse line. His intentions were thus of the best. But they were misunderstood – in part deliberately so.

For the Polish authorities took this as a further ground for winding up, entirely in line with Soviet propaganda at that time, their own campaign against alleged West German 'revanchism': a campaign intended to mobilise the Polish population behind the Jaruzelski regime. It was a curious reward for the government which, of all major Western governments had shown most understanding for General Jaruzelski's attempts at 'normalisation' and 'stabilisation'. In this way, the German minorities issue, linked to the frontier question, once again blighted relations between the Polish and West German states.

Nor was it only the Jaruzelski regime. With that exquisite sensitivity to the feelings of other nations which he was later to display in his remarks on Polish-Jewish relations, Primate Glemp preached a sermon in which he said, in effect, that there were no Germans left in Poland, and they should anyway be glad to be Poles. Proudly he reported his retort to an old lady in West Germany who had asked him that no injury should be done to the Germans remaining in Poland. 'What Germans, what injury?' he had replied. This in turn provoked outrage in West Germany. And so, forty years after the end of the war, the bitter cycle of recrimination continued.

In the second half of the 1980s the remaining German minorities produced yet another problem for the Federal Republic. This time, it was a problem of success. For years, for decades, the Bonn government had urged and paid the authorities in Warsaw, Moscow and Bucharest (not to mention in East Berlin) to let their Germans go. And now, suddenly, they came, not just in their tens of thousands but in their hundreds of thousands. The total number of out-settlers from the Soviet Union and Eastern Europe soared from just over 40,000 in 1986 to nearly 80,000 in 1987, over 200,000 in 1988, a staggering 377,055 in 1989 and nearly 400,000 in 1990. The main reasons for this growth were twofold: a fundamentally altered emigration policy of the Soviet Union under Gorbachev, embodied in a new decree of January 1987; and the virtually free-for-all travel policy of the Polish government, combined with an economic situation that was a powerful incentive to take up the 'German option'.

Here, surely, was a great success for German Ostpolitik. Was not this precisely what Chancellor Kohl had demanded, with renewed emphasis, in his government declaration of 1983, referring to those concerned not merely as 'people of German origin' but simply as 'Germans'? Yet the result of this great flood of Germans 'coming home' was not an outpouring of national welcome and public delight but, on the contrary, a growing public resentment and resistance, reflected in election successes for the new party of the far right: the *Republikaner*. The *Republikaner* were a curious phenomenon: an extreme right-wing, populist nationalist party one of whose main sources of electoral support was resentment against newly arrived German nationals.

In vain did politicians from the President and Chancellor down argue that many of these Germans had suffered long and hard just for being Germans. In vain did they recall that a ruined Germany had after the war welcomed and integrated many times this number of Germans from the East. In vain did ministers and economists point out that these mainly young, often well-qualified, highly-motivated people would be a net economic gain to a country whose own native-born German population was shrinking and ageing. What disgruntled voters in the big cities like Berlin or Frankfurt or the poorer parts of rural Bavaria saw was housing, jobs, and extra social security payments going to newcomers, even in preference to the locals.

To understand this reaction one must understand that this large increase in the number of out-settlers came at the same time, and partly for the same reasons, as a large increase in the number of Germans moving from East to West Germany, and of other East Europeans (for in the terms of Yalta Europe, the East Germans and the Germans in the East were also 'East Europeans') who came to visit, to stay illegally, or to seek political asylum. Here it is important to note that if in article 116 of its constitution, and the subsequent interpretation of that article in law and government practice, the Federal Republic had a remarkably generous definition of Germanity, then in article 16 of its constitution, and the subsequent interpretation of that article in law and government practice, the Federal Republic had a remarkably generous definition of asylum.

Mindful of the way in which Germans persecuted by the Nazis had been granted asylum in Scandinavia, America, Britain and other free countries, the drafters of the Basic Law said simply, sweepingly: 'Persons persecuted on political grounds shall enjoy the right of asylum.' In practice, even people with the barest claim to have been persecuted in Eastern Europe were not actually sent back. In the second half of the 1980s, the number of asylum-seekers from Eastern Europe, and particularly from Poland, soared, while, with the gradual *de facto* softening of the regime at home, the grounds on which they claimed asylum became ever thinner. Already in 1987, some eighty-five per cent of all those applying for asylum in the whole European Community were doing so in the Federal Republic. The total number of asylum-seekers topped the 100,000 mark in 1988, while at the end of that year some 200,000 Poles were registered as staying 'not just temporarily' in West Germany.

The cause for popular resentment was thus by no means only the Germans from the East, but rather a whole great influx of strangers of all shades and backgrounds. Even the Berliner who moved from one end of the Friedrichstrasse to the other was not immune to this resentment, and the tension between the so-called *Ossis* and *Wessis* – roughly, Easties and Westies – would become acute after the complete opening of the German-German frontier. But beyond this, opinion polls revealed a rough continuum of resentment from the (least resented) Germans from the GDR, through Germans from Romania or Russia, to Germans (or 'Germans') from Poland, to Poles, to the people known until the early 1990s as 'Yugoslavs', and thence to the (most despised) Gipsies, Africans and other lesser breeds without the D-mark. As one wit observed, the hostility was directed against everything beginning with A: *Asylanten*, *Ausländer*, *Aussiedler* (that is, asylum-seekers, foreigners, out-settlers).

Ironically, it was the Federal Republic's own interpretation of its own nationality and asylum laws which helped to create this continuum, especially by its treatment of that dubious middle ground represented above all by the inhabitants of Upper Silesia. For between the Silesian who suddenly rediscovered a German past, in order to secure his family a decent standard of living, and the Silesian who sought asylum as a Pole, in order to secure his family a decent standard of living, there was, in truth, scant difference. They were both, as the popular joke had it, less *Volksdeutsche* than *Volkswagendeutsche*. But then, could not that equally well be said of most ordinary West Germans? And why not?

As a result of this unexpected and disconcerting development, the position of the German minorities became, like so many other aspects of German Ostpolitik, simultaneously an issue of domestic and of foreign policy. In domestic policy, a major debate began about the right of asylum. In foreign policy, the Kohl government began to give new emphasis and urgency to the second possible line of policy towards the Germans in the East: that of helping them to stay rather than helping them to leave. Beside the individual human right – to leave – the Bonn government increasingly placed the group rights of minorities.

People qualified as Germans under article 116 of the Basic Law should, it was argued in Bonn, be able to live as Germans in whatever state they now found themselves. They should have German-language teaching, cultural life, journals, church services etc, and equal opportunities. The unique culture of Central Europe had been made by the tense yet seminal co-existence of Slavs, Germans and Jews. The Jews could never be brought back, but the Germans might still play their part. This was thus, at its best, neither an illiberal nor an unattractive vision. But so long as the states of Eastern Europe remained communist, it remained just that: a vision.

Hungary was the exception that proved the rule. Here, in a state with a small German minority, relatively unburdened historic ties with Germany, and increasingly warm relations with Bonn, János Kádár's regime recognised the advantages that could accrue from an exemplary treatment of its Germans. On the first visit by a President of the Federal Republic, in 1986, Richard von Weizsäcker was entertained by schoolgirls from the so-called Swabians of the Danube, dancing folk-dances in colourful folk-costumes, singing folk-songs and reciting folk-poems. It was, said the President, 'an occasion that moves the heart'. The exemplary folk-treatment did not only move the heart-strings of the Federal President. It also moved the purse-strings of the Federal Government. In giving an untied DM 1 billion credit to the Hungarian government in 1987, Bonn made it very plain that this was partly in recognition of the good treatment of the German minority. On a visit to Hungary in 1988, the Christian Democrats' foreign affairs spokesman, Volker Rühe, went so far as to say that 'the treatment of minorities plays a dominant role in my present conversations with the Hungarian leadership and the Association of Hungary Germans'.

What is more, politicians and policymakers in Bonn made no secret of the fact that this credit was to be understood as a signal to other states in the Soviet bloc: if Poland, Czechoslovakia, Romania or even the Soviet